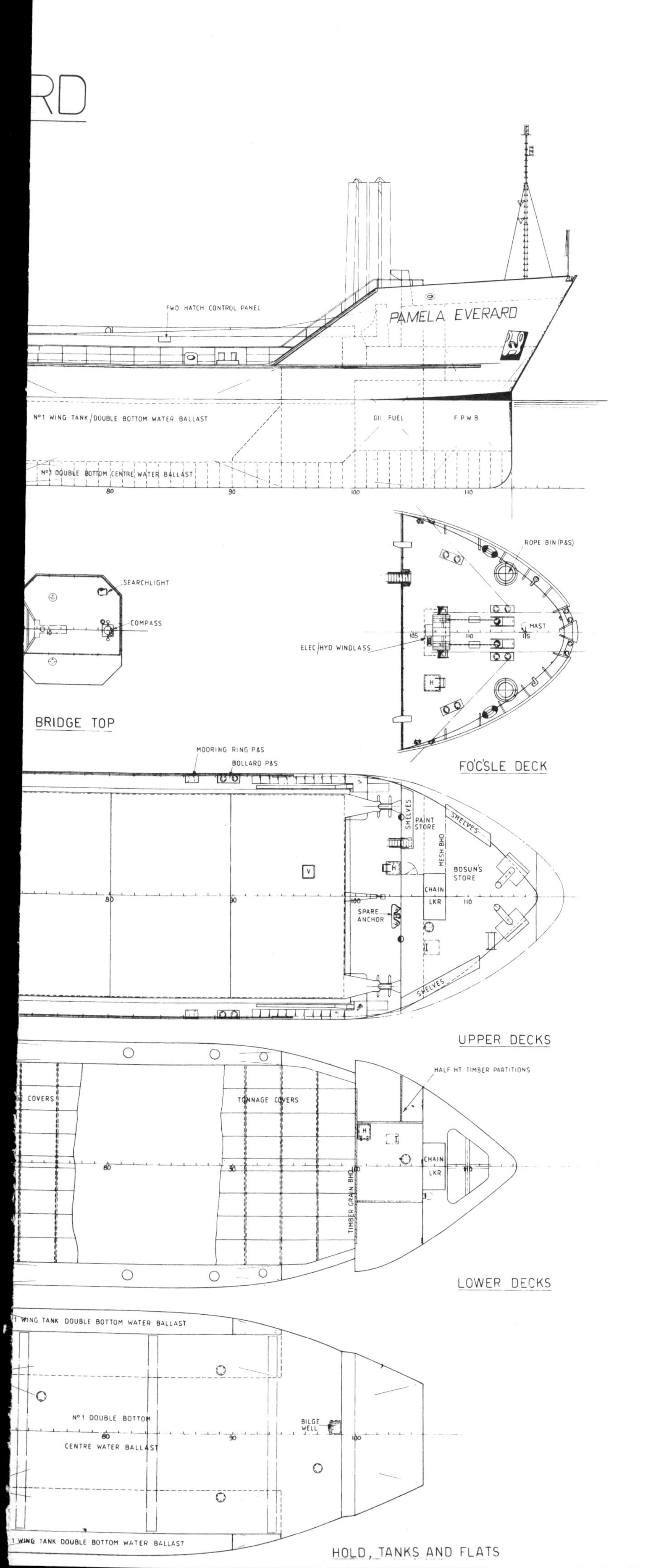

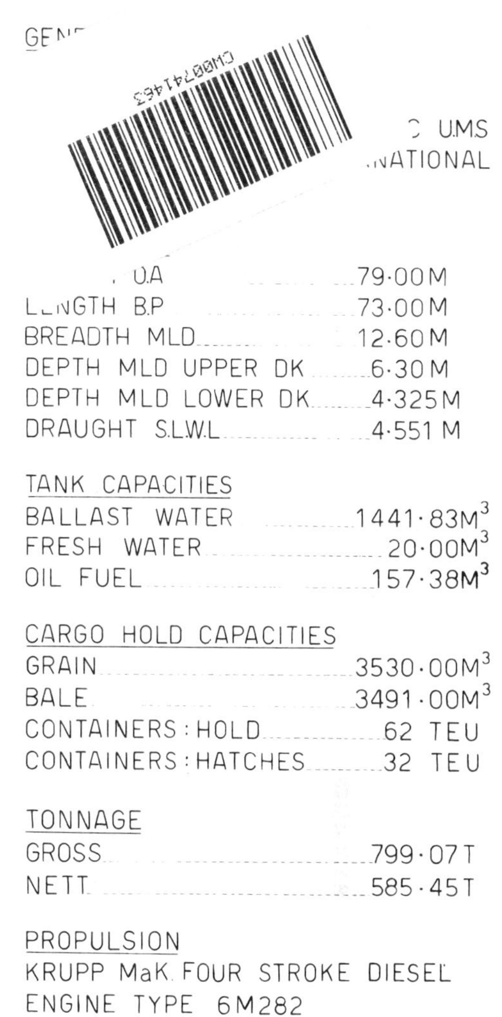

GEN[illegible]

[illegible] UMS

[illegible]NATIONAL

[illegible] O.A	79·00M
LENGTH B.P	73·00M
BREADTH MLD	12·60M
DEPTH MLD UPPER DK	6·30M
DEPTH MLD LOWER DK	4·325M
DRAUGHT S.L.W.L	4·551 M

TANK CAPACITIES

BALLAST WATER	$1441\cdot83M^3$
FRESH WATER	$20\cdot00M^3$
OIL FUEL	$157\cdot38M^3$

CARGO HOLD CAPACITIES

GRAIN	$3530\cdot00M^3$
BALE	$3491\cdot00M^3$
CONTAINERS: HOLD	62 TEU
CONTAINERS: HATCHES	32 TEU

TONNAGE

GROSS	799·07T
NETT	585·45T

PROPULSION

KRUPP MaK FOUR STROKE DIESEL
ENGINE TYPE 6M282

ISSUE	REMARKS	DATE
	MODIFICATIONS	

SUBMISSIONS	SUBMITTED	APPROVED

TITLE "AS FITTED" GENERAL ARRANGEMENT

YARD No. 558

RICHARDS (SHIPBUILDERS) LTD
CROWN WORKS,
LOWESTOFT, SUFFOLK.
TEL. No. 0502-3251

SCALES 1:100

DRAWING No.

DRAWN	CHECKED	APPROVED
W Gulley[?]		
PRINT No.		DATE

Greenhithe, Kent.

From a painting by Frank H. Mason

EVERARD OF GREENHITHE

K.S. GARRETT

THE WORLD SHIP SOCIETY
KENDAL

Endpapers: General arrangement drawing of the motor vessel **PAMELA EVERARD** (by kind permission of Richards (Shipbuilders) Ltd.)

Published in Great Britain by
The World Ship Society, Kendal, Cumbria LA9 7LT.

ISBN 0 905617 58 4

Typeset by Pat and Anne Murphy, 10, Bracken Way, Walkford, Christchurch, Dorset BH23 5LW

Printed by the Alden Press, Oxford

CONTENTS

The Founder Mr. Frederick T. Everard. *Company archives*

FOREWORD

The Everard Family is indebted to Captain Garrett for his history of the company. The objective approach has led to a story that is fascinating and particularly interesting for the present generation.

There have been tremendous changes in the shipping industry in the last hundred years and the sophisticated ships in our fleet today bear little resemblance to the wooden sailing barges built by my great grandfather but the spirit required to operate them remains the same.

Ethel, the only surviving member of the third generation, has assisted Captain Garrett greatly in establishing much that occurred in earlier years. The ships' descriptions, because there are so many, will have taken a great deal of painstaking research and provide an excellent historical guide to the fleet and the development of our ships.

I hope others find this book as interesting as I have done.

Michael Everard
Chairman
F.T. Everard & Sons Limited

Mr. Frederick M. Everard, Mrs. Rosemary A. Shotton and Mr. William D. Everard.

INTRODUCTION

It has been my pleasure to carry out the research and to talk to the many people who, in their own way, have made this book possible. It has also been a privilege to write about a surviving shipping company and, moreover, one which has continued for over one hundred years in the private ownership of four generations of the Everard family. What makes it virtually unique in these days of mergers and takeovers is the fact that the company's affairs continue to be actively directed by that same family. The spirit of the business has always been typified by the restless nature of the founder who could not bear not knowing what the barges he had built were doing. This provided the spur to build and trade a number of barges for himself. In the same way the company made the transition from sail to motor ships, determined to be in the forefront of developments in the constant endeavour to control and operate a fleet of ships.

It must have taken supreme optimism coupled with a compulsion to own ships that drove the company to embark on a building programme during the slump of the thirties when others could only think of scrapping or laying up their ships. Despite the economic situation, not only did the fleet increase but the business expanded with the acquisition of several companies whose activities were related to the main sphere of shipowning and operation.

The founder was once described as "impatient to get things done, yet very careful about what he does". This description exactly characterises the business today; that spirit which built ships during a depression, survived and rebuilt after the war, rode out the vicissitudes of post war trade, and is still alive and eager to accept the challenge of today's changing world.

Many people have been involved with the company over the years and some families have worked for the company for several generations both afloat and ashore. When planning the narrative a decision was made at an early stage that it would be invidious to name some but yet to apparently ignore others equally deserving of recognition. In the event it was decided to name only the members of the Everard family where, to avoid confusion, the modern spelling of the name, adopted in 1917, has been used throughout.

I would like to thank all the people who helped in the preparation of this book, and in particular my wife, Sheila, without whose encouragement and good natured forebearance it would never have been completed. While every effort has been made to ensure accurary and a balanced view, any errors contained herein and the opinions expressed are mine alone.

K.S. GARRETT
East Malling
December 1990

ACKNOWLEDGEMENTS

Many thanks are due to the Everard family and to all the present and former employees of the company who helped in the compilation of this history, in particular the following:

V. Allen, C. Alston, D. Bartholomew, I. Barnicoat, A. Bennett, W. Bowles, C. Burnett, E. Coker, L. Green, J. Harris, P. Humphreys, E. Kimber, A. Kirk, D. Lane, A. Luker, A. Matthews, C. Norman, J. Nunn, A. Scutt, R. South, C. Upfold, J. Urquhart, H. Wadhams and J. Wells.

Others outside the company also provided invaluable assistance and advice, not only the World Ship Society Central Record Team and Photograph Library, but also the following: R. Childs, R. Coates, C. Conway, T. Farnham, A. Hague, H. Higgs, B. Jones, W. Lind, L. Sawyer, R. Schmelzkopf, S. Scott, H. Smith, L. Spurling, D. and E. Wood.

Apart from the company archives, information was obtained from the following sources: World Ship Society Central Record, Lloyds Register of Shipping, National Maritime Museum, Guildhall Library, Port of London Authority Library, Public Record Office, the Registrars of Ships at Hull and London and the Society for Spritsail Barge Research.

The manuscript was kindly read by R. Fenton and K. O'Donoghue and the photographs were provided as acknowledged in the history.

VERONICA winning the 1963 Thames Barge Match. *Company archives*

EVERARD OF GREENHITHE

SAILING BARGE ORIGINS

The company as it is known today came into existence in 1922 with the formation of the limited company by the founder Mr Frederick T. Everard. His three sons, W.J. Everard, F.W. Everard, A.M. Everard, and his daugher, Miss A.E. Everard, joined him as directors of the company. The registered office was at Greenhithe on the site of Keep's barge yard where the founder had worked as the foreman shipwright. Originally he had worked at Keep's other yard at Battersea and when he first moved to Greenhithe he is reputed to have walked all the way with his tools over his shoulder. He had become the yard manager by 1880 when he acquired the yard for himself and continued to build and repair the traditional spritsail barges of the London river.

Content, at first, merely to build and repair these sturdy but elegant craft, the story goes that he became increasingly curious to know what happened to them when they sailed away from his yard. It is therefore not surprising that when faced with the prospect of a bad debt arising from some repair work, and here the story is probably apocryphal, he took a barge in payment and thus became a shipowner. Fanciful or not, the fact remains that in 1892 he acquired the barge INDUSTRY from Thomas Bevan, a cement manufacturer and bargeowner of Northfleet, and proceeded to trade her himself. Apart from being his first known venture into shipowning, the event is also significant because it shows an early contact with the cement industry which has always been important to the company.

It is more probable that the story is confused with the acquisition of his second barge, ELIZABETH. She had been sunk in a collision in 1889 and abandoned by her owner. The wreck was raised by the Thames Conservancy Board from whom the barge was subsequently purchased in 1895.

The first craft to be built at Greenhithe for the company's own account was the coastal sailing barge LORD KITCHENER of 1889. She was followed by several large barges for other owners, some of which were acquired by the company at a later date. Others, for example HERON, LARK and EMU, were owned by the Associated Portland Cement Manufacturers (1900) Ltd., known locally as the Combine, but unfortunately a complete building list does not appear to have survived. Two particularly noteworthy barges were the CAMBRIA and HIBERNIA of 1906, built simultaneously by Mr Will Everard and Mr Fred Everard in a spirit of brotherly rivalry. They had both trained as shipwrights at Greenhithe and at Fellows & Co. at Great Yarmouth. Their brother, Mr Alf Everard, trained as an engineer at Plenty & Son Ltd. at Newbury.

It is said that the HIBERNIA had an extra strake of deck planking on her port side and carried about five tons more cargo than her sister. She drove ashore in a gale off Cromer in 1937 and broke up; whereas CAMBRIA, the last barge to trade under sail alone, is still in existence and is preserved by the Maritime Trust.

The year 1906 also saw the purchase of three sailing barges that had been built in Sweden. Altogether four were built although the difficulties must have been daunting because the Swedes had no experience in building this peculiarly English traditional craft. The engineer in charge of the project at Berqvara had worked for a while in England but it is not known whether he ever visited Greenhithe. The attraction seems to have been the source of abundant and cheap timber for construction and also the bonus of a good paying cargo of timber for the delivery voyage to England. One of the barges remained in Sweden, but the other three were sailed to this country by Swedish delivery crews as the ESSEX, SUSSEX and KENT: all

Launch of **LADY MAUD**: note the Union Jack. *Company archives*

HIBERNIA stranded near Cromer in 1937. *Company archives*

owned by the Berqvara Syndicate Ltd. They were renamed LINA, MARGUERITE and SPENCER on their arrival in England in 1901 and saw long service, the last not being sold until 1950.

EARLY OIL AND STEAM

As the early years of the Twentieth Century passed, developments were taking place in marine propulsion and it must have seemed obvious that a total reliance on wind and tide was becoming a thing of the past. To keep abreast of progress the company's first motor vessel was built at Greenhithe and entered service in 1913. Called GRIT, she was known in the vernacular as a "boomy barge" although the purist description would be an auxiliary ketch with leeboards. She had a small Kromhout engine of 45 hp and like many innovations was viewed by some with suspicion. Her first skipper soon asked for a transfer but whether this was due to the accelerated pace of life or just because he didn't like sharing his cabin with an oil engine, is not certain.

The choice of name for this first motor vessel is interesting and there has been much speculation and many theories on the derivation but very little historical fact. The most promising if somewhat prosaic of these theories is that the word was in jingoistic vogue at the time and was meant to portray the enduring human quality needed to build, operate and sail the vessel. This theory is given some credibility by the names given to subsequent ships and a glance at the names of the early sailing barges purchased from Thomas Bevan gives a clue to the probable derivation of the theme. Another theory suggests that the first GRIT was intended to be one of a pair with the second vessel being called DETERMINATION. As things turned out the first vessel was lost before the second was completed and the latter therefore repeated the earlier name. A further theory referring to the lengthy building period suggests that the name was derived from the initial letters of the phrase Got Ready In Time, but this was almost certainly coined by some wag in the shipyard to suit the second vessel.

The first GRIT did not have a very long life and was sunk by the German submarine UB29 in the English Channel in 1916 when carrying military stores to France. The submarine commander, Oberleutnant zur See Pustkuchen told the crew in perfect English that he had been to school at Canterbury and allowed them to take to their boat within sight of Newhaven before he sank the ship by gunfire having first taken custody of the ship's register. Apparently it took a number of hits before the ship sank and at one stage he asked the survivors what materials had been used in her construction. He received the defiant reply "English oak". The name survived, however, and the last GRIT built in 1976 was the seventh vessel to bear the name. Unfortunately, experience has shown that, as a group, the GRITs have not been lucky ships and four out of the seven have been lost either in collision or by enemy action. Although the name has a powerful sentimental attraction, it is unlikely that, after the loss of GRIT (7) in collision in 1988, the name will be used again.

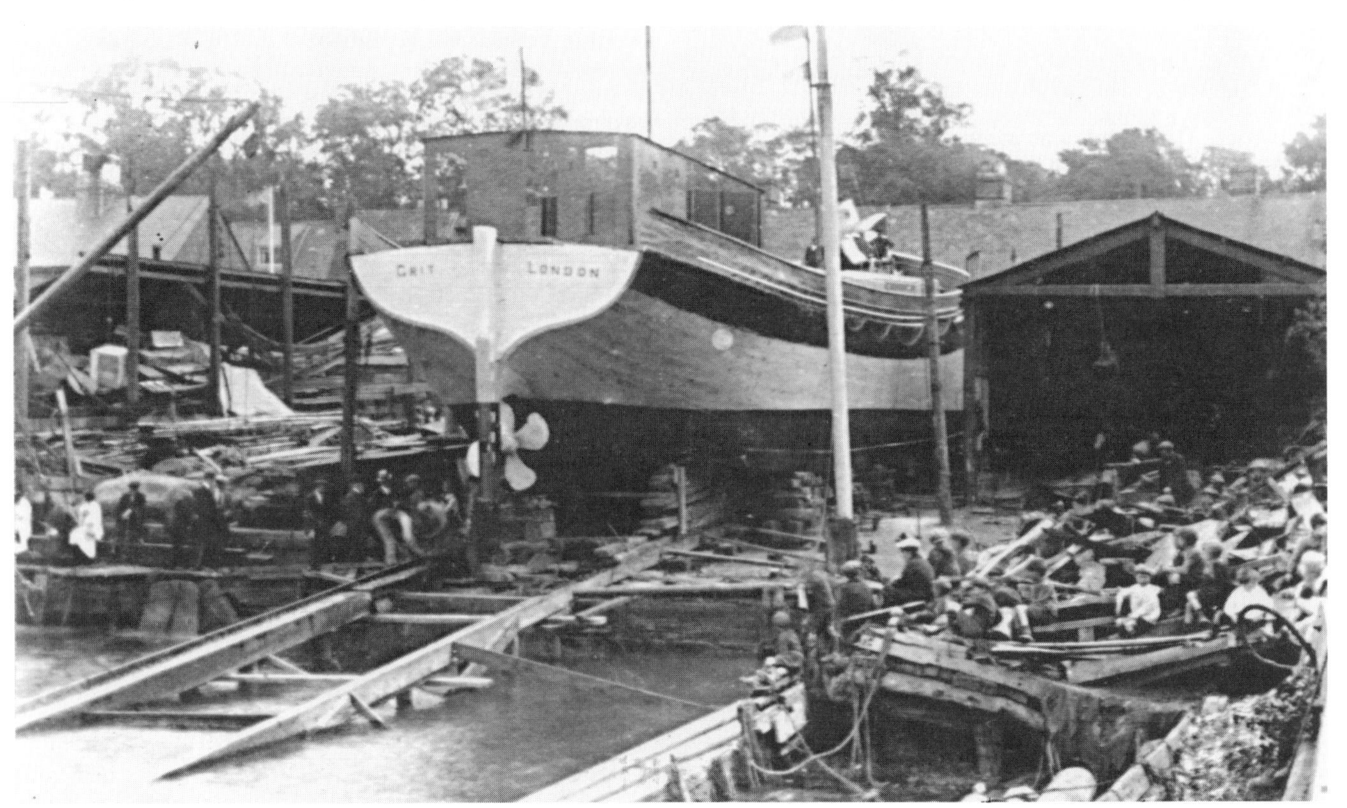

Launch of **GRIT (2)** at Greenhithe. *Company archives*

During the First World War three small dry cargo steam vessels – NORSEMAN, TOSCA and BELLAVALE – were purchased. They were kept busy during the war and in the short post war boom that followed but with the exception of TOSCA they were sold by 1920 to enable the company to concentrate on the development of the coastal motorship. These early steamers together with the sailing barges helped to forge a long term trading link with Van den Berghs Ltd., now part of Unilever plc, by carrying many of their raw materials and finished products, notably Blue Band margarine.

TOSCA was not sold until 1926 and she was replaced immediately by the slightly larger TIRYDAIL, and in 1929 by the GLEN MARY. The reason for buying these second hand steamers when motor ships were being built is not at all clear. It may have been to consolidate certain trades, or more likely, they might just have been bargains. Other dry cargo steamers have been bought, particularly after the Second World War, but it is interesting to note that the company has never built a dry cargo steamship. A number of coastal shipping companies based their whole operation on the purchase of cheap elderly steamships and their success or failure depended on still having some profit in hand after the expenditure on surveys and repairs. The problem was ever present but came to a head with the inevitable special survey when the crucial decision had to be made on whether to scrap or continue trading. However, these early Everard steamships do not seem to have fallen into this category until after their sale by the company.

The development of tankers, however, took a very different path. The work for Van den Berghs' was progressively built up and in 1919 the steam tanker ALCHYMIST was purchased. She had been built to carry wood tar for a firm of timber merchants and the steam heating coils in her cargo tanks were the result of fifty years of testing and experience. Cleaned up and slightly modified, it was found that the technology was transferable to the carriage of edible oils in bulk and the trade was instantly revolutionised by eliminating the need for barrels and all the associated handling costs and leakages. The ship proved very successful and over the next few years four new tankers were ordered whose design was based on the experience gained.

The Town Wharf at Greenhithe about 1910 with the steamer **LOUGHBROU** discharging coal. *E. Coker*

AGILITY was the first of these new tankers, built by George Brown & Co. of Greenock at a cost of £15,350. The link with George Brown was apparently formed during Mr W.J. Everard's wartime naval service in Glasgow and he is said to have stated his intention of building twelve vessels, if not a full baker's dozen, at the Garvel Shipyard. Time proved this to be a conservative statement and in the end no less than twenty-eight vessels were built for the company at Greenock, culminating in the tanker ATONALITY in 1949. After the war the company also purchased three EMPIRE tankers that had been built by George Brown.

The Garvel Shipyard at Greenock in 1939 with, from left to right, yard numbers 212, 211, 210 and 208. *D. Brown*

A family group at the launch of the steam tug **F.T. EVERARD** at Great Yarmouth 1928. From the left: Mr. Frederick T. Everard, Master Frederick A.J.B. Everard, Miss Annie E. Everard, Miss Ethel A. Everard and Mr. and Mrs. Frederick W. Everard.

NAMES

Not only was the AGILITY the first in a long line of tankers built for the company but she also marked the start of the now famous range of names ending in -ITY. These names were originally selected by Miss A.E. Everard from "Nuttalls Standard Pronouncing Dictionary" published by F. Warne & Co. circa 1872. The volume had belonged to her mother, Mrs S.A. Everard, and is still in existence: many of the original names can be seen underlined in pencil.

Since the series was started over one hundred different names have been used, many of them more than once, the majority beginning with A or S but some also with C, F or T. The etymological derivation of some is a little dubious and a few were quite definitely manufactured but nevertheless they created a house style and in retrospect none has turned out to be ridiculous. Some show quite a sense of humour, for example ship number 333 was being built by Fellows at Great Yarmouth where progress was very slow. On one of his regular visits to the yard, Mr W.J. Everard, when asked if he had decided upon a name for the ship, replied that it would be an antique before it entered service. On his next visit he found the name ANTIQUITY painted on the stern. Others like SCARCITY and AUSTERITY described the difficult period when the ships were built just after the Second World War.

Another example of the humorous touch was the name TANKITY which aptly described the little tanker that bore the name. Once the company had decided to adopt names beginning with the letter C the name CITY probably displayed an irresistible brevity. CENTURITY fitted into the scheme in a general way but was manufactured in 1956 for what was considered to be the hundredth ship in the fleet at the time.

All of the various shipping companies taken over by Everards had their own nomenclature but although a few ships had their names changed to fit in with the Everard scheme it is only some J. Hay & Sons Ltd. names that have been used subsequently. Latterly the choice has been confined to S names for the larger dry cargo ships, C names for smaller dry cargo ships and A names for tankers. Family names continue to be used in the dry cargo fleet and also until recently for tugs.

CENTURITY with original yellow hull. *M. Cassar*

Greenhithe about 1930 with the steamer **AGILITY (1)**, a steam tug (probably **FAVEROLLE**), the motor vessel **GRIT (2)** without her funnel and alongside her a Yorkshire keel. The stern of the training ship **WARSPITE** can be seen in the river. *Company archives*

BARGES, TUGS AND LIGHTERS

More sailing barges were purchased during and after the First World War and 1919 saw the peak year when altogether thirty-six were owned. The larger barges operated on coastal voyages mainly on the south and east coasts while their smaller sisters ran river cargoes, in particular cement from the works to big ocean going vessels in the docks for export all over the world. Between the wars a freight of 1/6d per ton was a typical rate for taking cement from Swanscombe or Thurrock to the Royal Docks. An extra charge of 10/-would be made if the barge was required to shift from one dock to another. Occasionally barges would be towed upriver over the tide, probably in response to a call to get the big ship loaded before the weekend, and for this the company would charge an extra £4-10s.

Other sailing barges, usually ones near the end of their useful lives, were engaged in the mud or clay trade. This arduous work of keeping the cement works supplied with one of their raw materials took heavy toll of both men and craft and continued until the mid-1930s. It involved sailing down to the mud holes in the estuary, loading the clay and sailing back to the cement works. Most of the clay was taken to the Tunnel Cement Works at West Thurrock, but the barge would have to take the clay to another cement works if the quality was not considered good enough.

Originally the loading was carried out by a gang of "muddies" using wooden shovels but later a Grafton steam crane, mounted on a pontoon and equipped with a grab, did the job. Although the work was very hard the barge crews, paid by the share system, could earn reasonable money and by working seven days some managed to carry five freights in a week.

Everything had to go just right to achieve this and a certain amount of bribery was involved to ensure the co-operation of the crane drivers at the mud workings and the cement works.

The end of the work came quite suddenly when the cement works obtained alternative sources of supply and the crews were naturally sorry because there was little other work available. The barges, however, were just about worn out and it has been said that after they were laid up at Greenhithe they let out an audible sigh when the ebb tide left them high and dry.

CAPABLE and **GRIT (2)** at Greenhithe. *Company archives*

Shortly after the First World War, two Government surplus steam tugs were purchased together with a number of dry cargo and tank lighters for the river work to augment the sailing barges. Some of the lighters were built in Holland and were purchased on the Thames in what was a Dutch auction in both senses, while others were built for the company at Faversham and Great Yarmouth. A few were specially designed to negotiate creeks and canals leading off the Thames, particularly in the upper reaches. These tugs and the early steamers could often be seen alongside the coaling pontoon with its Grafton steam crane at Greenhithe. The ships, in particular those returning from foreign voyages, would often leave little presents concealed in the crane for the lighterage foreman to ensure future favours.

Over the years other tugs have been acquired and also lighters, some from other lighterage companies who were unable to continue trading. The early demise of the Thames lighterage work has been confidently forecast for a number of years by many authorities but despite everything it still exists, albeit operating at only a fraction of the original level of activity.

In the mid-twenties Mr F.T. Everard demonstrated his passion and belief in sailing barges by ordering from Fellows & Co. Ltd. of Great Yarmouth the four largest barges ever built. They were enlargements of the GREENHITHE design, a barge originally laid down for R. & W. Paul Ltd. of Ipswich in 1923 but completed for Everards and rigged at Greenhithe. These fine barges were named WILL, FRED, ALF and ETHEL EVERARD and were known affectionately as the "iron pots" because of their steel hulls. Between them they put up a number of record passages and also performed very well in the Thames and Medway barge races. The ETHEL was abandoned at Dunkirk in 1940, and the FRED and ALF were cut down and converted into motor coasters. The FRED EVERARD was chartered by the Admiralty as a stores vessel during the war and, stationed at Scapa Flow, she supplied stores and ammunition to H.M.S. HOOD before her fateful last patrol.

Only the WILL EVERARD survived as a sailing barge and she had a small auxiliary engine fitted in 1950. She was sold in 1966 and with her name shortened to WILL is still actively engaged in charter work.

SAILING BARGE MATCHES

The annual barge matches on the Thames and Medway always caused great excitement and Mr F.T. Everard was very keen that his barges should put up a good show; a tradition carried on by his sons. Shortly before the matches in 1929, Mr Everard died and his five entries were withdrawn that year as a mark of respect. He was succeeded by his eldest son Mr F.W. Everard who remained as Chairman until his death in 1964. The success of the Everard barges can be seen by the impressive display of cups and trophies now decorating the boardroom. Up to the Centenary Matches in 1963, after which the Everard barges no longer competed, they had won twenty-two Thames races and twenty-three on the Medway in addition to many second and third places and other awards.

FRED EVERARD and **ETHEL EVERARD** with others on the hard at Greenhithe. *Company archives*

Final touches before the barge match. *Company archives*

Competition was intense with the arch rivals, Goldsmiths, Gills, Horlocks and many other smaller barge owners. The preparations were always very thorough and the competing barges were carefully slipped, cleaned, painted and re-rigged beforehand. The skippers vied with each other to be selected and were then able to choose their own racing crews. The VERONICA was very successful following her purchase in 1932 but was badly damaged in a collision in 1949 and laid as a hulk at Greenhithe for several years. Mr W.J. Everard, watching the 1955 Thames Match from the committee ship ROYAL SOVEREIGN, was very disappointed to see his barge SARA beaten by SIRDAR, and vowed that if the same happened in the following Medway Match he would rebuild VERONICA in time for next year's matches. In the event SIRDAR did win the match and Mr Everard kept his word with a vengeance. VERONICA won the Champion Bowsprit class in both the Thames and the Medway matches in 1956. She repeated the feat in the Centenary Matches in 1963 and was finally sold as a houseboat in 1966. SARA was equally successful and won many matches between her purchase in 1929 and her breaking up in 1964.

THE MOTOR VESSEL GROWS

The second GRIT came into service in 1923. She had taken a long time to build and in all probability she was laid down before the war. When she was launched at Greenhithe in 1921 her wooden hull leaked considerably and she had to be recaulked. She was larger than her predecessor but the essential difference was that she was a genuine, if small, motor coaster. She was not a sailing vessel with an auxiliary engine but a motor vessel that could set some sails to take advantage of a favourable wind.

The ship was relatively short-lived and was run down and sunk in thick fog by the Latvian steamer GAISMA off Hythe in February 1934. In the ensuing court hearing the GRIT was held to be 75 per cent to blame for the collision. The crew were all rescued by the Hythe lifeboat CITY OF NOTTINGHAM and were safely brought ashore at about five o'clock in the morning. Strangely, some of the survivors maintained for many years afterwards that the guilty vessel was in fact the large German passenger vessel EUROPA. It could be coincidence but a study of contemporary Lloyds Lists shows that the EUROPA must have passed through the area at about the right time when inward bound to Bremen from New York having made a short stop at Southampton.

Around the time in the early twenties, when the second GRIT came into service, a number of other small motor vessels were purchased. Amongst these were four ex-Government vessels known as X Lighters or "Beetles". Inspired by Admiral Sir John Fisher and Winston Churchill they had been designed by Walter Pollock and over two hundred were built in shipyards all over the country in 1915, many being used in the ensuing Dardanelles campaign. Their engines came from a number of sources including J. & C.G. Bolinders Co. of Stockholm where overtime had to be worked to complete the order, so great was the pressure to get the ships built. They were forerunners of the Second World War landing craft and were designed around the dimensions of the army howitzer carriage. When completed some were converted into tankers and given names, those purchased by Everards being LOBSTER, OYSTER, MUSSEL and SHRIMP. These shellfish names were changed to curiously pedestrian names and they became ROAM, WANDER, RAMBLE and SAUNTER. As completed they had flush decks and bowboards. The first two named foundered

Mr. Frederick W. Everard and Mr. William J. Everard.

Company archives

Greenhithe. *From an Ordnance Survey map of 1910*

in bad weather and it was thought that the bowboards were a contributory factor, holding the water on deck and preventing it from clearing in heavy seas. The remaining two had half height fo'c'sle heads built on to improve their seakeeping qualities.

Gradually the yard at Greenhithe was expanded by the purchase of adjacent properties and wharves. Its position with repair facilities poised midway between the estuary and the upriver wharves and the enclosed docks gave the company many natural advantages. Despite the deep economic depression the company still managed to expand the fleet of motor ships throughout the twenties and thirties. The majority of the new vessels came from the Garvel Shipyard of George Brown & Co. Ltd. at Greenock but a number were also built by Fellows & Co. Ltd. at Great Yarmouth. Everards had become financially associated with Fellows and also the neighbouring engineering works of Crabtree & Co. in 1931, although the controlling interest was not acquired until 1948. Both the companies at Great Yarmouth were sold in 1970.

Although the sailing barges were still carrying a considerable amount of cargo right up to the outbreak of war in 1939 their numbers were declining: the heyday of the Everard barges as trading vessels had occurred in the early twenties. Meanwhile the steamships and motor vessels were making an ever increasing contribution. Not being dependent upon the wind they made generally faster and more predictable passages and would negotiate narrow rivers unaided where a sailing barge would probably need the assistance of a tug. The new ships made a speciality of trading to places where it was said that it was only possible to get alongside the wharf if there had been a heavy dew.

CARGOES AND TRADES

The ships carried cement to builders' merchants up and down the coast, grain and cattlefeed, bricks from Belgium for the developing London suburbia, stone from the West Country for the new Lambeth Bridge, china clay and roadstone also from the West Country. But the largest single commodity carried at this time was coal. It was taken to gas works, power stations and to merchants for sale as domestic house coal in ports all around the coast.

An early coal contract was to supply the Margate Gas Works with coal from Keadby on the River Trent.

ACRITY, ACTIVITY, ASEITY and **SAGACITY (1)** discharging coal at the Norwich Power Station.

D. Brown

Everard ships at Bideford. *Company archives*

The trade from Keadby to Margate, Norwich, Exeter and elsewhere continued into the fifties when the ships, all of them small, were carrying over one million tons annually to various gas works. This work ended more or less overnight when, by new processes, gas was produced from oil instead of coal. This unbalanced other trades: for example, a cargo of coal to Norwich was often followed by a cargo of sugar from the factory at nearby Cantley, a trade that again had existed for a number of years but was now no longer viable.

Coal declined as a fuel for power stations and for domestic uses at about the same time but the trade did not completely cease. A number of factors meant that coal staged a recovery in the early eighties and is once again a major coastwise cargo.

Some ships were built to cope with the restrictions of particular trades or berths and when all went well they got on with the job and did not make any headlines. When things went wrong, however, the reverse could be embarrassingly true. A case in point was the AQUEITY, built in 1934 to carry coal up the Exeter Canal to the gas works. Unfortunately a mistake had been made in the dimensions and on her maiden voyage the ship stuck fast in the Countess Wear Bridge cutting. Two more vessels were hastily ordered and built to the correct dimensions to redeem the mistake.

The tankers were also busy, not only building on the success of carrying edible oils for Unilever but also with petroleum products for the major oil companies. They often traded away from the confines of the home coast to the Baltic and beyond. A further tanker innovation was the building of the ACCLIVITY in 1931. Her profile was kept very low to enable her to negotiate the bridges on the River Seine during her voyages with edible oil from Zwijndrecht to Paris. One of her special features was the provision of double bottom ballast tanks which was unusual in small ships at that time and particularly rare in small tankers. They were needed to overcome the problem of the low bridges and to ease the problem of cleaning the cargo tanks but nevertheless anticipated the general use of segregated ballast tanks in coastal tankers by nearly fifty years. Another feature of her design was the very large daily service fuel oil tank which enabled the ship to make the return passage from Le Havre to Paris without drawing fuel from the main bunker tanks and therefore incurring customs duty. Apart from the trade for which she was built, the ship carried edible oil cargoes to many ports on the east coast. Because of her low air draft she was known as the submarine and on voyages to the Thames was said to submerge at the Hook of Holland and surface again at Southend.

A look through some of the early motor ship journals is both nostalgic and interesting with their voyages, cargoes, freight earnings, demurrages and expenses all set out in remarkably legible handwriting which seems to convey much more feel and understanding than today's soulless computer print-out accounts. Oil cake from London to Truro at eleven shillings per ton, stone from Newlyn to Margate at five shillings, coal from Keadby to Norwich at five shillings and sixpence. The cargoes and ports are familiar but it is as well that the freight rates have improved.

Another familiar feature of these old journals are the names of the ships' agents in the various ports. Some, no doubt, are long departed and others swallowed up in mergers but many are still in business and are in extensive use today including Oughtred & Harrison of Hull, Smalls of Great Yarmouth, Whartons of Keadby, Garland & Flexman of King's Lynn, Cooks of Aberdeen, Watsons of Rochester, Sandells of Southampton, Tamlyns of Plymouth and Falmouth, Bennetts of Penzance and until recently, Harris of Par and Hannan, Samuel of Fowey.

The expansion of the fleet was steady rather than meteoric and was built on a sound financial base. The ships of the period were all purchased for cash with the company holding all the sixty-four shares – unlike the situation before the limited company was formed when individual family members held the shares of some of the ships. Once sufficient money had been accumulated the specification would be decided and an order would be placed for a new ship. Despite all the activity, money was very short and if the freight on a particular cargo had not been paid it was occasionally necessary to obtain a loan from local tradesmen to pay the wages at Greenhithe. The costings for new ships were also very tight and in 1933 a ship from George Brown was cancelled because the Chancellor of the Exchequer had increased the tax on fuel oil in his budget. However, all the ships were financed from the company's own resources and it was not until 1970, and the building of the SECURITY (2) at Hessle, that outside sources of finance were used.

LIFE ON BOARD

Life on the new ships might have been a little easier than on the sailing barges but by present day standards it was pretty tough. Many of the early vessels had open bridges known as "pneumonia wheelhouses" with only a canvas dodger as protection from the elements but in fairness some of the older seafarers preferred them and did not like to be boxed in. Accommodation was spartan and the crews provided their own bedding; often a straw filled bag and a couple of blankets. The sailors and firemen generally lived and ate in the fo'c'sle, which in bad weather could be very unpleasant and was frequently flooded: a keen eye coupled to nimble footwork was required to deliver cooked food from the galley. Lighting and heating was rudimentary with oil lamps providing the former and a temperamental coke stove sometimes known as a "bogie" provided heat and required more or less constant attention. Fresh water was precious and was pumped by hand to a tank above the galley from where it could be collected by bucket for washing or the weekly dhobie. Stokeholds were lit by evil smelling duck lamps that only provided the barest minimum of illumination.

Even taking inflation into account wages were poor by today's standards and following on from the barges the crews of the smaller ships were paid on the share system, a basic "payment by results" that probably had its origins with the Phoenicians. In this case, half of the freight earnings less half of the expenses were divided amongst the officers according to agreed percentages. The master not only got the highest percentage but also received a gratuity of one guinea for each cargo. Payments were made to the officers to compensate them for the extra fuel used if, as frequently happened, they were called upon to tow a sailing barge. The ratings received a weekly wage and everybody had to pay for their own food and insurance stamps. The Second World War brought many changes and improvements but much in the way of creature comforts had to wait for the occasional cyclical boom in the post-war years.

One of the features of life on board the vessels was the frequent visits made by one or other of the Everard family. Always eager to see their ships and to take any note of their condition they would arrive, unheralded, in the most unlikely places and usually at weekends. Many crews were caught unawares and disciplined for relaxing their efforts and none more so than the captain of the second GRIT who was enjoying himself in Par, the Cornish china clay port, one Bank Holiday Monday. Few would have had the imagination or temerity to make his reply. Mr W.J. Everard arrived with his family only to find that the captain was not on board, and the deck boy was despatched to summon him from the town. Eventually he arrived with what was described as "minimum ullage" having indulged himself freely at a local hostelry. Mr Everard could see the prospect of a lively interchange and quickly ushered his family into the motor car. Imagine his surprise when having remonstrated with the captain for his obvious insobriety, he heard himself being blamed for having placed the captain in such moral turpitude by leaving the ship in port over a bank holiday when it should have been at sea and earning money.

CAPABLE nears completion at Greenhithe. Note the compass adjuster on the open bridge. *Company archives*

A six cylinder 'P' type Mark 2 engine, the most powerful produced at Newbury.

Company archives

ENGINES FROM NEWBURY

All the new motor ships had engines built at the Newbury works of Plenty & Son Ltd., later known as Plenty-Still Oil Engines Ltd. The two early GRITs had Dutch designed Kromhout engines that were made under licence at Newbury between 1912 and 1920. The Plenty engines that followed these were very similar at first but much development took place in both auxiliary and propelling machinery. Everards had come to rely on Plenty for engines and spare parts when, in 1931, the engine builders were forced into liquidation. In 1932 the works were acquired by Everards and the name changed to the Newbury Diesel Co. Ltd., and further supplies of machinery were assured. The engines from Newbury were generally supplied by the company to a shipyard so that the price of a ship rarely included the cost of the engine.

Shortly after the takeover, production of the famous range of Sirron engines commenced, the first of which was works number 641 and was installed in the APRICITY built by George Brown in 1933. The name Sirron was simply the name of the designer spelt backwards. These engines were developed through various types until 1967 although the Newbury company continued in the field of control engineering until sold in 1987. Probably the most famous of the Sirron engines was the 'O' type which was in production from 1941 until 1967. The final engine, the four stroke 'T' type, did not get beyond the prototype stage when it had to be conceded that there were insufficient resources available for development to compete successfully with the large volume engine builders and reluctantly the building of engines ceased at Newbury. SUPREMITY, then building in Holland, was to have had the first 'T' type engines but instead received machinery by British Polar Engines Ltd.

ODD MEN OUT

Although the building programme was in full swing in the immediate pre-war years with new ships from the yards of George Brown and Fellows, the company still acquired the occasional ship from elsewhere. Two of these, the small dry cargo steamers SNOWCRETE and HARTFORD, were purchased from the Cement Marketing Co. Ltd. late in 1936. They were kept long enough to consolidate the trade they had been engaged in and were then sold in 1937.

Later that year the SEQUACITY came into service, an event perhaps not too noteworthy at the time but which had considerable historical significance because she was the first of the company's ships to be built at Goole. She was originally laid down as a speculative venture by the shipyard and was acquired at a late stage, the company having little influence on the design or the choice of engine. The ship herself was short lived and was sunk in May 1940 by the plunging shot from enemy shore batteries at Cap Gris Nez while on passage to Dunkirk to assist with the evacuation of the B.E.F. She was the prototype for the EMPIRE CLIFF class of 1940 and the slightly larger ABILITY and AMENITY of 1943.

Another acquisition just prior to the war was a ship quite outside the mainstream of development but which, nevertheless, survived as a successful unit of the fleet for twenty years. Originally laid down in 1932 as a steamer for their own account by R. Williamson & Son at Workington she had laid on the stocks incomplete since the yard closed until Everards purchased the hull. Apparently there was quite a lot of undergrowth to be cleared from around the ship before the ways could be prepared for her launch as SODALITY in April 1938. No engine had been installed and the stern tube was blanked off to make the ship seaworthy. As yard number 244, she was the last ship to be built by Williamson's yard whose closure meant the end of shipbuilding in the area although the purchase of the ship by Everards raised vain local hopes that the shipyard would be reactivated. The hull was towed around to Goole where she was completed.

SODALITY on trials off Grimsby in 1938. *Company archives*

Instead of the intended steam machinery the ship was fitted with a seven cylinder 'L' type engine from the Newbury Diesel Co. Ltd. This engine, works number 708, had been intended for the tug S A EVERARD then building at Great Yarmouth but instead the tug was fitted with a similar but more powerful eight cylinder unit. The ship's engine seatings had to be redesigned to take the diesel engine which had to be set higher than usual to line up with the shaft aperture and it was possible to pass underneath the engine to get from one side of the engineroom to the other.

Early in the war the ship took cargoes of cased petrol to France until the evacuation began. She then took food to Dunkirk and returned with soldiers. Returning again with food, it was too late because Dunkirk had fallen and she took her cargo to Ramsgate instead to feed the many survivors who had been landed there.

The ship survived the war and took part in the Normandy invasion. Towards the end of her life she was laid up at Greenhithe and was used by ships' crews in transit elsewhere; meanwhile many items were removed including the main engine which was reconditioned and later installed in the tug R A EVERARD. The ship's hull, for little else remained, was finally sold for scrap in 1958.

A notable casualty in pre-war days was the George Brown built motor vessel ACTUOSITY. She was launched on a Friday and was always considered to be an unlucky ship. No Everard ship has since been launched on a Friday and the name is most unlikely to be repeated. On the fateful voyage in November 1934 the ship had discharged at Cardiff and was bound, in ballast, to King's Lynn. Such a long voyage in ballast must in itself have been a dead loss commercially and illustrated the difficulties being experienced by coastal shipping at that time. The weather was bad with a south westerly gale when at about 0400 somewhere off Ilfracombe the crankshaft seized and the main engine was immobilised. Most of the crew had served in sailing ships and using their experience they jury-rigged some sails using hatch tarpaulins and the ship's derricks, with the idea of bringing the ship to a safe anchorage in the more sheltered waters to the east of Barry on the South Wales coast. Somehow they managed to get across the Bristol Channel using wind and tide but unfortunately the tide turned at a crucial moment and it became obvious that the ship was not going to reach shelter. About 1700 both anchors were dropped but due to the severity of the weather they dragged and eventually the ship ended up on a rocky shelf hard against a low cliff near Llantwit Major. She defied all attempts at refloating until eventually wooden ways were driven underneath, greased with huge quantities of tallow and she was finally launched broad-side on with the aid of hydraulic jacks. The ship was then towed into Swansea where repairs to the bottom and the engine were carried out. She was an early loss during the war and sank off Cromer after striking a submerged object in October 1940.

ACTUOSITY aground near Llantwit Major in 1934. *R. Seaman*

EVERARDS AT WAR

By the outbreak of war in 1939 the fleet had been built up to thirty-six motor ships, seven steamships, three tugs, twenty-four sailing barges and a large number of lighters and service craft. During the war over fifty ships were managed at one time or another for the Government. The company had no respite throughout the war and the ships were engaged in the Norwegian campaign, the evacuation from Dunkirk, many English Channel and North Sea convoys, the D-Day landings and the liberation of Europe. A total of twenty-two ships did not survive the war and two of the managed ships were also lost. A special memorial is maintained in the parish church at Greenhithe for those Everard employees who lost their lives during the war.

The London office was moved from Great Tower Street to Fenchurch Buildings after an air-raid in 1941 and the Chartering Department remained there until 1984 when more convenient accommodation was found in the Baltic Exchange Chambers in St Mary Axe. This move was relatively short lived and in 1989 the London office again moved, this time outside the City and from the prestigious but expensive EC3 to Elder Street in E1.

The Greenhithe office and the adjacent shipyard remained on the same site and there was a total commitment to repair war-damaged ships and to keep the fleet running efficiently. The shipyard also built two Mark 3 tank landing craft for the Government, 334 launched in early 1942 and 364 launched a year later. All of this was no easy achievement with the wartime shortages, air-raids, the demands of firewatching and duties with the local Home Guard to contend with. About this time some design work was carried out by Fellows' drawing office for the construction of three dry cargo coasters although no reference can be found to the proposed building yards. They were allocated the yard numbers 101, 192 and 193 which indicates that two yards were involved, neither of them being Fellows. The design was very similar to the George Brown-built SUMMITY and SUPREMITY, both of which entered service in 1939. These three ships were almost certainly never built and will probably remain a mystery but later, shortly after the end of the war, a similar vessel which could have been number 101 was laid down at Greenhithe using steel prepared at Great Yarmouth. Work proceeded very slowly, there rarely being more than two or three men allocated to the job, which was eventually abandoned with little more than the keel, some floors and intercostals and a few frames in position.

Everard ships were involved in the war right from the start. The SERENITY had the misfortune to be the first loss when she was attacked by enemy aircraft and sunk off Whitby in December 1939. A few months later, in May 1940, the ACCLIVITY had an incredible escape when she was discharging whale oil in Zwijndrecht, a port where she was a frequent visitor.

The guns of the invading German forces could be heard and it was decided not to wait to finish the discharge but to cut and run. The ship was fired upon as she passed through Rotterdam and out past the Hook of Holland where she probably sailed straight through a minefield. The captain had asked for details the day before but had been told that the Dutch charts had already been destroyed. The ship arrived in the Thames the next day largely unscathed and survived the war although she was in the thick of things on many occasions.

The ANTIQUITY was fitted out as a rescue ship early in the war with extra food stores and water tanks. The cargo hold was strewn with straw to afford a minimum of creature comfort. The ship was sent to Granville to pick up any British survivors but none could be found either there or at St Malo so the ship returned empty to Weymouth where she was given orders to proceed to St Helier.

The ship arrived during the afternoon of 20th June 1940 and people who had previously registered at the Town Hall as voluntary refugees were allowed to board. An unbelievable number of four hundred and seventy-five refugees embarked and the ship sailed for Weymouth later that evening. The captain gave his cabin to a lady who was in an advanced state of pregnancy and although all the necessary preparations were made the birth did not take place on board and the lady was taken to hospital as soon as the ship arrived back in Weymouth with the best wishes and undoubted relief of the whole crew. The ship returned to the Channel Islands but any further evacuation was refused because by that time the occupation of the islands was imminent and it was considered too dangerous. Later the ANTIQUITY took part in many convoys including CW8 in July 1940 that was so badly mauled by enemy aircraft in the Straits of Dover that the surviving ships were anchored in isolation off the Isle of Wight for a while in what was believed at the time to be an attempt to suppress the bad news.

ANTIQUITY after the war.

D. Hocquard

SUMMITY (1) on the beach at Dover in July 1940 after being bombed. Note the armoured wheelhouse and degaussing coils.

Company archives

Another member of that fateful convoy was the SUMMITY with a cargo of cement. She received a direct hit from a Stuka dive bomber and although the cement cargo deadened the explosion to a certain extent she was obviously going to sink so while she still retained steerage way the captain turned out of the convoy and managed to beach her under Shakespeare Cliff. She was later towed into Dover, what remained of the cargo discharged and the ship made seaworthy enough to be towed away for repairs.

Early in the war the ACRITY was requisitioned on a T99A charter for use as a naval stores vessel and at very short notice was loaded with ammunition and ordered to sail for Norway, regardless of the fact that none of the crew possessed the necessary certificates to proceed outside the Home Trade Limits. The ship, escorted by two armed trawlers, took a very circuitous route to Harstad Fjord and arrived during an aerial bombardment but discharged her cargo safely. She returned home and later spent two years at anchor loaded with ammunition as a floating reserve store.

The ARIDITY was mined in the Thames Estuary in October 1940 when inward bound with a cargo of wheat. The sea suction valves were blown in by the force of the explosion and the engine room was wrecked but all the crew managed to escape safely. The ship did not sink but drifted ashore and the SEDULITY was sent downriver to stand by her stricken sister until she could be towed up to Greenhithe by a tug. Later, repaired and with a new engine, the ship was present at the Normandy landings despite having been officially classified as a war loss.

SEDULITY herself was often in the thick of things, particularly on the East Coast. In early February 1942 bound from Cantley to Selby with sugar she was about to anchor for the night off Cromer when attacked by German aircraft. A bomb went right through the ship but the ensuing explosion lifted the steering quadrant off the rudder stock. The machine gunning that followed shot through the rod and chain steering gear in several places. Two wounded men were put ashore at Cromer and the ship proceeded towards Great Yarmouth under tow of the motor vessel CHARLES M. The steering gear had been temporarily repaired but unfortunately failed just in the harbour entrance, the two ships going on opposite sides of the pier, but all ended safely.

On another occasion at the Wells anchorage an aeroplane was sighted and identified as friendly. This turned out to be a big mistake and the German dropped a stick of four bombs close astern rocking the SEDULITY violently. No great damage was sustained but the blast disintegrated all the WC pans while in the galley a row of hanging cups was shattered leaving most of the handles still dangling from the hooks. The ship, on passage from Blyth to Norwich with coal, managed to get to Great Yarmouth for repairs.

Another early casualty was SUPREMITY. She entered service in November 1939 and thus did not appear in the company livery but spent her short life in wartime grey. She appears to have been a busy ship because in her thirteen months' existence she spent three weeks fitting defensive equipment and yet still carried thirty-nine cargoes. She took coal to Rouen on her maiden voyage and this was the only foreign port she ever visited. In early December 1940 she loaded coal at Blyth for London and proceeded south in convoy FS53. Entering the Thames Estuary on the afternoon of 6th December, she detonated a mine near the East Oaze Buoy and immediately began to settle. There were no casualties but later when the ship was being abandoned the chief engineer fell overboard and disappeared. The survivors managed to row to the wreck of a larger vessel, HOUSTON CITY, to seek shelter from the bitter weather and throwing blackout precautions aside a fire was kindled for warmth. The second engineer, clad only in his thin engineroom clothes was so numb with cold that standing too close to the fire he did not notice that his trousers had caught alight. At dawn they explored the wreck and found some flares which were seen by the approaching escort trawler HMS LARCH just before she used the wreck for some gunnery practice.

WARTIME MANAGEMENT

Everards managed over fifty vessels for the Ministry of Shipping and its successor the Ministry of War Transport from 1940 until after the end of the war. In general the company was concerned with the technical and personnel aspects while various ministries carried out much of the chartering. The first ships to be managed were two small Danish auxiliary schooners which, although put under the British flag in 1940,

EMPIRE CADET: the name ship of the class. *A. Dickson*

retained their Danish crews. The RUTH II at one time had an Australian army gunner on board to complete the cosmopolitan picture.

Other dry cargo vessels and tankers followed, mainly from Goole, and then in 1942 the company was appointed manager of EMPIRE DWELLER and a little later EMPIRE AUDREY. These tankers were built at Greenock by George Brown, a builder well known to the company. The lead ship of the class, EMPIRE RUBY, had originally been intended for Everards' management but was transferred to Elder Dempster Lines Ltd. The ship went out to the West African coast where a tanker was required and where Elder Dempsters had considerable influence and experience. The ship was yard number 217 which was originally intended for an Everard dry cargo coaster but wartime priorities had forced the cancellation of this in favour of the first of the three repeats of an earlier tanker design and built to the Ministry account.

EMPIRE CLIFF and EMPIRE FORELAND were based on the earlier SEQUACITY and were forerunners of the later ABILITY and AMENITY. Gradually the MOWT transferred these and other dry cargo vessels to the management of other owners, enabling Everards to concentrate on tankers. EMPIRE BOY from Goole was the first of a number of steam tankers with others coming from the Grangemouth Dockyard Co. Ltd. and A & J Inglis Ltd. of Glasgow, most of them being units of the EMPIRE CADET class. Another group were the six American T1-M-A1 tankers. They were given the names of American oilfields like WALNUT BEND and RIO BRAVO which all sounded quite exotic to British ears. They had engines, accommodation and the bridge aft, which had the appearance of being rather high and collectively they were given the nickname "Queen Annes Mansions" presumably after the tall London building of that name used by the Admiralty during the war. The survivors went to the Mediterranean and later to the Far East as the war moved on and in keeping with Ministry policy the management was transferred to companies with local experience. It was also Ministry policy to allocate ships for management that were much the same size as the company's own ships although there were many exceptions including in Everard's case EMPIRE PYM and EMPIRE GANGES, both of which were much larger than contemporary Everard vessels.

By far the largest group numerically were the somewhat prosaically named CHANTs. Of prefabricated construction, they were intended for the invasion of Europe and apparently the name was derived from Channel Tanker. It would appear that the original intention was to build sixty-eight of them, all named CHANT followed by a number (omitting 13). At an early stage it was decided to complete twenty-five of them as dry cargo ships and instead of CHANT numbers they were given FABRIC numbers, but these too were changed in favour of EMPIRE F names before the ships were completed. Although there was an undoubted demand for such vessels after the war, the Government refused to sell any of these basic little tankers for operation by British owners although a number were acquired by British brokers before being finally sold abroad. The reason behind this policy is unknown but it did not prevent Everards from purchasing two from their foreign owners in later years. With the names AUSPICITY and AVERITY, they traded for another eighteen years before disposal.

With the advance of the Allied forces a number of German vessels were taken as prizes and amongst these eight small naval tankers were given EMPIRE names and allocated to Everards for management although in some cases this management only extended to a voyage across the North Sea or perhaps organising the inward clearance with the customs. Shortly after the war, when an official distribution of the victors' spoils was made, four of these tankers were handed over to the USSR.

During the war, in 1943, the firm of Nash & Miller Ltd. was acquired together with Pelican Wharf at Wapping. The company also owned some elderly sailing barges of which only one, the MONA, was still active and she was sold in 1946. The company name was changed to Everard Maritime Services Ltd. in 1954 and the wharf itself was sold in 1969.

EMPIRE SHOAL at Dieppe in 1945.

H. Jones

Many of the company's vessels took part in the invasion of Europe in 1944 and a large composite painting by Frank H. Mason celebrates the occasion by showing them all with a few attendant escort vessels. One convoy alone, ETC8 which sailed from Southend on 13th June 1944, contained three Everard vessels, ABILITY, SIGNALITY and SEDULITY, bound for the Sword and Juno beaches.

PLANNING FOR PEACE

Eventually the war came to an end and the company could look forward and plan for the future. These plans were tinged with sadness for in 1945 Mr. Alf Everard, the youngest son of the founder, died. The post-war construction commenced with the building of ships at Goole and Grangemouth where contacts had been made during the war, whilst a number of EMPIRE ships were purchased from the Government, some of which had been managed for the Ministry of War Transport.

By far the largest group of former Government vessels were the nine dry cargo FABRIĊ or EMPIRE F class ships. As a departure from previous naming policy but, for obvious reasons, they were all given names beginning with the letter F. They served the company well and carried a wide variety of cargoes to many of the smaller coastal and upriver ports until 1961 when they began to be sold for scrap, it being considered too expensive to put them through their third special surveys. As often happens with a large class of ships, they tended to collect their own characters and folklore. Some of the most amusing yet plausible concern the skipper of one who must have been a frustrated farmer at heart. His wheelhouse was festooned with tomato plants and boxes of seedlings and when on passage upriver to Norwich he would often put his ship into the bank and jump ashore to set a few snares. He would collect his catch a day or two later on his way downstream. But he surely set his sights too high when he acquired a piglet which was housed in a small compartment at the stern. The animal was well fed and put on so much weight that it could not be extricated and had to be slaughtered *in situ* by a butcher at Keadby. However, his party piece concerned some chicks or ducklings (opinions vary) that he was raising in his cabin. Due to understandable complaints from the crew, they were banished to the forecastle space that also incorporated the chainlocker. Inevitably, shortly after their incarceration the anchor had to be let go in an emergency before the unfortunate birds could be caged. As the anchor cable roared out of the spurling pipe it was accompanied by a cloud of feathers and other fowl pieces. So many people claim to have seen the episode that it must have been performed in front of a large audience but nevertheless there is probably more than a grain of truth in the story.

One of the chief engineers also became something of a legend. For reasons best known to himself he always slept on the deck of his cabin and, a late riser in port, he would emerge resplendent in a dressing gown. By this time his breakfast would be thoroughly dried out in the hotpress and he incensed the cook by unceremoniously dumping it overboard. These were the days when crews had to buy their own food and he maintained that as he had paid for it he could do what he liked with it. Nevertheless he was a clever engineer and in his spare time he worked on a perpetual motion machine. He professed to have no faith in the internal combustion engine and as a precaution always hired two taxis to take him to the station when he went on leave.

Mr. Alfred M. Everard. *Company archives*

EMPIRE FANAL: a typical member of the class. *R. Dunston Ltd.*

The continuing personnel management of the LADY KATHLEEN for Concrete Maritime Ltd. meant that the company was, the first time, managing other owners' ships in peacetime. The ship was sold to Norwegian owners in 1948 and was wrecked off Riga after dragging her anchor in November 1951. The crew were saved from the perils of the sea only to be interned for a while before they were repatriated. Although many coastal companies were active in ship management in both pre- and post-Second World War days, Everards' efforts in this direction did not really start until the building of the DAVID and EDGAR DORMAN in 1978. Since then many ships have been managed for a variety of owners. In most cases, all three elements of management have been carried out, although in the case of a few ships where the owners had captive "in house" cargoes or charters only the technical and personnel elements have been involved.

The title of manager when applied to ships is capable of wide interpretation and there are several different forms of management depending upon the particular aspect of ship operation in question. There are three main elements of ship management; commercial, technical and personnel and while many owners carry out all three directly or through a subsidiary management company, there are other owners who subcontract particular elements to outside specialists. Each of these specialists can be said to be the ship's manager in the particular element or elements that they cover. Thus a ship can have more than one manager each dealing with his own element. In the absence of an accepted definition, classification societies often rationalise the situation by naming as the manager the company or individual who pays the survey fees and apparently requires the various classification certificates and other official documents, but there is little uniformity.

For British ships there is also a quite separate and distinct legal requirement to specify the ship's manager laid down in Section 59 of the Merchant Shipping Act 1894. The manager recorded in the Mercantile Navy List is the person who is responsible for ensuring that all safety and legal requirements are met and who, of course, can be arraigned if things go wrong.

As in earlier days, the Everard calendar was eagerly awaited each Christmas with its twelve reproductions of Frank H. Mason paintings of the company's ships. These calendars were distributed far and wide to shippers, brokers, agents, official organisations and others across the whole spectrum of coastal shipping. The painting of the month was also reproduced on the back cover of the well-known "Sea Breezes" magazine. It was said that newsagents placed the magazines face downwards on the counter to enhance their sales. Many of the paintings were also reproduced as postcards and were used to confirm cargo fixtures originally made by telephone. Thousands must have been sent out to agents and brokers all over the country. The postcards, like the calendars, became collectors' items and spread the company's name far beyond the confines of the industry. Today the calendars, still much in demand although larger in size, consist of only four illustrations.

YARMOUTH AND GOOLE

In 1948 the controlling interest was acquired in Fellows & Co. Ltd. and Crabtree (1931) Ltd., both of Great Yarmouth. With them came the associated shipping agency, Gorleston Port & Dock Co. Ltd., whose name was changed to Anglian Marine Services Ltd. in 1965. Ships were built and repaired at Great Yarmouth until the shipyard and works were sold in 1970. Fellows also built a number of tank and dry cargo lighters for the Thames lighterage business. On completion, these craft were towed around to London by the company's own ships. At one time Great Yarmouth probably ranked next to London in commercial importance to the company and, apart from the numerous ships passing close to the port on their way up and down the east coast or across the North Sea, many ships loaded and discharged their cargoes there. Many more passed through on their way to deliver coal to the power station at Norwich and then again on their way back out to sea with beet sugar from Cantley. This trade fell away in the late sixties and hence the decline in importance of Great Yarmouth to the company's operations. The convenient position of the port is still recognised and occasionally a ship which has discharged a cargo but is not fixed for the next will be instructed to proceed to Yarmouth Roads for orders. This gives the Chartering Department a little more time and the ship will be well placed to take advantage of whatever opportunity may present itself.

Due to their frequent visits to Great Yarmouth it is not surprising that a number of the crews were either local men or had married local girls. There is a story that a local widow with ten daughters often took them to a public house frequented by sailors. Eventually she managed to get them all married but there is no known record of how many became wives of Everard sailors.

During the disastrous East Coast floods of 1953 the SEDULITY and FLEXITY were alongside together at Great Yarmouth. The river was so high that baulks of timber pulled from the river had to be jammed between the ships and the quay to stop them from ending up on the dockside. The SIGNALITY with a crew of East Anglians was at anchor in the roads and they were worried about the situation ashore. The master of the SEDULITY managed to obtain news of their families and relayed this to them using the ship's radio.

HILARITY: tender to **SINGULARITY** at the 1953 Coronation Review at Spithead. *Company archives*

TRADE EXPANDS

Apart from the two large vessels, SUPREMITY and SUPERIORITY built at Goole, most of the post-war built ships had been relatively small and much the same as their pre-war sisters. However, in 1949 the building programme took a big step forward with the construction of the STABILITY at Goole. Although this ship and her sister SECURITY were originally painted black they were soon changed to yellow and with the other ten similar vessels of the class were collectively known as the "Yellow Perils".

In many respects they were diminutives of the two earlier vessels from Goole but they achieved a better aesthetic balance and were handsome looking vessels that set new standards in coastal ship design, crew accommodation and sea-keeping qualities. At about 1,800 deadweight tons they achieved a number of operational economies not enjoyed by their two larger predecessors by being measured at just below 1,600 gross tons. This is one of the important tonnage points in the SOLAS (Safety of Life at Sea) regulations beyond which a ship must carry additional crew and equipment. In this particular case it would have meant carrying a radio officer, a full radiotelegraphy station and a radio direction finder. A ship of 1,599 gross tons would normally be equipped with just a radiotelephone operated by the deck officers who would hold the necessary radiotelephony certificates.

Early in 1953 the SINGULARITY, built the year before at Goole, was taken in hand at Greenhithe and prepared to represent coastal shipping at the Coronation Review at Spithead. The holds were thoroughly cleaned out and temporary dormitory accommodation constructed to house all the company's guests. A motorboat, HILARITY, for use as a tender was also prepared down to the last detail with polished brass fairleads and goldleaf for the mast truck and name boards. The ship was finally painted white and looking very elegant sailed on a short cruise to Rouen before taking her place in the Review lines at Spithead.

In addition to the purely home trade work this class, together with the later GEORGINA V EVERARD and FREDERICK T EVERARD and some of the larger former EMPIRE ships, expanded the company's activities northwards to the Baltic with coal and homewards with timber and pulp. They also went south to North Africa returning home with phosphates from Casablanca. These relatively long voyages had to be carefully planned because the ships could easily run out of fresh water if they were neaped outside a discharge port.

The "Yellow Perils" were superb workhorses and proved themselves reliable and versatile ships which could carry a wide variety of coastal cargoes. Much was coal, of course, with the STABILITY at the time being the largest vessel to berth on the Camber Quay at Portsmouth with regular shipments of coal from Goole for the Portsmouth gas works. SIMILARITY spent many years carrying coal, also from Goole, to Kingsbridge in Devon. All the survivors at one time or another loaded roadstone at Arklow, Newlyn or Dean Quarry in Cornwall for the Thames and elsewhere.

One cargo that was vastly unpopular with the ships' crews was cement clinker. The majority of this was loaded at the Tunnel Portland Cement Co. Ltd. works at West Thurrock and was taken to the Rothesay Dock in Glasgow. The dust got everywhere and it was impossible to remove all the traces. Other cargoes of clinker were found for Drogheda and Denmark, for instance, and at one time the crews thought there was a plot to cover the world in a grey blanket. One master who spent a long time on the trade from West Thurrock to Glasgow kept a running total of the tonnage he had carried and by his reckoning it exceeded the half million mark.

Grain was also a frequent cargo and in the ships' later lives they joined in the transhipment trade with soya beans to the Erith Oil Works on the Thames. Everard ships were no strangers to the works that had been originally built by the Maypole Dairy Co. in 1915, later acquired by the British Oil & Cake Mills Ltd. and became part of Unilever Ltd. in 1929. It was quite usual to have one or two ships on the berth discharging, maybe two more on the buoy at Greenhithe waiting, one or two at Rotterdam loading and, of course, a couple at sea. Normally one ship followed another on to the discharging berth in strict rotation but occasionally the receivers would, for no apparent reason and at very short notice, alter the agreed rotation. If this happened in the evening when some crew members were ashore, confusion would ensue while one crew was mustered from those remaining aboard the other ships to take the chosen ship to Erith. The really difficult task came later in collecting everyone and getting them back to their own ships.

SINGULARITY (1) on trials off Grimsby. *Company archives*

Some of the smaller vessels also carried clinker in conjunction with other cargoes. The ABILITY, for example, was engaged for some time on a trade known colloquially as the "eternal triangle" carrying clinker from Drogheda to Glasgow, thence in ballast to Partington to load coal back for Drogheda. Other ships with a low air draft also loaded coal at Partington for Drogheda but then loaded peat for the gas works at Wandsworth. The trip up the Thames through the bridges had to be carefully planned and the ship needed to arrive off Cherry Garden Pier in good time to lower masts and other top hamper before proceeding upriver.

CEMENT IN NEW ZEALAND

After a lengthy investigation, the Tunnel Portland Cement Co. Ltd. of London decided to set up a subsidiary, New Zealand Cement Co. Ltd., to manufacture Guardian Portland Cement at Westport in South Island. As it was proposed to sell the cement in the Auckland area of North Island it was realised that ships would be required. The West River Shipping Co. Ltd. was formed jointly by Tunnel Cement and Everards. The French vessel FRONSAC was purchased in 1960 and, renamed WESTPORT, she arrived in New Zealand early in 1961. Later, in 1963, the ETHEL EVERARD was converted to a self discharging bulk cement carrier and renamed GUARDIAN CARRIER; she successfully discharged her outward cargo at a new silo at Onehunga in April 1964. The WESTPORT was also converted to carry bulk cargo in 1963 but soon reverted to carrying bagged cement. Meanwhile a manager had been sent out to New Zealand and an Everard office was established at Westport from where the operation of the two ships was efficiently managed. In 1966 the New Zealand Cement Co. Ltd. merged with the Milburn Cement Co. Ltd. of Dunedin to become New Zealand Cement Holdings Ltd. The new company purchased both ships in 1967 after which Everards had no further direct involvement and the West River Shipping Co. Ltd. was officially wound up in 1971.

TANKERS

The post-war expansion of the dry cargo fleet was far exceeded by that of the tankers although the growth was mainly achieved by the purchase of former EMPIRE and other ex-Government vessels with relatively few new-buildings. Altogether thirty-six tankers were purchased between 1945 and 1957. The sizes of these ships varied from the modest 180 deadweight tons of the former military oil barge ATTUNITY to the 5,127 deadweight tons of the second ASTRALITY, formerly the EMPIRE GANGES.

The work these ships were engaged upon depended not only on demand but also on their suitability, which varied considerably. Some, equipped with heating coils and with tanks in good condition, carried edible oils, molasses and lubricating oils. Others carried motor spirit and other clean petroleum products while others were "dirtied" and carried fuel oil for power stations

CANDOURITY (1)
awaiting conversion at Goole.

C. Hill

and bunkering. This last was a particularly arduous duty and was carried out, mainly on charter to the various major oil companies, in many ports and estuaries around the coast. Size, too, was an important factor since it governed the ports to which the ships could trade.

The five ex-Admiralty 'C' class coaling lighters purchased in 1956 formed an interesting group. Laid up in the Medway, they were first towed to Greenhithe and later to Goole where they were lengthened, widened and converted into tankers. Alone of the group, CITY traded for a short while as a dry cargo vessel before conversion. The conversion work, which nearly doubled their deadweight, was quite a challenge and the ships were cut along the centre line at deck level and the sides allowed to fall out nearly four feet before a new mid-body section was added. There was a very pronounced knuckle forward and aft where the widened mid-body met the original bow and stern sections. Together they had a varied trading life, CITY, CLANITY and COMMODITY being on bareboat charter to Shell-Mex & BP Ltd. for most of their lives.

CONFORMITY and CANDOURITY both spent some time running fuel oil from Coryton upriver through the bridges to Hammersmith but were also engaged on bunkering operations on the Thames, Medway and Bristol Channel. Their operational range was limited because of small bunker capacity and this occasionally led to difficulties. CLANITY, for example, experienced bad weather on a voyage and running very short of fuel only managed to get into Great Yarmouth by shutting down the boilers and drifting as far as possible towards the coast with each tide for a couple of days before lighting up for the final dash to safety.

Some small scale bunkering work was undertaken by four former military oil barges. Two of these, renamed APEXITY and ATTUNITY, were purchased in 1952 and the other two, TANKITY and TOTALITY, in 1956. They had been built by the Shipbuilding Corporation Ltd. for the Admiralty towards the end of the war but had been transferred to the Army and were operated by the Royal Army Service Corps. They were employed by Everards on estuarial and harbour work and the equipment and crew accommodation was rather basic. In fact, one skipper had the temerity to complain about having to live in the wheelhouse only to be informed that on the contrary he was lucky to have a cabin equipped with a wheel and telegraph. One of them was supplying some bunkers to the QUEEN MARY and was asked by an incredulous duty engineer to increase the pumping rate because his machinery was consuming oil at a faster rate than the little tanker was supplying it.

The larger ARGOSITY and ARDUITY were also lengthened and with good tanks and heating coils they alternated between vegetable oils, lubricating oils and clean petroleum products generally. ARDUITY made a number of trips to Iceland to pick up cargoes of fish oil for the Mersey. Her unlengthened sister vessel AMITY set a trend by successfully carrying the first cargo of bulk lard from Brussels to Liverpool. Having proved that it could be done, the carriage of lard and tallow then formed a very important part of the company's tanker operations.

When built, few of these EMPIRE tankers or indeed the pre-war tankers had a mainmast but were fitted later with a light pole mast to carry the second masthead light. This was required by the 1948 Regulations for the Prevention of Collisions at Sea when they came into force in 1954. The presence or otherwise of this mast can give a good clue as to the date of a photograph.

Until the late sixties most of the new-buildings were placed on time charter to the major oil companies for the carriage of clean petroleum products and fuel oil. The high point of all this work was undoubtedly from the mid-fifties to the mid-sixties after which, due to the age and condition of the ships and competition from the oil companies' own fleets, the number of Everard tankers declined rapidly. Most of the older tankers were sold for breaking up by 1970, leaving a smaller but modern fleet of versatile tankers to carry on.

ATTUNITY *J. Callis*

GROUP DIVERSIFICATION

Quite apart from the ships themselves the company developed in other directions in the post-war years, although most of these developments were based on shipping activities in one form or another. The shipbuilding and repairing facilities at Great Yarmouth have already been mentioned while further north the company became associated with J. Wharton (Shipping) Ltd. of Keadby in 1952. An oil storage installation was built at neighbouring Gunness in 1958 and was supplied by Everard tankers for a number of years. This association with Whartons was to have a continuing effect on the company's affairs as will be seen.

An early road tanker. *Company archives*

Meanwhile, at Greenhithe, Everard Transport Services Ltd. was formed and in 1955 took over the running of the road transport fleet from Everard Maritime Services Ltd. The building of the oil storage installation had started in 1954 and the idea was based on a concept of complete through handling with Everard ships bringing oil products to Greenhithe for storage and final delivery to customers by Everard road tankers. This concept only met with limited success and in reality the storage and road transport activities developed independently.

Later additions to the road transport section of the Group were G. Fox & Son Ltd. in 1968, Ridbridge Ltd. in 1977, and Thomason & Kelley Ltd. in 1980. Everards were operating a fleet of modern road tankers on both domestic and continental work when, in 1984, this section became a casualty of the ever worsening economic situation and ceased to trade. The vehicles were all sold and the familiar red and white houseflag is no longer to be seen on the main roads and motorways up and down the country.

The oil storage section developed with a tank farm in the old chalk pit at Greenhithe and other tanks on the Globe Wharf. Heating oils and other clean petroleum products always formed the largest volume in storage but several of the more exotic, expensive and specialist vegetable oils were also successfully stored. Some of these, for example illipenut oil and sheanut butter, required very special and careful treatment. The section was given a separate identity in 1974 and became F.T. Everard & Sons Kent Ltd. It was closed in 1986 when, although still making a profit, substantial investment was required to modernise the plant and little return could be envisaged for the capital outlay. The storage tanks were soon removed, making a considerable change to the Greenhithe landscape.

The shipyard at Greenhithe, the oldest part of the company, continued as a service to the fleet and carried out major and minor repairs to the ships, although many of the newer vessels were too large for the slipways and had to be drydocked elsewhere. A surprisingly comprehensive range of skills were employed and most of the tradesmen had served their apprenticeships in the yard. There were engineers, shipwrights, fitters, electricians, coppersmiths, blacksmiths, sailmakers and riggers. Between them they could equally install a new main engine in a motorship or make a main horse from a tree trunk by adze and run up a mainsail with its traditional red ochre dressing for a sailing barge. The management of the shipyard was split from the fleet in 1968 and in 1973 ships belonging to other owners came for repair for the first time. For a while all went well but eventually economics forced the closure of the yard in December 1982. Shortly afterwards the facilities were leased to South Thames Shiprepairers Ltd. who carried on with a much reduced labour force before they too bowed to the seemingly inevitable and the yard closed for the last time in July 1985.

Other developments included the purchase of Dean Quarries Ltd. in Cornwall in 1956, made with an eye to return cargoes from the south west. Another quarry was acquired in 1960 with the purchase of A. & F. Manuelle Ltd. of Guernsey and the associated Crown Wharf in Deptford Creek. The ships brought many thousands of tons of crushed granite for roadbuilding

SUMMITY (1) loading roadstone at Dean Quarry, Cornwall in 1965.

Company archives

AUTHENTICITY (1) discharging at the Globe Wharf, Greenhithe. *Company archives*

into the Thames and elsewhere. Both quarries and Crown Wharf were sold by 1970 although A. & F. Manuelle Ltd. continued trading until 1973 and was not finally wound up until 1978. Dean Quarries Ltd. remained as a dormant company for a few years until in 1974 its name was changed to F.T. Everard & Sons Kent Ltd. to take control of the oil storage installation at Greenhithe.

The Plymouth based wharfage and warehousing company of Cattedown Wharves Ltd. was purchased in 1957. The busy wharf and the adjacent warehouses exist as a separate and successful entity within the Group, the stevedoring and storage activities providing a valuable source of revenue. Many of the dry cargoes handled originate from local agricultural needs such as fertilizer and fish meal but a considerable volume of oil cargoes are also handled. For various reasons the company has become the owner or part owner of Everard vessels at different times, for example the motor vessels CLARITY and GILLIAN EVERARD. In much the same way as Great Yarmouth on the east coast, Cattedown Wharf at Plymouth has often provided a sorely needed haven of refuge for an ailing ship in the south west.

A further acquisition was the shipbroking firm of Matthews & Luff Ltd. in 1962. Established in 1845, the company had owned a number of sailing and steam ships but for a number of years had confined its activities to shipbroking. Totally absorbed into the Everard Chartering Department, it was wound up in 1985.

An interesting aspect of diversification took place in 1988 when the company acquired Ships Electronic Services Ltd. of Greenhithe. This company provides a whole range of services connected with the specification, development, supply, installation and subsequent maintenance of shipboard electronic equipment.

MORE SHIPPING COMPANIES

Over the years a number of other shipping companies have been acquired and absorbed into the Group, generally without leaving much trace. The first and smallest of these was Martins Coastal Steamships Ltd. of Plymouth. At the time of the purchase in 1950, the company operated two formerly Swedish-owned and Italian-built motor coasters, DALESMEET and WATERSMEET. In due course these became CAPACITY and CELEBRITY and the company itself became Everard Shipping Co. Ltd. A number of other ships, particularly tankers, were purchased for or transferred to this company but it had been dormant for a few years when its name was changed in 1974 to F.T. Everard & Sons Greenhithe Ltd. for the operation of the repair yard at Greenhithe.

The next acquisition, in 1956, was the old established shipping company of J. Hay & Sons Ltd. of Glasgow with whom the company had had contacts

WATERSMEET later **CELEBRITY (1)** with the original goalpost masts. *T. Rayner*

The spectacular sideways launch of **THE DUCHESS** at Faversham.

Company archives

for a number of years through the carriage of cement clinker from West Thurrock to Rothesay Dock in Glasgow. Seven elderly steam coasters with their salmon pink funnels were integrated into the fleet but all had been sold or scrapped by 1963. The name of J. Hay & Sons Ltd. was maintained as a shipowning company for a number of years and alone of the purchased companies the Hay nomenclature survived for a while after the demise of the original ships. The last ship to bear a Hay name was the motor vessel THE DUCHESS built in 1963 and sold in 1981 while the company itself was wound up in 1985.

Towards the end of 1961 the company acquired Glen & Co. Ltd., another Glasgow-based company. Although Glen had owned a few ships over the years its main sphere of activity was as the managing owner for the ships of a variety of shipping companies for the most part engaged in transatlantic and Scandinavian trading. At the time of the purchase only two of these, Clydesdale Shipowners Co. Ltd. and Scottish Navigation Co. Ltd., were still active and between them owned six vessels. They had red funnels with a black top and the Everard funnel mark was soon painted at the bottom of the black top. All the ships were sold by 1967 and none of their names have been subsequently employed.

SPECIALITY (2) in heavy weather on passage from Uddevalla to Chatham in February 1990. *A. Richards*

With the purchase of Glen & Co. Ltd. the company also acquired J.T. Salvesen & Co. Ltd. and David Traill & Sons Ltd. of Grangemouth plus Urban Korner A/B of Gothenburg and thus became established in the liner trade between Scandinavia, the UK and Ireland. Some of the Glen trades have gone, several new ones have been tried and discarded but for some years the regular trade has settled down to voyages between Sweden and Ireland and Sweden to Gunness and Chatham. Much of the westbound cargo consists of timber, hardboard, paper and other forest products but a number of containers have also been carried. Eastbound ships frequently carry coal, silver sand for glass manufacture or some other bulk cargo because of the imbalance of the general cargo trade.

The association with Whartons made Gunness a natural choice for the import of timber and regular shipments have been made since 1967. Grangemouth had been an important port for Glens but gradually the cargo bookings declined and the port was taken off the regular schedule. Following an attractive offer from the Forth Ports Authority the stevedoring company of David Traill & Sons Ltd. was sold in 1977. J.T. Salvesen & Sons Ltd., who had been shipowners since 1843 and had also been involved in the Scandinavian liner trade, remained in business as forwarding and general ships' agents for a while but the company was finally sold in 1985. Perhaps Johan Theodor Salvesen's major claim to fame was to have installed his youngest brother Christian as manager of his office at Leith in 1851.

Although by no means a purchase or a takeover, the company acquired a number of shares in the London and Rochester Trading Co. Ltd. in 1955 and Mr. W.J. Everard became a director. Together the joint fleets would have been a truly dominant force in coastal tramp shipping but there do not seem to have been any moves towards integration. One tangible result was that a few of the contemporary London and Rochester Trading Co. Ltd. vessels were built with engines from the Newbury Diesel Co. Ltd. Everards disposed of their share holding about the time that the Rochester company became involved with the Proprietors of Hays Wharf, after which the two companies went their own ways.

Miss Ethel A. Everard. *Company archives*

Mr. Frederick A.J.B. Everard. *Company archives*

Mr. W.J. Everard died in 1958 leaving his brother Mr. F.W. Everard the last surviving son of the founder to carry on until he died in 1964. As a mark of respect many ships had a blue mourning band painted around their hulls. He was succeeded by his nephew Mr. F.A. Everard as Chairman and Miss E.A. Everard became the Managing Director. The new Chairman's eldest daughter, Mrs. R.A. Shotton, became a Director in 1969, followed by his two sons Mr. F.M. Everard and Mr. W.D. Everard in 1974.

NEWBUILDINGS: DRY CARGO

The sister vessels ACTUALITY and APRICITY were ordered in 1966 especially for the timber trade from Scandinavia to Gunness. They were equipped with Gotaverken steel hatches, hydraulic winches for the swinging derricks and steel stanchions for the deck cargoes of timber. To maximise their deadweight carrying capacity their construction was kept as light as possible and when they entered service they were considered to be the largest ships that could safely navigate the lower Trent making them ideal vessels for Gunness with their deadweight of 1,160 tons. They were soon eclipsed and nowadays ships with a deadweight well in excess of 3,000 tons are regular visitors.

Much of the top hamper of derricks and winches was removed from the two ships in 1976 to improve their stability after the relatively heavy Newbury diesel engines were removed and replaced by lighter Mirrlees Blackstone units. By this time they had reverted to general coastwise trading with various bulk cargoes and both were sold in 1982.

Altogether, during the sixties, a total of twenty-two vessels was built and another twelve were purchased including two tugs and those vessels acquired with the purchase of Glen. The dry cargo ships varied from the 2,500 deadweight ships built by Clelands and at Goole all with family names, the two low air draft vessels

ACTUALITY (3) as completed. *J. Callis*

from J. Pollock Sons & Co. Ltd. at Faversham and the five small vessels from Clelands and Fellows. Four tankers came from Goole and towards the end of the decade four typically Dutch-looking tankers from Groningen.

The large dry cargo vessels were not only engaged on normal coastwise trading but also ventured further afield and took over some of the Baltic work from their smaller sisters. After their new engines were fitted in the mid-seventies they went south to the Mediterranean on various charters, usually loaded with generals, containers and vehicles on the outward passage, returning home with various bulk commodities such as phosphate, emerystone, bentonite, perlite or pumice. Later they reverted to coastwise trading and were all sold by 1984.

The two sister vessels CAPACITY and THE DUCHESS were built with low air drafts to enable them to negotiate the Seine bridges to reach Paris. Although the CAPACITY made a few voyages as far as St. Etienne the trade did not materialise. CAPACITY seemed to have a more varied life than her sister vessel and became involved in liner runs from Felixstowe to Zeebrugge, later from Silloth to Drogheda and from Preston to the Isle of Man. In between times she inaugurated the regular service with East Anglian malting barley to the whisky distillery at Port Ellen on the island of Islay. This trade was continued by the larger CLARITY and later still COMMODITY.

The small 'F' type vessels were built with limited coastwise trading in mind and being of 199 gross tons they fell just below the threshold of the major international conventions. The first pair, FRIVOLITY and FESTIVITY, were built at Great Yarmouth in 1963 and were followed by the slightly improved FIXITY in 1966. Experience gained from these ships later formed the basis of Cleland's standard XL400 design. FUTURITY and FORMALITY were built to this design and a number of sister vessels were also built for other owners at Wallsend and in Malta. In 1963 FRIVOLITY started the bulk cement trade from Northfleet, where the original cement works of Thomas Bevan had stood, to Cowes in the Isle of Wight.

For this trade the ships were equipped with special portable bulkheads to reduce the cubic capacity of the holds for safety reasons to ensure that the cement cargo which can, under some circumstances, run like water came well up into the hatch coamings. The work was to continue with FUTURITY taking over for a number of years and finally FORMALITY until 1987 when Blue Circle Industries plc made the decision to supply the needs of the island by lorries using the ferry.

FESTIVITY achieved a sort of notoriety when she became the subject of a formal inquiry after being abandoned in the North Sea during a gale in November 1971. The inquiry appeared to have some difficulty in reaching any particular conclusions — nevertheless some of them were used to influence the operation of small coastal vessels in general. These five little ships almost formed a "fleet within a fleet" as each aspect of their operation was somewhat different to that of their larger sisters. The last was sold in 1987.

FUTURITY (2)

Company archives

Most former **EMPIRE** tankers were sold for scrap but **ALLEGRITY** came to an unfortunate end in 1961. *Company archives*

NEWBUILDINGS: TANKERS

The new tankers were to have different careers from their predecessors. The large fleet of former EMPIRE tankers and other older vessels was being rapidly sold off or broken up as their charters came to an end, some of these quite abruptly and prematurely as the changes of trade patterns dictated. Many of these tankers had been engaged on long term charters to one or other of the major oil companies and they had all been very hard worked, particularly those that had been involved in bunkering.

The AGILITY was the first of the more modern type of tanker to enter service. She had been laid down at Goole to the shipyard's own account and was purchased by Everards at a late stage which accounts for her British Polar main engine rather than a Newbury unit which would undoubtedly have been the company's choice. Initially she carried motor spirit and gas oil from Coryton to Gunness for Mobil Oil Co. Ltd. but this work ceased when the Associated Petroleum Terminal came on stream at Immingham. Later she went on time charter to ICI and carried their motor spirit from the Tees to the Tyne for a number of years before being replaced by a larger vessel in 1976.

AGILITY (2) after launching at Goole. *C. Hill*

The next tanker, ANNUITY, also from Goole, was nearly twice the size and although throughout her service with the company she spent periods on general coastwise trading, she was mainly engaged in carrying lubricating oils from Rotterdam to Barton on the Manchester Ship Canal and later from Rotterdam to Silvertown on the Thames for Gulf Oil (Great Britain) Ltd.

ASSIDUITY was built around a specification drawn up by Mobil Oil Co. Ltd. but when placed on charter to them was never completely satisfactory and in due course she was relieved by the AUDACITY for the trade from Coryton up the east coast to Ipswich and King's Lynn. In 1973 the ship came to Greenhithe where she was completely refitted with a new engine, cargo pumps and pumproom.

Very early in life the ALACRITY was converted into a chemical tanker to carry a limited range of products and went on charter to Esso Petroleum Co. Ltd., transferring shortly to Essochem Belgium NV and then to Panocean Storage & Trading Co. Ltd. The introduction of stringent international regulations for chemical tankers in the early seventies coupled with considerable over-tonnaging in the coastal chemical market forced her return to clean petroleum work as conversion would have been uneconomic. Never as flexible or equal in performance to later tankers, she was always the first to be laid up for a period if work fell off in the summer months. She was eventually sold in 1986 to a Liberian owner who, it seems worthy of mention, was actually based in Liberia.

The year 1967 saw the first two deliveries of a series of four similar tankers from Groningen. The first, AUTHORITY, came out slightly smaller than anticipated and the second vessel, ASPERITY, was made slightly larger to make up the deficit. Unfortunately, the hard trading conditions of the early eighties forced the sale of AUTHORITY because, although her operating costs were the same as her larger sister, her earning power was considerably less. Purchased in 1985 by a Greek owner she had a garage constructed on deck to house road tankers used to distribute the ship's cargo ashore on islands in the Greek Archipelago. The second pair, ACTIVITY and ALLURITY, were more or less identical and followed in 1969. All four vessels spent periods on charter to the major oil companies carrying clean petroleum products and between charters carried many spot cargoes of a similar nature and also edible oils, lard and molasses, proving themselves very versatile in operation. ALLURITY carried a number of experimental cargoes of carbonate slurry to Sweden for use in the paper industry. ACTIVITY and ALLURITY, temporarily converted, spent a number of months during the period 1984 to 1986 on charter as standby anti-pollution vessels for offshore oil drilling rigs.

The summer of 1988 proved to be a particularly difficult period for tankers, probably because it followed a relatively mild winter, and both ACTIVITY and ALLURITY were taken out of service to complete their special surveys and were then laid up at Greenhithe before being sold.

The AUDACITY entered service in 1968 between the two pairs of Dutch tankers. She was the Goole answer to the Groningen tankers and in fact for the same gross tonnage she did better on deadweight and was certainly more heavily constructed than the minimum scantling "built down to a figure" Dutch vessels. Initially she went on to time charter to Shell-Mex & B.P. Ltd. and carried motor spirit and gas oil from Shellhaven to ports on the south and east coasts before relieving ASSIDUITY on the Mobil Oil Co. Ltd. charter from Coryton to Ipswich and King's Lynn. While on this work she would regularly carry more than one hundred cargoes in a year. Eventually the charter came to an end and the ship went onto general trading with clean petroleum products, mainly centred on Milford Haven. In 1972 the Newbury main engine was removed and replaced by a Deutz unit similar to those installed in the Groningen built tankers. Shortly afterwards, while negotiating the tortuous King's Lynn channel, the new engine seized and the ship, fully laden with motor spirit, went aground. Two tugs were sent to assist on the next tide and shortly after the towing operation was under way the ship took a sudden sheer with the result that one tug went aground on each side of the channel and the ship eventually settled in the middle of the fairway. All went well on the next tide and the ship was safely brought into King's Lynn, discharged, and later towed to Goole for engine repairs.

A much smaller Goole-built tanker, ACCLIVITY, also entered service in 1968: like her earlier namesake she had been built with a low air draft for trading to Paris with edible oils. This work did not develop as promised and she went instead onto general coastwise trading but eventually settled down to a regular run carrying lard from the continent to London and in particular to Bow Creek. Taken off the work in 1981, she was soon sold to Moroccan owners based in Casablanca.

Two much larger tankers joined the fleet in 1971 when the company purchased Thun Tankers Ltd. which was the British subsidiary of a Swedish company. The name was changed to Thames Tankers Ltd. and the ships were renamed AMITY and ANTERIORITY. In terms of deadweight they were just below the ASTRALITY of 1955 which therefore retained the distinction of being the largest tanker ever owned by the company.

They were very well equipped vessels although their pipeline system was rather basic and did not permit easy segregation of various grades of cargo. The system also relied on hydraulic valves which proved unreliable in service. ANTERIORITY's cargo system was altered shortly after purchase to make the ship more versatile but although similar plans were made for the AMITY she was sold before they were carried out.

ANTERIORITY spent some time on general coastwise trading including trips to the Mediterranean and the Black Sea and then undertook four voyages around the Cape of Good Hope to Jeddah. These voyages took place against a background of oil shortages and Middle Eastern conflicts but despite considerable misgivings nothing untoward occurred although there were a few operational problems. The work came to an end with the re-opening of the Suez Canal when Jeddah could be supplied with special lubricating oils more economically by larger parcel tankers on their way elsewhere. When purchased, the AMITY was engaged on time charter to Svenska BP A/B carrying fuel oil to various Baltic ports from Gothenburg. When the time charter came to an end in 1975 she was placed on bareboat charter to a French company. Unfortunately the French did not keep up the charter payments and eventually the ship was arrested. The legal proceedings to recover the ship took over a year and shortly after these had been completed in 1977 she too was sold.

ALLURITY (2) on trials. *Company archives*

SKORPIOS formerly **APRICITY (1)** still going strong after half a century.

Company archives

FLEET MODERNISATION

The 1970's saw a large building programme underway, mostly dry cargo ships but ending with the first two of a group of three tankers. The first of the dry cargo ships was SUPREMITY (3) from Groningen. She was a tween decker, equipped with a twenty-five ton crane and was specially designed for the liner trade between Scandinavia and Ireland. It was intended for the ship to be powered by the first pair of the new four stroke 'T' type Newbury engines. However, development work on the engine was not completed and the decision was made to install a British Polar unit instead. This decision effectively spelt the end of diesel engine manufacture at Newbury. An identical sister vessel was cancelled before completion due to concern that the volume of trade might not support two such specialist ships.

SUPREMITY continued in the liner trade until 1980 when she was sold to a Welsh company after a short time charter. Probably unique amongst Everard vessels, she never visited Greenhithe. There then followed a series of eight gearless dry cargo ships of 1,599 gross tons all built with various levels of investment grants. The first two came from Richard Dunston Ltd. of Hessle closely followed by two of similar size from Goole. These were immediately followed by the four FRED EVERARD class vessels which for the same gross tonnage managed to achieve an additional 400 tons of deadweight by extending loopholes in various paragraphs of international tonnage regulations.

Engaged at first on general coastwise trade, these fine vessels were soon pressed into Mediterranean work with steel and china clay cargoes outward bound, returning with phosphates or other bulk minerals. During the summer season they were to be seen on voyages around the North Cape to Archangel to load timber. They were often used on the liner trade from Sweden with timber, generals and containers. A lack of crew accommodation, air conditioning and refrigeration prevented them from venturing further afield to West Africa and beyond. They were strong, reliable and versatile ships which managed to cope very well with the needs of a number of diverse trades despite being originally conceived as coastal bulk carriers. The wheel eventually turned its circle and the Mediterranean work fell off with the result that the ships were brought back to their original north west European coastal trade. The mid-eighties were a particularly difficult time and after short lay-ups they were all sold by 1987 with the exception of the SAGACITY which lasted a little longer. The MAIRI EVERARD of similar size was built in 1974 and was the company's first vessel to have a box hold where all the ship's frames are contained within wing ballast tanks which gives flush and unobstructed sides to the hold. This facilitates cargo stowage, trimming and subsequent cleaning and is much in favour with charterers. Although particularly suitable for carrying grain, the ship started on the timber trade from Sweden, later went on charter to carry steel pipes from Glasgow for North Sea oil operations and eventually reverted to timber although interspersed with carrying occasional bulk cargoes.

Later, in 1975 and early 1976, the company took delivery of six smaller dry cargo vessels, two from Wivenhoe and four built at Groningen to a more or less standard design produced by Conoship BV. These were replacements for the ageing SONORITY and CENTRICITY type vessels that were being gradually sold off. The Dutch built ships were slightly smaller than their British built counterparts and with the same running costs carried about seventy tons less cargo. They compensated for this in some measure by having a better hull form and were therefore more economical on fuel and, being better sea ships, they could often make their passages when the larger pair could not. It was originally anticipated that the Dutch built vessels would carry on the trade to Selby and although the first two, CONFORMITY and CANDOURITY, both made successful voyages and passed through the toll bridge several times, all without incident, a limit was placed on the beam of ships permitted to pass through the bridge. This effectively precluded them and a number of similar ships from visiting the port. At first this exclusion was seen as a very serious matter but shortly afterwards the Olympia Oil & Cake Mills Ltd. at

Launch of **SAGACITY (3)** at Goole. *C. Hill*

SINGULARITY (2) on trials. *Company archives*

Selby changed from crushing imported soya beans to concentrate on locally produced rape seed. Although protests had been made it was not thought worthwhile to pursue the matter, and the toll bridge, vital to the local community but ever a problem to coastal shipping, was left to bask in the protection afforded by its Act of Parliament of 1791. Despite all this, the ships being of a very handy size soon found successful places in general coastwise trading. The COMMODITY spent a number of years taking malting barley to Port Ellen on the island of Islay and had the distinction of having a lady chief officer. Eventually production declined and the distilleries were kept supplied with their barley by lorries using the regular ferry. COMMODITY then joined CELEBRITY on the same general coastwise trading as their foreign built sisters.

After the six small vessels were completed there was only a short breathing space before orders were placed for four much larger vessels. With the same hull form, two were gearless and the other two were geared, and while they were all below 1,600 gross tons their deadweight exceeded 4,000 tons. This was achieved by using a number of loopholes in the tonnage regulations including one which allowed a non load-bearing tween deck. Even this deadweight was increased in later years by extending the notional tween deck and increasing the height of the fo'c'sle head thus permitting deeper loading. This practice was much in vogue in contemporary German vessels and the British Government gave their approval to extend the advantage to British ships. The four Everard ships ended up with probably the highest deadweight for any 1,599 gross ton ships anywhere.

The building contract for three of the vessels was awarded to Swan Hunter Shipbuilders Ltd. The first ship, SINGULARITY, was built by their Readhead Shipyard at South Shields and the two gearless ships, STABILITY and SPECIALITY, were built at Goole. The fourth vessel, JACK WHARTON, was built for J. Wharton (Shipping) Ltd. by Richards (Shipbuilders) Ltd. at Lowestoft. Everards superintended the building and on completion bareboat chartered the vessel which appeared in Everard's livery until sold in 1987.

SINGULARITY had the misfortune to be the last ship built at the Readhead Shipyard and her departure was to mark the closure of the yard. Towards completion, progress was plagued by industrial action and a "work to rule" which made sea trials and the handover date uncertain. The ship had been nominated to represent coastal shipping at the 1977 Jubilee Review at Spithead but as the date approached there were still some doubts about her completion and so the FRED EVERARD, then carrying out special survey at the neighbouring Tyne Dock Engineering Co. Ltd., was prepared and made a fitting substitute.

Meanwhile the JACK WHARTON was being built at Lowestoft where, because of a temporary imbalance of steel workers and outfitting tradesmen, the yard concentrated on the after end of the ship with the engineroom and all the accommodation; so much so that at one time the construction looked more like a block of high rise flats than a ship.

The two geared ships were each equipped with one twenty ton crane amidships that could plumb both holds but only had the outreach to lift full twenty foot containers two lines fore and aft of amidships. This meant that they were not totally self-sustaining on container work which proved to be a handicap that considerably limited their usefulness. The five ton swinging derricks at each end could only handle smaller general cargo and ships' stores.

CELEBRITY (2) on trials. *Company archives*

STABILITY (2)

FotoFlite

As originally designed the ships should have had a bulbous bow but this was deleted from the final design. By giving more buoyancy forward it would probably have enabled them to cope better with head seas and also reduced their propensity to end up with a trim by the head when loading homogeneous cargoes. The bulb should also have given a better hull form which would have reduced the wash and almost certainly reduced the fuel consumption.

The two geared vessels pushed out the limits of Everards' trading pattern to a considerable extent, as had been intended. They were soon engaged on voyages to the Mediterranean and West Africa and also to Archangel during the summer season. These voyages, although considered adventurous enough for a British coastal company, were soon eclipsed by transatlantic voyages to Canada, the USA, West Indies, Guyana and the Azores. SINGULARITY undertook two voyages in 1979 to Brazil and ventured one thousand miles up the Amazon to Manaos. Later, in 1981, she passed through the Panama Canal on her way to Buenaventura in Colombia. At the other extreme, JACK WHARTON made a voyage through the Suez Canal and down the Red Sea to Yenbo.

The JACK WHARTON was involved in a drama in 1978 which, although it had a happy ending, was very worrying at the time. The ship was at anchor off the island of Lipari where she was waiting to load pumice and one evening the master and the third engineer had gone ashore in the inflatable rubber boat. On their return they were approaching the ship when the propeller of the outboard motor became fouled and the motor stopped. At this point a sudden squall blew up and the small boat was soon lost to sight. The ship got underway and searched down wind but in vain. A search by helicopter was initiated at dawn but equally had no success. Meanwhile the captain had waited for the weather to abate before attempting to clear the fouled propeller. Eventually they managed to restart the motor and heading south they beached the boat soon after dark at a spot near Milazzo in Sicily. Leaving the engineer to look after the boat, the captain walked along the foreshore until he found a house. The occupants were naturally surprised but had heard about the missing men on the local radio and made them very welcome.

The voyages of the two gearless ships were more modest in comparison. SPECIALITY started life on the regular run between Ireland and Sweden and although she did some transatlantic work she was placed on time charter to the Central Electricity Generating Board in 1985 to carry coal to power stations. STABILITY was even more restricted and started out on the soya bean trade from Rotterdam to Erith going later onto the Swedish service and also onto a CEGB time charter. Both ships later reverted to general coastwise trading, the Swedish timber trade to Chatham and also seasonal timber cargoes from Archangel.

SPECIALITY and STABILITY achieved a certain notoriety when the company obtained an injunction against the National Union of Seamen to stop their secondary industrial action in support of the miners' strike in January 1985. The legal process was successful and both ships sailed from Workington with cargoes of open cast coal. The company, having made its point, did not press for damages and let the matter rest.

As built, all four ships ran on marine diesel distillate fuel or gas oil. This was becoming increasingly expensive in the late seventies particularly with the longer sea passages that the ships were making and in 1980 they were hastily converted to burn the heavier but cheaper IFO 30. Unfortunately the price differential was already narrowing and with supply problems and the higher maintenance costs associated with burning the heavier oil the potential savings were never fully achieved and it was not long before they all reverted to the original fuel.

In 1983, shortly after the end of the Falklands conflict, both SINGULARITY and JACK WHARTON, together with LINCOLNBROOK and LEICESTERBROOK, made regular voyages to Ascension and Port Stanley carrying military stores, equipment, refrigerated containers, helicopters, vehicles, munitions, buildings — in fact everything required to support and maintain the forces in the islands. Although the ships were not ideally suited for this sort of work, by improvisation and dedication, probably never fully recognised, they made a useful contribution. The fitting of fully load-bearing tween decks in 1984 made them more flexible in operation as general cargo and stores ships but had its own penalty when they reverted to bulk cargoes.

FRED EVERARD (4) at the 1977 Jubilee Review at Spithead.

A. Richards

Eventually the Falklands work fell off and in early 1987 the geared ships were both sold. JACK WHARTON was by this time owned by F.T. Everard Shipping Ltd. and was to have been renamed SIMILARITY but the change did not take place. Apart from the flurry of the Falklands work with relatively high initial freight rates it is probably quite true to say that in the end the simpler SPECIALITY and STABILITY, uncluttered with cranes and derricks, proved to be the more successful pair. They have good timber intake and with a slightly higher deadweight they can carry good freights of coal and other coastal cargoes and can also cope with grain cargoes more successfully than the geared ships.

Almost as soon as the four large cargo ships were in operation the company started the design studies for some new tankers. These were more sophisticated than earlier tankers and were equipped with deepwell pumps in each pair of cargo tanks. Most important for fast turnrounds in port, they have segregated ballast tanks, enabling ballast water to be pumped out or taken in while cargo is being loaded or discharged whereas in the older tankers the majority was taken in cargo tanks and had to be pumped ashore and the tank mopped dry before cargo could be loaded.

Three ships of about 2,400 tons deadweight were ordered and built at Goole, the lead ship being the ABILITY which entered service in March 1979 and was the first Everard vessel to sport two funnels. After a few teething problems they soon settled down to successful trading on charter to major oil companies, contracts of affreightment and spot cargoes. Although perfectly capable of carrying a wide range of oil cargoes, in practice they have been confined for various reasons to carrying clean petroleum products and lubricating oils in the north west European area. In service they have proved particularly reliable vessels and rarely stop for any repairs between their scheduled maintenance periods thereby amply repaying the time and care that was put into their design and specification.

ABILITY (3)

Company archives

COMBEN LONGSTAFF & CO. LTD.

Between the delivery of the second and third vessels of the tanker building programme a fairly momentous event took place in April 1980 when the company purchased Comben Longstaff & Co. Ltd., together with its subsidiaries County Ships Ltd., Williamstown Shipping Co. Ltd., and Gowan Shipping Ltd. The fleet consisted of five 'S' brook vessels, four more modern 'L' brook vessels and the two much larger 'D' brook vessels. The last two vessels were not part of the deal but Everards managed them for a short period while they were being sold by Longstaff's former parent company Consolidated Gold Fields Ltd.

The ships were soon integrated into the Everard fleet and gradually their funnel marks were changed although they retained their names and colour schemes. Longstaffs had been serious competitors on the coastal scene in earlier years but by the time of the purchase all their ships were trading further afield. They had also been involved in managing ships for other owners for many years but had withdrawn from all such arrangements before the purchase. The last of these ships had been the NORTHRIDGE which Longstaffs had managed for North Africa Line Ltd. of London from 1977 until a couple of months before the purchase in 1980 when the ship was transferred to Everards' management.

The 'S' brook ships were conventional, geared, two hold cargo ships and continued on Mediterranean, Baltic and Russian trading for a while but all were sold by mid-1983. Although only about ten years old they had proved somewhat troublesome in operation, in particular their DC electrical installations became very difficult to maintain.

The four blue painted 'L' brook ships had been built to a much more modern design and were really the main attraction. They all had single box holds with single hatches which made them good ships for grain although portable bulkheads had to be rigged for safety and stability reasons with heavier cargoes. They also had portable beams for rigging a load-bearing tween deck. Two of the ships were also equipped with a pair of travelling cranes that could be used either singly or in tandem.

The gearless LANCASTERBROOK and LONDONBROOK with their grain bulkheads in place were soon engaged on the regular trade from Rotterdam to Erith with soya beans. Their box holds reduced the discharging time considerably and later they even had their own small bulldozers to assist. Eventually, however, in spite of all the economies, the work came to an end when the mill stopped crushing the imported soya beans. The ships then went onto general trading, the regular Swedish trade and also spent periods on time charter to the CEGB.

The geared pair, LINCOLNBROOK and LEICESTERBROOK, went onto general trading: summer voyages to Archangel and the regular Swedish run. Their cranes were, generally speaking, of no great importance during this period but they came into their own when the ships were put onto the Falkland Islands work. Their cargoes were similar to those carried by the SINGULARITY and JACK WHARTON but they were particularly successful in carrying the large Chinook helicopters. These aircraft were taken both out and home because their major overhauls were carried out in Great Britain and a method had to be devised with the Royal Air Force for loading them in the Falklands. The ship was made ready by battening down the hatches and running the cranes to each extremity. The helicopter would then land on the hatch, no mean feat when one considers the size of the ship. It would then be temporarily lashed down while the rotor blades were removed and stowed in the cabin and the lifting wires secured. The cranes would be hooked on, one at each end, the lashings removed and the helicopter lifted clear of the hatch covers, then when these were rolled back, the aircraft would be carefully lowered into the hold and secured for the voyage. Shortly after the Falklands work came to an end one of each pair was sold, leaving LANCASTERBROOK and LEICESTERBROOK to carry on for a little longer.

SOLENTBROOK *Company archives*

LINCOLNBROOK inward bound to Gunness with timber from Uddevalla in April 1986 passes **LEICESTERBROOK** in the Trent outward bound for Ridham Dock to load for Ascension and Port Stanley. *C. Hill*

SHIP MANAGEMENT EXPANDS

During this busy period Everards became increasingly active in the sphere of ship management. This had started in 1978 with the DAVID and EDGAR DORMAN of Shamrock Shipping Co. Ltd. Both ships and the owning company were later acquired by J. Fisher & Sons plc of Barrow, and Everards retained the management for a while until the ships were placed on bareboat charter to J. & A. Gardner & Co. Ltd. of Glasgow in 1984. Everards were superintending the building of two further ships, the SHAMROCK ENDEAVOUR and SHAMROCK ENTERPRISE, which were also taken by Fishers with Everards carrying on with the management until this was transferred to Coe Metcalf Shipping Ltd., a subsidiary of Fishers, in 1986. Everards became involved with yet more Fisher acquisitions when the Barrow company purchased the fleet of Onesimus Dorey (Shipowners) Ltd. of Guernsey in 1983. The three vessels, BELGRAVE, PERELLE and ROCQUAINE, were managed until they were handed over to demise charterers in 1986.

Late in 1979 Blue Circle Industries plc bought the LIGAR BAY, a self discharging cement carrier that was laid up in New Zealand. Everards sent out a delivery crew and brought the vessel back to the UK where she carried bulk cement from the Thames up the east coast to Aberdeen and Lerwick. She was joined by the Dutch-registered MERCURIUS in 1980 and the Jersey-registered FARNESE in 1983. The MERCURIUS was transferred to the UK register early in 1988 and renamed BC MERCURIUS but unfortunately did not last very long and was sold for scrap before the end of the year after an engine room fire. FARNESE too was transferred to the UK register in 1988 at the request of the Jersey Registrar because she was no longer beneficially owned by a Jersey based company. This seemed a particularly strange move when at the time most other island or off-shore registries were seeking ways to expand their activities.

After superintending the building of the RIVER DART and RIVER TAMAR in 1981 Everards took over the technical and personnel management of the two vessels for the General Freight Co. Ltd. After a few years of successful operation, the parent company, Unilever plc, decided to rationalise their operations by disposing of all their transport interests and both the ships were sold in 1985.

In 1982 the Panamanian-registered DORIS I became the first tanker to be managed since the EMPIRE tankers of the wartime days. The ship was relatively elderly having been built in 1964 and was specially equipped to carry edible oils including lard and was required to maintain supplies to the Pura Food Group's factory in Bow Creek.

FOUR NEW DRY CARGO VESSELS

After the AMENITY in 1980 there was a gap of nearly four years before the company took delivery of another new vessel. This ship, the SELECTIVITY, was the first of a class of four vessels of 799 gross tons whose keels were laid before the new London Tonnage Rules came into force. If the ships had been measured according to the new rules, their gross tonnage would have been much greater.

The design and specification of any vessel is always a compromise between what is desirable and what is possible but notwithstanding a few minor mistakes and some teething problems, these four vessels gave the chartering department more flexibility and economy than any other class of dry cargo ships. Their single box holds have tank tops strengthened to carry heavy cargoes such as steel coils having a high point loading, but the most important features are the two portable steel bulkheads. These can be moved into various positions giving considerable variations in the space between them. It is therefore possible, provided that the shipper's estimate of stowage factor is correct, to adjust the bulkheads to ensure that grain cargoes come high enough up the hold to obviate the necessity for topping off with bagged grain for stability reasons. At one time topping off bulk grain cargoes with bags was a regular occurrence on coastal vessels but stricter international and domestic regulations coupled with the grain shippers' ability to drive a hard bargain has completely reversed the picture. The shipowner is often faced with having to guarantee that his ship can load without the need for bags with the corollary that if the calculations go wrong and in the event bags are required, the shipowner will have to pay for them. The problem is not usually so much the cost of the bags as the time and the labour costs incurred in doing the job.

These bulkheads have also been used to separate different grades of coal and other bulk cargoes and also to provide the necessary separation between the engine room and a cargo of explosives. Two of the class, SELECTIVITY and PAMELA EVERARD, were built to the account of Investors in Industry plc and leased to the Company while the other pair, WILLONIA and STEVONIA, were built for J. Wharton (Shipping) Ltd. of Gunness. Everards superintended the building of both ships and managed the WILLONIA from new. The original plan was that they should manage the ship

SELECTIVITY (2) *Company archives*

for two years and then, when the STEVONIA was delivered, both ships would revert to their owner. However, in 1986 a complicated deal was arranged, described at the time as a de-merger. Basically, Everards relinquished their share of the Gunness operation in return for the five ships of the Wharton fleet, ANGELONIA, LIZZONIA, WILLONIA, STEVONIA and JACK WHARTON. To achieve this the new F.T. Everard Shipping Ltd. was formed to take over the ships. The de-merger did not affect the Trent Lighterage Co. Ltd. whose sole remaining ship ECCTONIA was coincidentally sold shortly afterwards. The agreement required that the ships be renamed although the change was deferred until the ships' next docking because it makes the task so much easier to accomplish if the ship is lying idle for a few days. Strangely enough, it was the latest vessel, STEVONIA, which was the first to be changed when she docked for repairs to some bow damage sustained in a collision.

MORE SHIPS FOR MANAGEMENT

The company acquired the management of the small dry cargo vessel GWYN of Graig Shipping Co. Ltd. of Cardiff in July 1985. She was one of the largest of the Yorkshire Dry Dock Co. Ltd. standard designs and although still built to a frugal specification she was more of a ship and less of a barge than some of the earlier models. Unfortunately the ship came to an untimely end when she sank in the North Sea in November 1985. All the crew were rescued safely but the ship was not raised until September 1986. She was declared a constructive total loss and was eventually sold for conversion to a suction dredger.

The commercial management of the six vessels in the Eggar Forrester (Holdings) Ltd. fleet was acquired in 1985 and was followed in early 1986 by the full technical and personnel management. Three ships were early Yorkshire Dry Dock designs and the other three were built in Denmark to a similar concept. Never considered to be objects of great beauty, they were nevertheless functional and in good hands performed to their design parameters. The ships' names frequently gave rise to ill-informed comment but they were in fact derived from nicknames used in the family of the owner.

All six were sold by 1988 with the Danish-built trio being sold "en bloc" to the Liberian arm of a Yugoslav company. It is, apparently, a feature of Yugoslav financial policy that to build a ship domestically or to buy ships from abroad becomes prohibitively expensive whereas owners are free to set up a foreign company that can buy ships and charter them to the home-based parent. The ships were handed over to their new owner at Greenhithe and sailed the following day, renamed and with five pointed red stars painted on their funnels.

The management of two other vessels was taken over during 1986. First came the dry cargo vessel COTINGA belonging to Hadley Shipping Co. Ltd. followed by the CHARLES CRUZ which although owned by J.E. Hyde Shipowners Ltd. was on charter to Pegasus Line of Gibraltar. Originally the ship was engaged on regular runs between Gibraltar, North Africa, Spain and the UK and was later used as a feeder vessel in the western Mediterranean for the Pegasus container operations until sold in 1989.

LATER DEVELOPMENT

1988 proved to be quite a varied year for the company. One particularly sad note was the death of the Chairman Mr. Fred Everard in June. The attendance list at his funeral at Southfleet read like a 'Who's Who' of the shipping world and bore adequate testimony to his personal standing and influence in the industry. He was succeeded as Chairman by his eldest son Mr. F.M. Everard.

Two Japanese tankers were purchased during the year as replacements for the ageing Dutch built tankers. Renamed AVERITY and AMITY and wearing the Bahamas flag, one went on charter to Burmah Petroleum Fuels Ltd. carrying motor spirit on the east coast and the other went into general coastwise trade mainly on the west coast of the UK.

After a considerable amount of preparatory work, an order was announced in October 1988 for two tankers from Richards (Shipbuilders) Ltd. of Lowestoft. A very high specification included deepwell cargo pumps, segregated ballast tanks, a free fall lifeboat and the most up to date communications and electronic equipment. The first, AGILITY, was delivered in March 1990 with the second, named ALACRITY, following later in the year. Both are the third ships of the company to bear these names. It is interesting to compare the building period of eighteen months and the price of over £4 million each, with the five months and £15,350 of the first AGILITY back in 1924.

Following the closures of the shipyard, oil storage and road transport sections the company found themselves with much unused land on the Greenhithe site. Planning permission was obtained for residential development and the land was soon sold. The office, standing more or less on the spot where the business had started in 1880, was closed and everything was moved to temporary prefabricated accommodation located a little way to the west by the old slipways at the foot of the former Plaster Products Co. Ltd. jetty. Shortly afterwards the bulldozers moved in and, in a surprisingly short time, all traces of a century of endeavour had been removed.

Another milestone was passed in early 1990 when the river lighterage section, F.T.E. Lighterage Ltd., together with the lighters and two remaining tugs were the subject of a management buy-out. Since the demise of the shipyard in 1983, the river lighterage operation had been the oldest surviving activity within the group. The new company took the name HCH Services Ltd. and still operates from Greenhithe.

A significant break with tradition came in 1989 when the STABILITY was placed under the Bahamas flag. This move was prompted by an acute shortage of British seafarers, in particular officers, and the new flag considerably widened the scope for recruitment. In the event the ship was manned by a complete crew of Polish seamen who soon seemed to settle down. The move was not lightly taken and was predictably misunderstood in several quarters although the company derives little benefit other than to keep the ship operating efficiently with qualified staff. The sister ship SPECIALITY and the lone survivor of an earlier class, SAGACITY, followed during 1990 but both retained their British crews.

In another break in tradition, in 1989 the company became involved in a business expansion scheme and a new company, Short Sea Europe p.l.c., was formed.

Launch of **ALACRITY (3)** at Lowestoft. *B. Ollington*

Capital was quickly subscribed and in July 1989 the vessel RIVER TRADER was purchased for which Everards provided the ship's husbandry. The ship was soon put to work trading across the North Sea but has the ability to trade much further afield. The venture proved successful and sufficient additional capital was subscribed in 1990 to order two new 3,000 tonne dry cargo vessels from Cochrane Shipbuilders Ltd. of Selby for delivery in 1991.

Orders were also placed early in 1990 for two vessels for the account of Scottish Navigation Co. Ltd. The first of these is a sister to those ordered by Short Sea Europe p.l.c. from Cochranes at Selby. The trio will be equipped with free fall lifeboats and hydraulically operated lowering wheelhouses to keep the air-draft to a minimum for negotiating up-river bridges. The dimensions of the ships are close to the maximum for the builders and also for entry into such inland ports as Goole due to the constraints imposed by twisting rivers, locks and bridge cuttings. The second vessel will be the largest ever built for Everards and the first to be built for the company by Appledore Shipbuilders Ltd.; who won the order in a close and keenly fought contest. She will be nearly two thousand tonnes larger than the Selby ships and has been planned around the operating parameters of Gunness on the Trent. There, the riverside berths present different problems to those experienced at a locked-in port and the important dimensions become the overall length for swinging in the river and the draft. The high deadweight has been achieved by designing a beamy ship able to arrive with a good cargo even on neap tides.

The celebrations marking the centenary in the autumn of 1980 seem only a short while ago, and yet already ten of the second hundred years have elapsed. Many things have changed and the company has altered considerably in those difficult few years. One thing has not changed and that is the dedication to survival which has helped the company to weather many storms and bodes well for the future.

F. T. EVERARD & SONS, LTD., **22 & 23, GT. TOWER STREET, LONDON, E.C. 3.**

And **THE WHARF, GREENHITHE, KENT.**

Telephones :	*Telegrams :*
ROYAL 5922 (3 lines)	EVERASHIP, BILGATE, LONDON
GREENHITHE 3	EVERASHIP, GREENHITHE.

STEAM AND MOTOR SHIPOWNERS.

TANK STEAMERS AND TANK BARGES.

COASTING AND RIVER SAILING BARGES.

TUG AND LIGHTER OWNERS.

SAILING VESSELS

NOTES:

The notation '1' or '2' in brackets after a vessel's name indicates that she was the first or second vessel of that name in the fleet. The dates following the name are those of entering and leaving Everard ownership. The histories are in chronological order, according to acquisition or to the date of completion for new vessels. Before 1922 the individual family member owning a vessel is shown but after the formation of the Limited Company in April 1922, to which all vessels were transferred, the registered owner of a vessel is only quoted when it is a member of the Everard Group other than F.T. Everard & Sons Ltd.

The vessels are all wooden spritsail sailing barges unless otherwise described. On the first line is given the vessel's Official Number in the British Registry followed by her tonnages, gross (g), net (n) and burden (b) which is an indication of the carrying capacity and according to the Thames Watermens and Lightermens Act 1893 is obtained by multiplying the registered tonnage by five thirds. Alternatively, for some of the larger barges, the deadweight tonnage is quoted.

The tonnages are followed by the dimensions; registered length × breadth × depth expressed in decimal feet.

Ships' histories have been corrected to December 1990.

S1 INDUSTRY (1892–1912)

O.N. 54763 38g 38n 63b 72.8 × 14.7 × 4.7 feet.

10.1866: Completed by Thomas Bevan, Northfleet for John Messer Knight & Thomas Bevan, Northfleet. *4.1892:* Acquired by F.T. Everard. *8.1912:* Vessel broken up.

S2 ELIZABETH (1) (1895–1899)

O.N. 20688. 35g 35n 58b 73.1 × 14.6 × 4.4 feet.

4.1858: Completed by George Smeed, Sittingbourne for his own account. *1875:* Owners became Smeed, Dean & Co. Ltd., Sittingbourne. *30.10.1889:* Sank near Lower Hope Point in River Thames after collision with the steamship MADELINE 1,282/74 while on passage from Sittingbourne to Bow with a cargo of flints. Wreck abandoned by the owner. Later raised and possessed by the Thames Conservancy Board. *11.1895:* Acquired and rebuilt by F.T. Everard. *9.1899:* Vessel broken up.

S3 DESPATCH (1897–1920)

O.N. 73607 42g 42n 70b 74.8 × 15.1 × 4.9 feet.

1.1876: Completed by Edmund George Watson, Rochester for Thomas Bevan, Northfleet. *8.1896:* Sold to Robert, Edmund & Wilfred Bevan, Northfleet. *11.1897:* Acquired by F.T. Everard. *10.1920:* Vessel broken up.

S4 PROMPT (1898–1903)

O.N. 73743 42g 42n 70b 74.1 × 14.8 × 4.8 feet.

12.1876: Completed by Edmund George Watson, Rochester for Thomas Bevan, Northfleet. *7.1896:* Sold to Robert, Henry & Wilfred Bevan, Northfleet. *8.1898:* Acquired by F.T. Everard. *1.1903:* Sold to Horace A. Waller, Greenhithe. *1.1922:* Vessel broken up.

S5 LORD KITCHENER (1899–1926)

O.N. 110073 80g 56n 93b 84.0 × 20.4 × 6.0 feet.

3.1899: Completed by F.T. Everard, Greenhithe for his own account. *17.1.1926:* Wrecked in heavy weather in Redlap Cove near Dartmouth while on light passage from Poole to Par.

S6 ENERGY (1899–1903)

O.N. 56870 40g 40n 66b 72.5 × 14.6 × 4.9 feet.

10.1867: Completed by Thomas Bevan, Northfleet for John Messer Knight & Thomas Bevan, Northfleet. *7.1896:* Sold to Robert, Edmund & Wilfred Bevan, Northfleet. *8.1899:* Acquired by F.T. Everard. *25.3.1903:* Sunk near Cold Harbour Point in Erith Rands, River Thames after collision with the steamship SOUTHERN CROSS 5,137/92 while on passage downriver with a cargo of coal. *30.3.1903:* Vessel raised and towed to Greenhithe, declared a total loss and broken up by the owners.

S7 LIVELY (1900–1924)

O.N. 60972 41g 41n 68b 72.6 × 14.7 × 5.0 feet.

8.1869: Completed by Thomas Bevan, Northfleet for John Messer Knight & Thomas Bevan, Northfleet. *7.1896:* Sold to Robert, Edmund & Wilfred Bevan, Northfleet. *4.1900:* Acquired by F.T. Everard. *1.1924:* Vessel broken up.

S8 ALERT (1900–1929)

O.N. 63664 40g 40n 66b 73.0 × 14.5 × 4.8 feet.

10.1870: Completed by Thomas Bevan, Northfleet for John Messer Knight & Thomas Bevan, Northfleet. *8.1896:* Sold to Robert, Henry & Wilfred Bevan, Northfleet. *7.1900:* Acquired by F.T. Everard. *11.1929:* Vessel broken up.

S9 LUCY (1901–1903)

O.N. 52678 44g 44n 72b 67.0 × 17.2 × 5.1 feet.

3.1865: Completed by an unknown builder at Lambeth for Benjamin Ranyard, London. *11.1883:* Sold to John Bazley White & Bros. Ltd., London. *10.1900:* Sold to Associated Portland Cement Manufacturers (1900) Ltd., London. *12.1901:* Acquired by F.T. Everard. *3.1903:* Sold to Thomas Rayfield, Gravesend. *3.1906:* Vessel broken up.

S10 A.K. (1901–1903)

O.N. 77051 53g 53n 88b 69.7 × 18.9 × 5.1 feet.

4.1876: Completed by Alfred Keep, Greenhithe for his own account. *10.1881:* Sold to John Bazley White & Bros. Ltd., London. *10.1900:* Sold to Associated Portland Cement Manufacturers (1900) Ltd., London. *12.1901:* Acquired by F.T. Everard. *3.1903:* Sold to John Thomas Rayfield, Gravesend. *8.1908:* Vessel broken up.

S11 BRITISHER (1902–1941)

O.N. 115802 95g 68n 113b 87.0 × 22.2 × 6.9 feet.

4.1902: Completed by F.T. Everard, Greenhithe for his own account. *4.11.1941:* Sunk by a mine with all hands in the Thames Estuary off the Maplin Sands while on passage from Great Yarmouth to London with a cargo of empty bottle cases.

S12 ANGLO-AMERICAN (1902)

O.N. 115854 93g 67n 110b 85.5 × 22.2 × 6.9 feet.

6.1902: Completed by F.T. Everard, Greenhithe for his own account. *9.1902:* Sold to Richard Lano and Henry Sansom, Portland. *10:1910:* Henry Sansom became sole owner. *4.11.1915:* Struck the breakwater at Alderney in thick fog while on light passage from Portland to Alderney. Abandoned but subsequently drifted and became a total wreck at Hope's Nose about 3 miles east of Torquay.

BRITISHER discharging on the Trent. *T. Farnham*

S13 HILDA (1902–1934)

O.N. 87054 72g 72n 120b 83.0 × 17.0 × 6.0 feet.

2.1881: Completed by Robert Webb, Henley-on-Thames for John Bazley White & Bros. Ltd., London. *10.1900:* Sold to Associated Portland Cement Manufacturers (1900) Ltd., London. *12.1902:* Acquired by F.T. Everard. *12.1934:* Vessel broken up.

S14 SCOTIA (1903–1929)

O.N. 118634 109g 77n 129b 89.6 × 22.9 × 7.1 feet.

12.1903: Completed by F.T. Everard, Greenhithe for his own account. *6.10.1929:* Anchor dragged in heavy weather and vessel drove ashore and was wrecked on North Beach, Great Yarmouth while on passage from Keadby to Maldon with a cargo of basic slag.

SCOTIA

National Maritime Museum

S15 GERTY (1904–1933)

O.N. 108259 91g 71n 115b 81.0 × 21.0 × 7.2 feet.

10.1897: Completed by James R. Piper, East Greenwich for Lewis A. Glover, Greenhithe and James R. Piper, East Greenwich. *2.1901:* Lewis A. Glover became sole owner. *11.1902:* Sold to Edward A. Glover, Forest Hill & Mary A. Hayne, Rosherville. *7.1904:* Acquired by F.T. Everard. *14.7.1933:* Vessel and cargo of wool caught fire at Deptford buoys. Beached at Millwall and fire extinguished but vessel eventually sank. *28.7.1933:* Vessel raised and towed to Greenhithe, declared a total loss and broken up by the owner.

S16 CAMBRIA (1906–1966)

O.N. 120676 109g 79n 131b 91.1 × 21.9 × 7.3 feet.

3.1906: Completed by F.T. Everard, Greenhithe for his own account. *1.1966:* Sold to Alfred W. Roberts, Pin Mill. *2.1971:* Sold to Coutts & Co., London. *11.1971:* Sold to the Maritime Trust Corporation Ltd., London. Still in existence (1990).

GERTY: a swimhead barge. *National Maritime Museum*

CAMBRIA in trade. *T. Farnham*

HIBERNIA

National Maritime Museum

S17 HIBERNIA (1906–1937)

O.N. 120677 109g 79n 131b 91.1 × 21.7 × 7.3 feet.

3.1906: Completed by F.T. Everard, Greenhithe for his own account. *9.11.1937:* Drove ashore in bad weather and wrecked at East Runton, near Cromer while on passage from Goole to Sittingbourne with a cargo of coal.

Launch of **CAMBRIA** or **HIBERNIA**. *Company archives*

MARGUERITE *National Maritime Museum*

S18 MARGUERITE (1906–1953)

O.N. 114808 77g 63n 106b 83.0 × 19.6 × 5.6 feet.

1901: Completed by Engelskavarvet, Bergqvara, Sweden for the Bergqvara Syndicate Ltd., London as SUSSEX. *12.1901:* Renamed MARGUERITE. *5.1906:* Acquired by Mrs S.A. Everard. *3.1911:* Transferred to F.T. Everard. *12.1953:* Vessel broken up at Greenhithe by the owner.

S19 SPENCER (1906–1949)

O.N. 114755 78g 64n 106b 83.8 × 19.8 × 5.6 feet.

1900: Completed by Engelskavarvet, Bergqvara, Sweden for the Bergqvara Syndicate Ltd., London as KENT. *9.1901:* Renamed SPENCER. *5.1906:* Acquired by Mrs S.A. Everard. *3.1911:* Transferred to F.T. Everard. *10.1949:* Vessel broken up at Greenhithe by the owner.

S20 LINA (1906–1938)

O.N. 114768 78g 63n 106b 83.4 × 19.8 × 5.7 feet.

1901: Completed by Engelskavarvet, Bergqvara, Sweden for the Bergqvara Syndicate Ltd., London as ESSEX. *10.1901:* Renamed LINA. *5.1906:* Acquired by Mrs S.A. Everard. *3.1911:* Transferred to F.T. Everard. *17.11.1938:* Sunk in collision with the Danish steamship HENRY TEGNER 1,457/14 in Blackwall Reach off Enderby's Wharf, Greenwich with a cargo of cement. *18.11.1938:* Raised and towed to Greenhithe, declared a total loss and broken up by the owner.

S21 PRIDE OF THE COLNE (1909–1924)

O.N. 58170 50g 50n 83b 73.1 × 18.1 × 5.8 feet.

12.1869: Completed by unknown builder at Ipswich for Benjamin Beckwith, Colchester. *2.1880:* Sold to Joseph H. Beckwith, Colchester. *4.1908:* Sold to Wm. Claxton Dines, Grays. *2.1909:* Acquired by F.T. Everard. *11.1924:* Vessel broken up.

S22 ELIZABETH (2) (1910–1924)

O.N. 77023 44g 41n 68b 73.9 × 16.0 × 5.1 feet.

10.1877: Completed by Peter Blaker, Crayford for John J. Coleby, Ealing. *11.1900:* Sold to Arthur T. Viney Blaker, Crayford. *8.1901:* Sold to Mrs Emily Blaker, Crayford. *2.1910:* Acquired by F.T. Everard. *11.1924:* Vessel broken up.

S23 LANDWICK (1910–1923)

O.N. 85121 42g 42n 70b 73.8 × 17.5 × 5.4 feet.

3.1882: Completed by Peter Blaker, Crayford for Edward Rutter, Great Wakering. *4.1905:* Sold to Arthur T. Viney Blaker, Crayford. *2.1910:* Acquired by F.T. Everard. *1.1923:* Vessel converted into a lighter and register closed.

S24 BRITON (1910–1923)

O.N. 114752 82g 65n 106b 85.0 × 21.2 × 6.4 feet.

9.1901: Completed by F.T. Everard, Greenhithe for Wm. T. Clifford, London. *4.1910:* Acquired by F.T. Everard. *20.12.1923:* Drove ashore in heavy weather on West Sands near Blakeney and wrecked while on passage from Boston to Sandwich with a cargo of coal.

S25 SCOT (1910–1934)

O.N. 112845 76g 60n 100b 85.0 × 19.7 × 6.1 feet.

5.1901: Completed by F.T. Everard, Greenhithe for Wm. T. Clifford, London. *4.1910:* Acquired by F.T. Everard. *13.7.1934:* Run down and sunk by the Danish steamship ENGLAND 2,767/32 while at anchor off Harwich during a passage from London to Great Yarmouth with a cargo of rice in bags. Wreck subsequently blown up.

S26 FRED (1910–1921)

O.N. 67116 42g 42n 70b 76.3 × 16.7 × 4.8 feet.

1875: Completed by Reckitt & White, Brentford for J. Clarke, Rochester. *6.1879:* Sold to Gibbs & Co. Ltd., Thurrock. *4.1885:* Sold to Herbert Keep, London. *5.1897:* Sold to Cecil Chancellor & Harry Keep, London. *4.1904:* Sold to Alfred H. Keep Ltd., London. *12.1910:* Acquired by F.T. Everard. *4.1921:* Vessel broken up at Greenhithe by the owner.

SCOT *T. Farnham*

JANE *T. Farnham*

S27 JANE (1912–1947)

O.N. 102828 67g 57n 94b 81.5 × 19.0 × 5.6 feet.

12.1893: Completed by Robert Mark Shrubsall, Sittingbourne for George West, South Benfleet. *9.1894:* Sold to Ambrose Ellis, Stanford-le-Hope. *4.1899:* Sold to George & Alfred Vandervord, Southend. *1.1901:* Alfred Vandervord became sole owner. *10.1912:* Acquired by F.T. Everard. *2.6.1947:* Crushed in the Royal Albert Dock, London by the United States steamship TITAN 7,486/43 while carrying a cargo of cement and subsequently broken up at North Woolwich.

S28 MABEL (1913–1949)

O.N. 104309 56g 50n 83b 73.8 × 17.5 × 5.4 feet.

1894: Completed by Frederick Sollit, Rochester for Miss Edith C. Haymen, Rochester. *4.1913:* Acquired by F.T. Everard. *1949:* No further trace.

S29 NILE (1914–1920)

O.N. 81642 48g 41n 74b 75.7 × 16.4 × 5.2 feet.

5.1880: Completed by Peter Blaker, Crayford for Edward Rutter, Great Wakering. *4.1905:* Sold to Arthur T. Viney Blaker, Crayford. *2.1910:* Sold to Percy James Sanders, Greenhithe. *1.1914:* Acquired by William J. Everard. *10.1920:* Vessel converted into a lighter and register closed.

S30 QUEEN BEE (1915–1947)

O.N. 98079 70g 70n 106b 80.5 × 18.2 × 6.1 feet.

4.1890: Completed by Richard Talbot & Sons, Chiswick for Alfred Wimble, Northfleet. *1914:* Sold to Charles Charleton, London. *1915:* Acquired by F.T. Everard. *1947:* Sold to A. Youngman. *1948:* Sold to Thomas D. Griffin, Belvedere. *1.1978:* Vessel broken up at Kingston-on-Thames.

S31 I. BROUNCKER (1915–1925)

O.N. 94568 56g 49n 81b 75.0 × 16.6 × 5.5 feet.

4.1889: Completed by George H. Curel, Frindsbury for James Little, Strood. *1.1890:* Sold to William Watson, Rochester. *9.1904:* Sold to James Little, Strood. *5.1905:* Sold to Henry R. Surridge, Poplar. *7.1915:* Acquired by F.T. Everard. *1.1925:* Vessel broken up by the owner.

S32 JOSEPH AUGUSTUS (1915–1925)

O.N. 108277 54g 40n 67b 76.1 × 17.2 × 5.4 feet.

12.1897: Completed by Horace Shrubsall, Ipswich for Henry Augustus Mears, Fulham. *3.1910:* Sold to Joseph Theophilus Mears, Fulham. *8.1915:* Acquired by F.T. Everard. *7.1925:* Sold to Ephraim Dowsett, North Woolwich. *6.1927:* Sold to Horace A. Cunis, Southwark. *1932:* Sold to Horace C. Cunis, Southwark. *9.6.1937:* Sunk off Kent Works at Stone when she went athwart the bow of the anchored steamship FARFIELD 468/21 when bound upriver with a cargo of ballast. *6.1937:* Vessel broken up.

S33 ANNE (1915–1921)

O.N. 67037 38g 38n 63b 73.7 × 14.4 × 4.5 feet.

5.1872: Completed by George Weedon, Rochester for John W. Kemp, Rochester. *11.1873:* Sold to John Charleton, London. *5.1885:* Sold to Charles Charleton, London. *12.1915:* Acquired by F.T. Everard. *4.1921:* Vessel broken up.

S34 LADY MARJORIE (1915–1950)

O.N. 102783 73g 66n 110b 80.6 × 18.3 × 6.1 feet.

1893: Completed by Richard Talbot & Sons, Chiswick for Charles Dinham, London. *1896:* Sold to Charles Charleton, London. *12.1915:* Acquired by F.T. Everard. *9.1950:* Sold for use as a houseboat.

LADY MARJORIE

T. Farnham

S35 LADY MARY (1915–1957)

O.N. 112692 67g 49n 82b 84.5 × 18.3 × 5.6 feet.

1900: Completed by F.T. Everard, Greenhithe for Charles Charleton, London. *12.1915:* Acquired by F.T. Everard. *8.1957:* Sold to the Thames Barge Sailing Club, London, but subsequently condemned and dismantled at Erith.

S36 LADY MAUD (1915–1959)

O.N. 118305 76g 59n 98b 84.0 × 20.0 × 5.8 feet.

1903: Completed by F.T. Everard, Greenhithe for Charles Charleton, London. *12.1915:* Acquired by F.T. Everard. *1959:* Vessel broken up at Greenhithe by the owner.

S37 SPRING (1915–1924)

O.N. 67030 40g 40n 66b 73.3 × 14.6 × 4.5 feet.

1.1872: Completed by George Weedon, Rochester for John Charleton, London. *5.1885:* Sold to Charles Charleton, London. *12.1915:* Acquired by F.T. Everard. *12.1924:* Vessel broken up by the owner.

S38 MINNIE (1916–1923)

O.N. 43995 46g 46n 77b 73.1 × 17.8 × 5.6 feet.

2.1862: Completed by an unknown builder at Portsmouth for John Charleton, London. *5.1885:* Sold to Charles Charleton, London. *2.1916:* Acquired by F.T. Everard. *10.1923:* Partially dismantled for use as a mooring barge and register closed.

LADY MARY *W.S.P.L.*

LADY MAUD at Wivenhoe 1952.

R. Smith

S39 EVELYN (1916–1923) Ketch

O.N. 105103 103g 85n 87.45 × 27.1 × 7.6 feet.

1.1900: Completed by George & Thomas Smith Ltd., Rye for George Coote and others, Rye. *7.1916:* Acquired by F.T. Everard. *28.9.1923:* Sailed from London bound for Poole with a cargo of cement. Last seen by the master of the sailing vessel GARSON 69/1864 on *3.10.1923* about 10 miles south of the Royal Sovereign Light Vessel. Presumed lost.

S40 ROYALTY (1917–1940)

O.N. 109919 101g 85n 141b 86.4 × 21.3 × 6.2 feet.

10.1898: Completed by William Higham & Co., Rochester for Miss Edith C. Haymen, Rochester. *4.1907:* Sold to Thomas Watson, Rochester. *1.1915:* Sold to David J. Bradley, Rochester. *3.1917:* Acquired by F.T. Everard. *1.6.1940:* Beached and abandoned at Malo-les-Bains, France during the evacuation of the British Expeditionary Force from Dunkirk and became a total loss.

ROYALTY in the Royal Docks, London. *W.S.P.L.*

S41 SUNBEAM (1917–1921)

O.N. 90991 76g 59n 98b 84.5 × 18.6 × 6.0 feet.

10.1886: Completed by George H. Curel, Frindsbury for J. Dixon Lee, Frindsbury. *6.1910:* Sold to David J. Bradley & Thomas W. Germany, Rochester. *1.1911:* David J. Bradley became sole owner. *4.1917:* Acquired by Frederick W. Everard. *22.11.1921:* Struck a wreck, probably that of H.M.S. ARETHUSA, on the Cutler Bank off Orfordness and sank while on passage from London to Great Yarmouth with a cargo of wheat.

S42 MARTHA (1917–1941)

O.N. 106530 103g 86n 143b 86.7 × 21.6 × 6.7 feet.

3.1897: Completed by William Higham & Co., Rochester for Miss Edith C. Haymen, Rochester. *3.1907:* Sold to Thomas Watson, Rochester. *12.1911:* Sold to David J. Bradley, Rochester. *5.1917:* Acquired by F.T. Everard. *9.1918:* Tonnages became 109g 92n 155b. *19.1.1941:* Lost anchor in heavy weather, drove ashore and broke up on Albion Beach near Walton-on-the-Naze while on passage from London to Ipswich with a cargo of ground nuts.

MARTHA *T. Farnham*

S43 JOHN BAYLY (1918–1937)

O.N. 104760 66g 56n 96b 81.2 × 18.7 × 5.6 feet.

7.1895: Completed by W.M.H. Felton, Sandwich for the Margate Hoy Co. Ltd., Margate. *4.1918:* Acquired by Alfred M. Everard. *7.1937:* Vessel broken up at Greenhithe by the owner.

JOHN BAYLY *National Maritime Museum*

MARY GRAHAM at Ipswich in 1935. *J. Burrows*

S44 HER MAJESTY (1918–1947)

O.N. 109106 62g 53n 88b 82.0 × 18.7 × 5.7 feet.

1897: Completed by W.A. White, Sittingbourne for the Margate Hoy Co. Ltd., Margate. *5.1918:* Acquired by William J. Everard. *5.1947:* Sold for use as a houseboat and subsequently broken up at Chiswick.

S45 AGNES MARY (1919–1953)

O.N. 89870 65g 55n 91b 81.5 × 18.6 × 5.4 feet.

1894: Completed by W.M.H. Felton, Sandwich for William Waters Tritton and others, Faversham. *10.1901:* Tonnages became 65g 50n 80b. *7.1913:* S.A. Gray, Faversham became managing owner. *2.1919:* Acquired by Miss Alice E. Everard. *3.1953:* Vessel broken up at Greenhithe by the owner.

S46 HARRIETT HOWARD (1919–1930)

O.N. 73731 54g 48n 80b 75.6 × 18.5 × 5.4 feet.

11.1876: Completed by Robert M. Shrubsall, Milton for John & Israel Howard, Great Wakering. *4.1888:* Sold to Harriett Howard, Great Wakering. *5.1892:* Tonnages became 54g 44n 73b. *4.1919:* Acquired by F.T. Everard. *6.1930:* Partially dismantled for use as a mooring barge and register closed.

S47 NELLIE MARY (1921–1949)

O.N. 89862 55g 44n 73b 80.0 × 18.3 × 5.4 feet.

1889: Completed by John Taylor, Sittingbourne for John Horsford, Sittingbourne. *12.1899:* Sold to Esther Chrisfield & William F. Drake, Sittingbourne. *8.1900:* Sold to William Sellen, Faversham. *8.1918:* Sold to George G. Watson, Rochester. *9.1919:* Sold to James Carter, London. *1.1920:* Sold to S.S. Nimrod Ltd., London. *10.1921:* Sold to Albert W. Schooley, London. *12.1921:* Acquired by F.T. Everard. *10.1949:* Vessel broken up at Greenhithe by the owner.

S48 MARY GRAHAM (1922–1937)

O.N. 127261 67g 47n 79b 80.2 × 18.6 × 5.9 feet.

11.1913: Completed by Medway Barge Builders & Carriers Ltd., Rochester for George Elijah Johnson, Rochester. *1.1916:* Sold to Herbert J. Haste & James O. Fison, Ipswich. *5.1919:* Sold to Francis L., John R. & Martin T. Payne, London. *8.1920:* Sold to the British & Foreign Glass Bottle Co. Ltd., London. *3.1921:* Sold to Payne Bros. Ltd., London. *10.1922:* Acquired by the company. *30.10.1937:* Drove ashore at Great Yarmouth with a broken sprit while on passage from London to Great Yarmouth with a cargo of wheat. Became a total loss.

S49 ASH (1922–1947)

O.N. 118230 63g 49n 82b 79.0 × 18.1 × 5.7 feet.

7.1907: Completed by William Higham & Co., Rochester for Solomon J. Brice, Rochester. *7.1917:* Sold to Henry R. Surridge, London. *4.1920:* Sold to the British & Foreign Glass Bottle Co. Ltd., London. *3.1921:* Sold to Payne Bros. Ltd., London. *11.1922:* Acquired by the company. *4.1947:* Sold to Brian P. Probyn, London for use as a houseboat.

ASH *T. Farnham*

S50 GREENHITHE (1923–1963) Steel

O.N. 147562 116g 89n 180d 87.2 × 21.1 × 7.25 feet.

11.1923: Completed by Fellows & Co. Ltd., Great Yarmouth (Yard No. 300) for the company and rigged at Greenhithe. *5.1963:* Broken up at Grays by T.W. Ward Ltd.

S51 MARTINET (1923–1941) Ketch

O.N. 128880 126g 101n 95.2 × 22.8 × 8.0 feet.

11.1912: Completed by George & Thomas Smith Ltd., Rye for Richard Earnshaw and others, Goole. *3.1913:* Tonnages became 126g 99n. *6.1917:* Frederick Fish, Goole became managing owner. *6.1923:* Acquired by the company. *26.2.1941:* Struck an underwater object off Aldeburgh near the Hook Whiting Buoy. Started to take water and sank on *27.2.1941*. She was on passage from Swanscombe to Norwich with a cargo of cement.

S52 FAIR WIND (1923–1930)

O.N. 108509 45g 45n 74b 74.5 × 14.9 × 5.2 feet.

9.1897: Completed by Gill & Sons, Rochester for William H.S. Peters, London. *10.1900:* Sold to Thomas Watson, Rochester. *2.1912:* Sold to David J. Bradley, Rochester. *4.1918:* Sold to A.R. & S. Sales Ltd., Woolwich. *12.1923:* Acquired by the company. *10.1930:* Sold to Joseph H. Argent, Chiswick. *6.1938:* Vessel broken up.

GREENHITHE *T. Farnham*

MARTINET *National Maritime Museum*

WILL EVERARD on trials.

Company archives

S53 WILL EVERARD (1925–1966) Steel

O.N. 148677 187g 148n 190d 97.6 × 23.1 × 9.6 feet.

7.1925: Completed by Fellows & Co. Ltd., Great Yarmouth (Yard No. 308) for the company. *10.1950:* Fitted with a 6-cyl. 2SA auxiliary oil engine made by the Newbury Diesel Co. Ltd., Newbury. *12.1966:* Sold to Vernon S. Harvey, Royston and renamed WILL. *1971:* Sold to John R. Hobbins. *1974:* Re-engined with a 6-cyl. 4SA auxiliary oil engine made by L. Gardner & Sons Ltd., Manchester. *11.1976:* Sold to Overseas Containers Ltd., London. *1986:* Sold to P & O Containers Ltd., London. *1987:* Owner became P & O Steam Navigation Co., London. Still in service (1990).

S54 ALF EVERARD (1925–1943) Steel

O.N. 148691 187g 148n 190d 97.6 × 23.1 × 9.6 feet.

10.1925: Completed by Fellows & Co. Ltd., Great Yarmouth (Yard No. 309) for the company. *6.1943:* Converted to a motor coaster (See No. 61).

ALF EVERARD leading **HAUGHTY BELLE** in the 1930 Thames Barge Match. *Company archives*

FRED EVERARD and **ETHEL EVERARD** *Company archives*

S55 ETHEL EVERARD (1) (1926–1940) Steel

O.N. 149723 190g 158n 190d 97.6 × 23.1 × 9.6 feet.

9.1926: Completed by Fellows & Co. Ltd., Great Yarmouth (Yard No. 315) for the company. *1.6.1940:* Beached and abandoned at La Panne, France during the evacuation of the British Expeditionary Force from Dunkirk and became a total loss.

S56 FRED EVERARD (2) (1926–1938) Steel

O.N. 149743 190g 158n 190d 97.6 × 23.1 × 9.6 feet.

9.1926: Completed by Fellows & Co. Ltd., Great Yarmouth (Yard No. 316) for the company. *12.1938:* Converted to a motor coaster (See No. 54).

ETHEL EVERARD in the 1927 Thames Match. *Company archives*

ETHEL EVERARD abandoned at Dunkirk. *German propaganda*

SARA *Company archives*

S57 SARA (1929–1964)

O.N. 115858 68g 50n 84b 84.6 × 18.9 × 5.8 feet.

8.1902: Completed by Alfred White, Conyer Quay for Samuel Horlock, Mistley. *8.1907:* Sold to Albert H. Horlock, Mistley. *1.1929:* Acquired by the company. *1964:* Vessel broken up at Greenhithe by the owner.

S58 VERONICA (1932–1966)

O.N. 120691 70g 54n 89b 85.0 × 19.2 × 5.9 feet.

4.1906: Completed by Horace Shrubsall, East Greenwich for Clement Parker, Bradwell-on-Sea. *7.1932:* Acquired by the company. *6.1966:* Sold to Frank A. Kennedy & Jean Bell, Queenborough for use as a houseboat and renamed VERONICA BELL. *11.1976:* Broken up at Queenborough.

S59 PRINCESS (1935–1953)

O.N. 116171 74g 58n 96b 85.3 × 19.2 × 6.3 feet.

12.1902: Completed by Horace Shrubsall, East Greenwich for Robert R. Horlock, Mistley. *3.1903:* Robert A., Edmond A. & Horatio F. Horlock became joint owners. *7.1935:* Acquired by the company. *3.1953:* Vessel broken up at Greenhithe by the owner.

VERONICA *W.S.P.L.*

PRINCESS *National Maritime Museum*

S60 MIRA (1943–1949)

O.N. 118459 60g 45n 74b 76.4 × 18.0 × 5.9 feet.

1904: Completed by Nash & Miller, Battersea for Robert Miller, Battersea. *12.1913:* Owners became Robert & Hugh Miller, Battersea. *2.1936:* Owner became Hugh Miller, Pelican Wharf, Wapping. *6.1943:* Owner became Beatrix Miller, Wapping. *6.1943:* Transferred to Nash & Miller Ltd. (W.J. Everard, manager), London. *1949:* Vessel broken up.

MIRA *National Maritime Museum*

S61 MONA (1943–1945)

O.N. 118404 63g 47n 78b 77.0 × 18.4 × 5.9 feet.

3.1904: Completed by Nash & Miller, Battersea for Robert Miller, Battersea. *12.1913:* Owners became Robert & Hugh Miller, Battersea. *2.1936:* Owner became Hugh Miller, Pelican Wharf, Wapping. *6.1943:* Owner became Beatrix Miller, Wapping. *6.1943:* Transferred to Nash & Miller Ltd. (W.J. Everard, manager), London. *8.1945:* Sold to George A. Nunnelly, Maidenhead for use as a houseboat.

S62 MONICA (1943–1947)

O.N. 123699 66g 54n 90b 80.0 × 18.6 × 5.7 feet.

9.1906: Completed by Nash & Miller, Battersea for Robert Miller, Battersea. *12.1913:* Owners became Hugh & John Miller, Battersea. *2.1936:* Owner became Hugh Miller, Pelican Wharf, Wapping. *6.1943:* Owner became Beatrix Miller, Wapping. *6.1943:* Transferred to Nash & Miller Ltd. (W.J. Everard, manager), London. *10.1947:* Vessel broken up.

S63 MYRTLE (1943–1947)

O.N. 112792 58g 46n 76b 77.0 × 17.7 × 5.5 feet.

1.1901: Completed by Nash & Miller, Battersea for Charlotte A. & Robert Miller, Battersea and William Higgs, Clapham. *11.1903:* Owner became Robert Miller, Battersea. *12.1913:* Owners became Hugh & John Miller, Battersea. *2.1936:* Owner became Hugh Miller, Pelican Wharf, Wapping. *11.1942:* Owner became Beatrix Miller, Wapping. *6.1943:* Transferred to Nash & Miller Ltd. (W.J. Everard, manager), London. *12.1947:* Vessel broken up.

DREADNOUGHT *Company archives*

S64 DREADNOUGHT (1957–1964)

O.N. 123849 85g 70n 113b 87.1 × 20.1 × 6.6 feet.

6.1906: Completed by Alfred White, Sittingbourne for Edward J. & Walter Goldsmith, London. *6.1947:* Sold to the Successors to Thomas F. Wood (Gravesend) Ltd., Gravesend. *4.1953:* Sold to Imperial Chemical Industries Ltd., London. *8.1957:* Acquired by the company. *9.1957:* Transferred to Everard Shipping Co. Ltd. *3.1964:* Broken up at Greenhithe by the owner.

Greenhithe about 1948 with a collection of sailing barges awaiting their fates. The **CUTTY SARK** and **H.M.S. WORCESTER** can be seen in the background.
Company archives

STEAM AND MOTOR VESSELS

NOTES

The notation '1', '2', etc. in brackets after a ship's name indicates that she is the first, second, etc., ship of that name in the fleet. The dates following the name are those of entering and leaving Everard ownership or management. The histories are in chronological order according to acquisition or to the date of completion for new ships. Hulls are steel unless otherwise stated.

On the first line is given the ship's Official Number in the British Registry followed by her tonnages, gross (g), net (n), and where known, her deadweight (d). From ship numbers 237 and M84 the gross and net tonnages have been calculated according to the International Convention on Tonnage Measurement of Ships (1969) and are considerably higher than for the same size ship measured under the previous rules. Dimensions given are registered length × breadth × depth expressed in decimal feet for ships numbers 1 to 130, M1 to M49 and T1 to T20. The dimensions for all other ships are the overall length × breadth × summer draught expressed in metres.

On the second line is a description of the engine and the name of the engine builder. In the case of engines built by the Newbury Diesel Co. Ltd. and predecessors the type is also given. T.3-cyl. denotes a triple expansion three cylinder steam engine and C.2-cyl. denotes a compound two cylinder steam engine. For motor vessels the number of cylinders is given and whether the machinery is two or four stroke, single or double acting (e.g. 4SA, 2SA etc.).

Before 1922 the individual family member owning a vessel is shown but after the formation of the Limited Company in April 1922 to which all vessels were transferred, the registered owner is only quoted when it is a member of the Everard Group other than F.T. Everard & Sons Ltd. The other members of the Group with the approximate dates of their ship-owning activities with Everards are as follows:

Everard Shipping Co. Ltd.	1950–1974
J. Hay & Sons Ltd.	1956–1985
Cattedown Wharves Ltd.	1957–1967
West River Shipping Co. Ltd.	1960–1967
Clydesdale Shipowners Co. Ltd.	1961–1984
Scottish Navigation Co. Ltd.	1961–1980 and 1990–date
Thames Tankers Ltd.	1971–1985
County Ships Ltd.	1980–1985
Gowan Shipping Co. Ltd.	1980–1985
F.T. Everard Shipping Ltd.	1986–date

To avoid unnecessary repetition the manager has been omitted for all vessels owned within the Everard Group of companies.

Ships' histories have been corrected to December 1990.

1. GRIT (1) (1913–1916) Wooden auxiliary ketch

O.N. 135249 147g 79n 200d 94.0 × 23.0 × 8.9 feet.
2-cyl. 2SA oil engine by Plenty & Son Ltd., Newbury.

7.1913: Completed by F.T. Everard, Greenhithe for his own account. *21.10.1916:* Sunk by gunfire from the German submarine UB29 about 25 miles south of Beachy Head while carrying military stores to Le Havre, France.

GRIT (1): the first motor vessel.

Author's collection

2. NORSEMAN (1916–1918)

O.N. 119150 352g 145n 142.0 × 24.1 × 10.6 feet.
C.2-cyl. steam engine by Renfrew Bros. & Co., Irvine.

8.1904: Completed by Irvine Shipbuilding & Engineering Co. (1902) Ltd., Irvine (Yard No. 31) for J. Kennedy & Sons, Glasgow. *7.1916:* Acquired by F.T. Everard. *10.1918:* Sold to Cullen, Allen & Co. Ltd., Belfast. *1920:* Sold to J.J. Murphy, Waterford. *5.1923:* Sold to Rose & Tate Ltd., Newcastle-on-Tyne. *7.1923:* Owners became Tate Shipping Co. Ltd., Newcastle-on-Tyne. *12.6.1925:* Sank off Great Yarmouth in position 52.45N, 01.53E following a collision in fog with the steamship BURNSIDE 916/20, while on passage from London to Newcastle in ballast.

TOSCA (the middle ship).

R. Anderson

3. TOSCA (1916–1926)

O.N. 99738 449g 169n 550d 155.4 × 25.6 × 12.5 feet.
C.2-cyl. steam engine by Ailsa Shipbuilding Co. Ltd., Troon.

6.1908: Completed by Ailsa Shipbuilding Co. Ltd., Ayr (Yard No. 208) for Mrs. G.A. Smith (W.W.C. Smith & Co., managers), Glasgow. *10.1916:* Acquired by F.T. Everard. *9.1926:* Sold to W.A. Wilson, Southampton. *12.1933:* Sold to G.B. Figari, Antonio Maggiola & Co., Genoa, Italy. *1940:* Sold to G.M. Scotto, Genoa, Italy. *24.4.1943:* Torpedoed and sunk by H.M. Submarine SAHIB south of Lipari.

4. BELLAVALE (1917–1920)

O.N. 129630 448g 176n 160.6 × 25.0 × 9.4 feet.
C.2-cyl. steam engine by Muir & Houston Ltd., Glasgow.

1.1910: Completed by Mackie & Thomson Ltd., Glasgow (Yard No. 385) for Samuel Kelly, Belfast. *1911:* Owners became John Kelly Ltd., Belfast. *1913:* Sold to Wilson & Reid, Belfast. *1914:* Sold to Henry Burden Junior & Co. Ltd., Poole. *1917:* Acquired by F.T. Everard. *1920:* Sold to Spillers Steamship Co. Ltd., Cardiff and renamed WHEATVALE. *1927:* Owners restyled Spillers Milling & Associated Industries Ltd. *1927:* Sold to Ald Shipping Co. Ltd., Bristol and renamed BURRINGTON COMBE. *1939:* Sold to D.P. Barnett, London. *1939:* Sold to Zubi Shipping Co. Ltd., London. *1940:* Sold to S. William Coe & Co. Ltd. (W.J. Ireland, manager), Liverpool. *1943:* Sold to H. Harrison (Shipping) Ltd. (same manager), Liverpool. *1945:* Sold to G.A. Sheves, Fraserburgh and renamed ARCHVALE. *1952:* Sold to Rose Line Ltd. (T. Rose & Co., managers), Sunderland and renamed DALESIDE. *12.11.1956:* Arrived at Dordrecht en route for Hendrik Ido Ambacht, Holland where she was broken up by Holland Scheepsloperij & Machinehandel N.V.

BELLAVALE with earlier funnel marking. *J. Clarkson*

GRANA at Rouen.

G. Dines

5. GRANA/CAPABLE (1) (1920–1935) Auxiliary schooner/motor coaster

O.N. 144446 214g 158n 108.6 × 23.0 × 10.1 feet.
2-cyl. 2SA oil engine by Kromhout Motorenfabriek, Amsterdam, Holland.

1918: Completed by Gebroeder Zwolsman Scheepsbouwmeesters, Ijlst, Holland for their own account as the schooner GRANA. *1919:* Sold to A/S Mercur (C.B. Nielsen, manager), Skien, Norway. *3.1920:* Acquired by F.T. Everard and fitted with a 2-cyl. 2SA auxiliary engine made by Plenty & Son Ltd., Newbury. *4.1925:* Converted to a motor coaster, fitted with a 4-cyl. 2SA oil engine made by Plenty & Son Ltd., Newbury and renamed CAPABLE. Tonnages became 216g, 128n and 275d. *12.1935:* Sold to John D. Sullivan, Westcliff-on-Sea. *5.6.1940:* Struck a mine and sank 2.8 miles from Horsesand Fort at Spithead while on passage from Alderney to Portsmouth with a cargo of stone.

CAPABLE on trials after conversion.

Author's collection

6. ROAM (1921–1926) Tanker

O.N. 145222 129g 105n 105.6 × 21.1 × 7.3 feet.
2-cyl. 2SA oil engine by J. & C.G. Bolinders Co., Stockholm, Sweden.

1915: Completed by Osbourne, Graham & Co., Hylton as dry cargo lighter X42 for the Admiralty. On completion converted to a tanker and given the name LOBSTER. *12.1920:* Sold to F.H. Connor, London. *5.1921:* Acquired by F.T. Everard and renamed ROAM. *26.10.1926:* Foundered in bad weather off the North East Goodwins while on passage from London to Bruges with a cargo of tar.

ALCHYMIST *A. Duncan*

7. ALCHYMIST (1) (1922–1950) Tanker

O.N. 105770 382g 209n 400d 147.5 × 24.1 × 12.8 feet.
T.3-cyl. steam engine by North Eastern Marine Engineering Co. Ltd., Newcastle.

12.1895: Completed by W. Dobson & Co. Ltd., Newcastle (Yard No. 81) for Thomas Burt Haywood, London. *7.1910:* Owners became Burt, Boulton & Haywood Ltd., London. *3.1922:* Acquired by F.T. Everard. *3.1950:* Sold to BISCO and allocated to T.W. Ward Ltd. for breaking up at Grays.

Note: The Limited Company was formed on *1.4.1922* and became known as F.T. Everard & Sons Ltd. The ownership of all vessels was transferred to the Company.

8. WANDER (1922–1928) Tanker

O.N. 146683 130g 83n 105.6 × 21.1 × 7.4 feet.
1- or 2-cyl. 2SA oil engine by J. & C.G. Bolinders Co., Stockholm, Sweden.

1915: Completed by Ropner & Sons Ltd., Stockton-on-Tees (Yard No. 514) as dry cargo lighter X3 for the Admiralty. On completion converted to a tanker and given the name OYSTER. *2.1922:* Sold to F.H. Connor, London. *12.1922:* Acquired by the company, renamed WANDER and re-engined with a 2-cyl. 2SA '2P50' oil engine made by Plenty & Son Ltd., Newbury. *23.11.1928:* Foundered in bad weather in the North Sea while on passage from Great Yarmouth to Hull with a cargo of molasses.

PAMELA HOPE

Author's collection

9. PAMELA HOPE (1923–1933) Wood

O.N. 146189 160g 113n 200d 89.9 × 22.0 × 9.2 feet.
4-cyl. 2SA oil engine by Sulzer Frères, Winterthur, Switzerland.

11.1921: Completed by Strand Shipbuilding Co., Chiswick for Hope Lighterage Co. Ltd. (A.R.C. Johnston, manager), London. *1.1923:* Acquired by the company. *1931:* Re-engined with a 2-cyl. 2SA 'P50' oil engine made by Plenty-Still Oil Engines Ltd., Newbury. *31.10.1932:* Anchor cable parted in bad weather and vessel drove ashore between Burnham Overy and Wells while on light passage from London to Wells. *24.11.1932:* Refloated and towed to Wells for temporary repairs and later to Greenhithe where she arrived *22.12.1932*. *31.1.1933:* Declared a constructive total loss and subsequently sold for use as a stores hulk.

FENCIBLE

Author's collection

10. FENCIBLE (1923–1929)

O.N. 132905 71g 36n 79.0 × 17.2 × 6.2 feet.
2-cyl. 2SA oil engine by Plenty & Son, Ltd. Newbury.

1913: Completed by Rennie Forrestt Shipbuilding, Engineering & Drydock Co. Ltd., Wivenhoe for W. Fieldgate, Brightlingsea. *10.1915:* Sold to the Admiralty for use as a boom defence stores vessel. *1.1923:* Acquired by the company. *10.1929:* Sold to J.J. Prior Ltd., London. *2.1934:* Sold to A. Batchelor, Halling, Rochester. *1936:* Sold to S. Goldthorpe, Grimsby. *1950:* Owner became S.L. Goldthorpe Ltd., Grimsby. *1969:* Broken up in the Humber area.

11. GRIT (2) (1923–1934) Wood

O.N. 147531 193g 110n 250d 105.8 × 23.5 × 8.9 feet.
4-cyl. 2SA oil engine by Plenty & Son Ltd., Newbury.

8.1923: Completed by F.T. Everard & Sons Ltd. at Greenhithe for their own account. *22.2.1934:* Sank after collision in fog with the Latvian steamship GAISMA 3,077/00 off Hythe while on passage from Keadby to Exeter with a cargo of coal.

GRIT (2) on trials off Greenhithe. *Author's collection*

12. AGILITY (1) (1924–1958) Tanker

O.N. 147633 522g 183n 700d 160.3 × 26.2 × 12.3 feet.
T.3-cyl. steam engine by Wm. Beardmore & Co. Ltd., Coatbridge.

4.1924: Completed by George Brown & Co., Greenock (Yard No. 141) for the company. *1958:* Sold to BISCO and allocated to T.W. Ward Ltd. for breaking up at Grays. Broken up by 12.1958.

AGILITY (1): the first 'ITY'. *W.S.P.L.*

13. AUDACITY (1) (1925–1942) Tanker

O.N. 148704 589g 242n 700d 172.8 × 26.7 × 12.7 feet.
T.3-cyl. steam engine by Wm. Beardmore & Co. Ltd., Coatbridge.

11.1925: Completed by George Brown & Co., Greenock (Yard No. 149) for the company. *1.3.1942:* Sunk by a mine south of the Humber Light Vessel in position 53.34N, 0.23E while on passage from Selby to Purfleet with a cargo of palm kernel oil.

AUDACITY (1) *J. Clarkson*

14. **RAMBLE (1925–1959)** Tanker

O.N. 148606 151g 63n 106.4 × 21.4 × 7.5 feet.
Oil engine of unknown make but possibly by the shipbuilder.

1915: Completed by Wm. Beardmore & Co. Ltd., Dalmuir as the dry cargo lighter X161 for the Admiralty. On completion converted to a tanker and renamed MUSSEL. *1920:* Re-engined with a 2-cyl. 2SA '2P50' oil engine made by Plenty & Son Ltd., Newbury. *12.1922:* Sold to Dashwood & Partners, London. *5.1925:* Acquired by the company and renamed RAMBLE. *1933:* Re-engined with a 2-cyl. 2SA 'SID' oil engine made by the Newbury Diesel Co. Ltd., Newbury. *1959:* Broken up at Greenhithe by the owner.

RAMBLE *W. Fry*

15. **STANLEY BALDWIN (1926–1946)**

O.N. 148506 149g 99n 107.2 × 20.9 × 7.5 feet.
1-cyl. 2SA oil engine by J. & C.G. Bolinders Co., Stockholm, Sweden.

1915: Completed by Wm. Beardmore & Co. Ltd., Dalmuir as the dry cargo lighter X167 for the Admiralty. *5.1920:* Sold to All Seas Marine & Salvage Co., London. *11.1925:* Sold to P.I. Woodcock, J.T. Brenton & P. Hakewill (P. Hakewill, manager), Falmouth. *7.1926:* Acquired by the company and renamed STANLEY BALDWIN. *1926:* Re-engined with a 2-cyl. 2SA 'P50' type oil engine made by Plenty & Son Ltd., Newbury. *1938:* Re-engined with a 2-cyl. 2SA 'P50' type oil engine re-conditioned by the Newbury Diesel Co. Ltd., Newbury. *12.1946:* Sold to M.P. Almlund, Ommel, Denmark and renamed LAIKA. *1952:* Sold to J. Kristensen, Marstal, Denmark and renamed ELMO. *1952:* Re-engined with a 2-cyl. 2SA oil engine by A/B Bolinder-Munktell, Eskilstuna, Sweden. *1956:* Sold to A. Otte & G. Jacobs, Hamburg, West Germany. *1965:* Sold to W. Holzman, Hamburg, West Germany and renamed GUTHOLZ. *1985:* Believed to have been broken up at Hamburg, West Germany.

STANLEY BALDWIN *S. Shipman*

16. **SAUNTER (1926–1946)** Tanker

O.N. 146604 143g 96n 105.4 × 21.1 × 7.4 feet.
2-cyl. 2SA Kromhout oil engine by Plenty & Sons Ltd., Newbury.

1915: Completed by Jos. T. Eltringham, Willington Quay-on-Tyne as the dry cargo lighter X106 for the Admiralty. On completion converted to a tanker and renamed SHRIMP. *6.1920:* Sold to M.S. Hilton, London. *7.1922:* Sold to James Dredging, Towage & Transport Co. Ltd., London and renamed BOTLEY. *11.1926:* Acquired by the company and renamed SAUNTER. *1927:* Re-engined with a 2-cyl. 2SA '2P50' oil engine made by Plenty & Son Ltd., Newbury. *4.1938:* Re-engined with a 2-cyl. 2SA 'SID' oil engine made by the Newbury Diesel Co. Ltd., Newbury. *8.1946:* Sold to W.G.S. Crouch & Sons Ltd., Greenhithe. *3.1970:* Broken up at Greenhithe by the owners.

SAUNTER as **BOTLEY**

Author's collection

17. PROWESS (1926–1961) Tanker

O.N. 149707 207g 77n 250d 106.1 × 23.2 × 9.1 feet.
4-cyl. 2SA 'P50' type oil engine by Plenty & Son Ltd., Newbury.

8.1926: Completed by George Brown & Co. Ltd., Greenock (Yard No. 154) for the company. *1938:* Re-engined with a 4-cyl. 2SA 'F' type oil engine made by the Newbury Diesel Co. Ltd., Newbury. *1961:* Sold to A.E. Peirce, Canvey Island. Resold to N.V. Machine & Scheepsloperij 'De Koophandel' for breaking up at Nieuw Lekkerland, Holland. Broken up by *3.1962*.

PROWESS *A. Duncan*

18. TIRYDAIL (1926–1946)

O.N. 136149 650g 363n 900d 176.0 × 27.6 × 11.8 feet.
T.3-cyl. steam engine by Plenty & Son Ltd., Newbury.

3.1918: Completed by C.H. Walker & Co. Ltd., Sudbrook (Yard No. 231) for Cleeves Western Valleys Anthracite Collieries Ltd. (T.D. John, manager), Swansea. *1920:* Manager became V.M. Williams. *1926:* Acquired by the company. *2.1946:* Sold to Williamstown Shipping Co. Ltd. (Comben Longstaff & Co. Ltd., managers), London and renamed LINCOLNBROOK. *7.1947:* Sold to Duff, Herbert & Mitchell Ltd., London and renamed JOSEPH MITCHELL. *9.2.1950:* Foundered off Ballycotton after striking submerged rocks while on passage from Garston to Cork with a cargo of coal.

TIRYDAIL *W.S.P.L.*

19. HEATHER PET/ASSURITY (1) YTIRUSSA (1927–1959) Wood

O.N. 146049 164g 94n 217d 94.0 × 23.5 × 8.0 feet.
2-cyl. 2SA oil engine by Vickers-Petters Ltd., Ipswich.

1921: Completed by Wills & Packham Ltd., Sittingbourne for Vickers-Petters Ltd. (H. Hillcoat, manager), London as HEATHER PET. *10.1923:* Sold to R.A. Gray, Steeple. *10.1923:* Sold to C.E. Mann, Kings Lynn. *3.1927:* Acquired by the company. *8.1934:* Renamed ASSURITY and re-engined with a 2-cyl. 2SA 'SID' type oil engine made by the Newbury Diesel Co. Ltd., Newbury. *1942:* Re-engined with a 6-cyl. 2SA 'C' type oil engine made by the Newbury Diesel Co. Ltd., Newbury. *1956:* Engine removed and hull used for training, renamed YTIRUSSA. *1959:* Broken up at Greenhithe by the owner.

ASSURITY (1) *Author's collection*

Greenhithe about 1957 with the **AGILITY (1)**, probably waiting for her voyage to the breakers, the **YTIRUSSA** and the hulk of the **LADY MAUD**. *J. Hines*

ABILITY (1)

A. Duncan

20. ABILITY (1) (1928–1940)

O.N. 149982 262g 125n 250d 115.1 × 23.2 × 8.7 feet.
5-cyl. 2SA 'P50' type oil engine by Plenty & Son Ltd., Newbury.

1.1928: Completed by Fellows & Co. Ltd., Great Yarmouth (Yard No. 319) for the company. *1938:* Lengthened to 136.8 feet, tonnages became 293g, 162n and 300d. *18.11.1940:* Sunk by a mine, six miles east of Clacton in position 51.45N, 01.12E while on passage from Greenhithe to Great Yarmouth with a cargo of cement.

AUTHORITY (1)

D. Brown

21. AUTHORITY (1) (1928–1965) Tanker

O.N. 160484 616g 274n 761d 179.8 × 26.7 × 12.7 feet.
T.3-cyl. steam engine by Wm. Beardmore & Co. Ltd., Coatbridge.

5.1928: Completed by George Brown & Co., Greenock (Yard No. 161) for the company. *11.1965:* Sold to A.E. Peirce, Canvey Island, resold to Brugse Scheepsloperij, Bruges, Belgium and arrived at Bruges for breaking up *5.3.1966.*

AMENITY (1)

R. Craig

22. AMENITY (1) (1928–1940)

O.N. 160543 262g 125n 250d 115.1 × 23.2 × 8.7 feet.
5-cyl. 2SA 'P50' type oil engine by Plenty & Son Ltd., Newbury.

7.1928: Completed by Fellows & Co. Ltd., Great Yarmouth (Yard No. 320) for the company. *1936:* Lengthened to 135.2 feet, tonnages became 297g 165n and 300d and re-engined with a 3-cyl. 2SA 'SBD' type oil engine made by the Newbury Diesel Co. Ltd., Newbury. *15.11.1940:* Struck a mine off the Humber in position 53.33N, 00.09E while on passage from Goole to Margate with a cargo of coal. The wreck was subsequently sunk by gunfire.

23. ASPERITY (1) (1929–1941) Tanker

O.N. 161300 699g 305n 760d 187.4 × 28.2 × 13.4 feet.
T.3-cyl. steam engine by Wm. Beardmore & Co. Ltd., Coatbridge.

9.1929: Completed by George Brown & Co., Greenock (Yard No. 170) for the company. *29.11.1941:* Sunk by a torpedo from a German E-boat in position 53.11N, 01.07E while on passage from London to Hull in ballast.

GLEN MARY

G. Osbon

24. GLEN MARY (1929–1940)

O.N. 145864 394g 148n 350d 143.2 × 24.6 × 10.5 feet.
T.3-cyl. steam engine by the shipbuilder.

8.1921: Completed by Crabtree & Co. Ltd., Great Yarmouth (Yard No. 183) for Wilson Bros. Bobbin Co. Ltd. (E.W. Turner, manager), Liverpool. *1929:* Acquired by the company. *1940:* Sold to G. Couper & Co. Ltd., Helmsdale. *1947:* Sold to J. & A. Gardner Ltd., Glasgow and renamed SAINT KEARAN. *6.4.1957:* Arrived at Port Glasgow to be broken up by Smith & Houston Ltd.

25. TARTARY (1929–1938) Tanker

O.N. 147548 300g 134n 130.3 × 23.2 × 9.8 feet.
C.2-cyl. steam engine by the shipbuilder.

10.1923: Completed by Crabtree & Co. Ltd., Great Yarmouth (Yard No. 182) for Burt, Boulton & Haywood Ltd., London. *11.1929:* Acquired by the company. *14.2.1938:* Grounded on the Haisborough Sands in bad weather. Refloated but foundered on the Barber Sands off Winterton where she exploded. She was on passage from Zaandam to Hull with a cargo of linseed oil.

TARTARY *W.S.P.L.*

26. ASSIDUITY (1) (1930–1960)

O.N. 162508 350g 186n 412d 135.3 × 24.6 × 8.7 feet.
5-cyl. 2SA 'P50' type oil engine by Plenty-Still Oil Engines Ltd., Newbury.

11.1930: Completed by George Brown & Co., Greenock (Yard No. 174) for the company. *1954:* Re-engined with a 6-cyl. 2SA 'F' type oil engine made by the Newbury Diesel Co. Ltd., Newbury. *6.1961:* Sold to BISCO and allocated to T.W. Ward Ltd. for breaking up at Grays where work commenced *20.6.1961.*

ASSIDUITY (1) *D. Brown*

ANNUITY (1)
aground near Rowhedge.

R. Smith

27. LEELEE/ANNUITY (1) (1931–1960)

O.N. 139195 144g 65n 210d 89.0 × 19.1 × 9.1 feet.
2-cyl. 2SA oil engine by J. & C.G. Bolinders Co., Stockholm, Sweden.

6.1916: Completed by Rennie Forrestt Shipbuilding, Engineering & Drydock Co. Ltd., Wivenhoe (Yard No. 1269) for James Pollock Sons & Co. Ltd., Faversham as LEELEE. *1925:* Sold to H.R. Gilbert, Brightlingsea. *1931:* Acquired by the company. *1933:* Re-engined with a 3-cyl. 2SA 'SID' type oil engine made by the Newbury Diesel Co. Ltd., Newbury and renamed ANNUITY. *1952:* Re-engined with a 6-cyl. 2SA 'C' type oil engine made by the Newbury Diesel Co. Ltd., Newbury. *9.6.1960:* Arrived at Grays for breaking up by T.W. Ward Ltd.

ARIDITY

T. Rayner

28. ARIDITY (1931–1966)

O.N. 162607 336g 172n 366d 130.0 × 24.6 × 8.9 feet.
5-cyl. 2SA 'P50' type oil engine by Plenty-Still Oil Engines Ltd., Newbury.

7.1931: Completed by Fellows & Co. Ltd., Great Yarmouth (Yard No. 330) for the company. *19.10.1940:* Sunk by a mine in the Thames Estuary 40 yards north east of the Oaze Light Vessel whilst inward bound to London with a cargo of wheat. Salved and declared a constructive total loss. Subsequently repaired at Greenhithe and re-engined with a 6-cyl. 2SA 'F' type oil engine made by the Newbury Diesel Co. Ltd., Newbury. *20.3.1942:* Re-entered service. *7.1966:* Sold to M. Gigilinis & D. Kalkasinas, Thessalonika, Greece and renamed SOULA. *1971:* Sold to C. Soulanis and others, Samos, Greece. *1974:* Sold to E. Drakatos, Piraeus, Greece. *1976:* Sold to Yellow Sea Marine Co. Ltd., Limassol, Cyprus and renamed STAR 1. *1988:* Deleted from Lloyds Register due to lack of information.

ACTIVITY (1)

A. Duncan

29. ACTIVITY (1) (1931–1966)

O.N. 162654 358g 182n 452d 135.2 × 24.6 × 9.1 feet.
5-cyl. 2SA 'P50' type oil engine by Plenty-Still Oil Engines Ltd., Newbury.

10.1931: Completed by George Brown & Co., Greenock (Yard No. 181) for the company. 1946: Re-engined with a 5-cyl. 2SA 'O' type oil engine made by the Newbury Diesel Co. Ltd., Newbury. *1962:* Re-engined with a 6-cyl. 2SA 'G' type oil engine made by the Newbury Diesel Co. Ltd., Newbury. *2.1966:* Sold to M. Gigilinis & D. Kalkasinas, Thessalonika, Greece and renamed GIANKAROS. *1971:* Sold to J. Calafatis, Piraeus, Greece and renamed IOANNIS K. *1977:* Sold to P. Panagopoulos, Piraeus, Greece. Believed still in existence but no owner recorded in Lloyds Register since 1985.

30. ACCLIVITY (1) (1931–1952) Tanker

O.N. 162667 389g 174n 499d 164.0 × 24.6 × 8.6 feet.
5-cyl. 2SA 'P50' type oil engine by Plenty-Still Oil Engines Ltd., Newbury.

12.1931: Completed by George Brown & Co., Greenock (Yard No. 182) for the company. *5.1942:* Re-engined with a 4-cyl. 2SA 'O' type oil engine made by the Newbury Diesel Co. Ltd., Newbury. *20.1.1952:* Sank five miles east by south of Dunstanburgh Castle after striking a submerged object while on passage from Thameshaven to Newburgh with cargo of linseed oil. She had been taken in tow by the motor vessel MAGRIX 454/38 but the tow rope parted.

ACCLIVITY (1)
fitting out at Greenock.

D. Brown

31. ACTUALITY (1) (1933–1940)

O.N. 163314 311g 149n 340d 129.2 × 24.7 × 8.9 feet.
4-cyl. 2SA 'SID' type oil engine by the Newbury Diesel Co. Ltd., Newbury.

2.1933: Completed by Fellows & Co. Ltd., Great Yarmouth (Yard No. 332) for the company. *8.12.1940:* Sunk by a mine in the Thames Estuary three miles south west of the Mouse Light Vessel while on passage from London to Norwich with a cargo of cement.

ACTUALITY (1) *Gainsborough Library*

ACTUOSITY

D. Brown

32. ACTUOSITY (1933–1940)

O.N. 163316 359g 177n 430d 135.3 × 24.6 × 9.1 feet.
5-cyl. 2SA 'SID' type oil engine by the Newbury Diesel Co. Ltd., Newbury.

2.1933: Completed by George Brown & Co., Greenock (Yard No. 183) for the company. *1937:* Re-engined with a 4-cyl. 2SA 'SID' type oil engine made by the Newbury Diesel Co. Ltd., Newbury. *3.10.1940:* Sank off Cromer in position 52.57N, 01.29E after striking a submerged object while on passage from Newcastle to London with a cargo of wheat.

APRICITY (1)

E. Taylor

33. APRICITY (1) (1933–1965)

O.N. 163393 402g 200n 525d 142.8 × 25.6 × 9.3 feet.
5-cyl. 2SA 'SBD' type oil engine by the Newbury Diesel Co. Ltd., Newbury.

10.1933: Completed by George Brown & Co., Greenock (Yard No. 184) for the company. *8.1965:* Sold to M. Gigilinis & D. Kalkasinas, Thessalonika, Greece and renamed SKORPIOS. *1972:* Sold to A. Tzitzifas & Co. (M. Gigilinis, manager), Thessalonika, Greece. *1974:* Sold to A. & C. Aronis, Piraeus, Greece. Still in service (1990).

ANTIQUITY

J. Callis

34. ANTIQUITY (1933–1965)

O.N. 163400 311g 148n 340d 129.2 × 24.7 × 8.9 feet.
4-cyl. 2SA 'SID' type oil engine by the Newbury Diesel Co. Ltd., Newbury.

11.1933: Completed by Fellows & Co. Ltd., Great Yarmouth (Yard No. 333) for the company. *1942:* Re-engined with a 6-cyl. 2SA 'G' type oil engine made by the Newbury Diesel Co. Ltd., Newbury. *8.1965:* Sold to D. & L. Taylor Ltd., London. *1966:* Deleted from Lloyds Register as no longer sea-going. *1975:* Broken up.

ACRITY

W.S.P.L.

35. ACRITY (1934–1963)

O.N. 163438 403g 200n 520d 142.8 × 25.6 × 9.3 feet.
4-cyl. 2SA 'SBD' type oil engine by the Newbury Diesel Co. Ltd., Newbury.

2.1934: Completed by George Brown & Co., Greenock (Yard No. 185) for the company. *12.1963:* Sold to A.E. Peirce, Canvey Island. Resold to Metaal Handel & Sloopwerken H.P. Heuvelman for breaking up at Krimpen-aan-den-Ijssel, Holland where work was completed by *9.1964.*

36. ANGULARITY (1) (1934–1941)

O.N. 163479 501g 260n 600d 160.5 × 26.7 × 9.4 feet.
5-cyl. 2SA 'SBD' type oil engine by the Newbury Diesel Co. Ltd., Newbury.

6.1934: Completed by George Brown & Co., Greenock (Yard No. 187) for the company. *6.2.1941:* Sunk by a German E-boat in the Shipwash Channel while on passage from Ipswich to Newcastle with a cargo of phosphates. One of the crew was taken prisoner.

ANGULARITY (1) at the 1935 Spithead Review. *W.S.P.L.*

ANGULARITY (1)

D. Brown

GRIT (3) *D. Brown*

37. GRIT (3) (1934–1943)

O.N. 163519 501g 254n 600d 160.5 × 26.7 × 9.4 feet.
5-cyl. 2SA 'SBD' type oil engine by the Newbury Diesel Co. Ltd., Newbury.

9.1934: Completed by George Brown & Co., Greenock (Yard No. 188) for the company. *5.11.1943:* Sunk in collision with the United States steamship THOMAS SULLY 7,725/43 one mile south by east of Tyne Piers while on passage from Kings Lynn to Newcastle with a cargo of wheat.

AQUEITY (1) *E. Taylor*

38. AQUEITY (1) (1934–1940)

O.N. 163551 301g 143n 375d 116.0 × 26.1 × 9.8 feet.
3-cyl. 2SA 'SBD' oil engine by the Newbury Diesel Co. Ltd., Newbury.

12.1934: Completed by Fellows & Co. Ltd., Great Yarmouth (Yard No. 336) for the company. *1936:* Lengthened to 137.0 feet, tonnages became 370g, 194n and 465d. *17.12.1940:* Sunk by a mine in the Yantlet Channel in the River Thames between Sea Reach No. 1 and No. 2 Buoys while on passage from West Thurrock to Sunderland with a cargo of cement.

ASEITY *A. Duncan*

39. ASEITY (1935–1966)

O.N. 163574 416g 213n 502d 142.9 × 26.7 × 8.7 feet.
5-cyl. 2SA 'SBD' oil engine by the Newbury Diesel Co. Ltd., Newbury.

3.1935: Completed by George Brown & Co., Greenock (Yard No. 189) for the company. *6.1966:* Sold to M. Gigilinis & D. Kalkasinas, Thessalonika, Greece and renamed DIMITRIOS A. *1972:* Sold to Andrias Bros. & Co., Thessalonika, Greece. *1974:* Sold to G. Kekatos, Thessalonika, Greece. *1975:* Sold to D. Kalkasinas, Thessalonika, Greece. *1977:* Sold to G. Kekatos, Thessalonika, Greece. Still in service (1990).

ARDUITY (1) *D. Brown*

40. ARDUITY (1) (1935–1942)

O.N. 164509 304g 143n 360d 116.2 × 25.5 × 8.8 feet.
3-cyl. 2SA 'SBD' type oil engine by the Newbury Diesel Co. Ltd., Newbury.

8.1935: Completed by George Brown & Co., Greenock (Yard No. 192) for the company. *16.5.1942:* Sunk by a mine five miles off Mablethorpe in position 53.22N, 00.30E while on passage from Keadby to Cantley with a cargo of coal.

ACCRUITY

C. Hill

41. ACCRUITY (1935–1965)

O.N. 164548 456g 237n 565d 150.7 × 27.7 × 8.9 feet.
5-cyl. 2SA 'SBD' type oil engine by the Newbury Diesel Co. Ltd., Newbury.

10.1935: Completed by George Brown & Co., Greenock (Yard No. 190) for the company. *5.1965:* Sold to A.C. Doucas & T.A. Vianellis, Thessalonika, Greece and renamed VOLOS. *7.12.1967:* Sprang a leak in the engine room and was beached in Derna Harbour where she foundered in heavy weather. She was on passage from Piraeus to Derna with a cargo of bagged cement.

42. ADAPTITY (1) (1935–1940)

O.N. 164549 372g 183n 465d 136.1 × 26.1 × 9.8 feet.
3-cyl. 2SA 'SBD' type oil engine by the Newbury Diesel Co. Ltd., Newbury.

12.1935: Completed by Fellows & Co. Ltd., Great Yarmouth (Yard No. 337) for the company. *5.10.1940:* Sunk by a mine off Harwich in position 51.44N, 01.17E while on passage from London to Grimsby with a cargo of ground nuts.

43. ANONITY (1) (1936–1941)

O.N. 164587 303g 141n 360d 116.2 × 25.5 × 8.8 feet.
3-cyl. 2SA 'SBD' type oil engine by the Newbury Diesel Co. Ltd., Newbury.

3.1936: Completed by George Brown & Co., Greenock (Yard No. 194) for the company. *4.3.1941:* Sunk by a mine 1.5 miles south east of Skegness Pier while on passage from Billingham to Boston with a cargo of fertilizer.

ANONITY (1)

D. Hocquard

44. SAGACITY (1) (1936–1940)

O.N. 164623 490g 249n 600d 153.2 × 27.7 × 9.6 feet.
5-cyl. 2SA 'SBD' type oil engine by the Newbury Diesel Co. Ltd., Newbury.

5.1936: Completed by George Brown & Co., Greenock (Yard No. 195) for the company. *28.10.1940:* Sunk by a mine two miles south east of the Spurn Lighthouse while on passage from King's Lynn to Newcastle with a cargo of wheat.

SEDULITY

A. Duncan

45. SEDULITY (1936–1967)

O.N. 164663 490g 249n 642d 153.2 × 27.7 × 9.6 feet.
5-cyl. 2SA 'SBD' type oil engine by the Newbury Diesel Co. Ltd., Newbury.

7.1936: Completed by George Brown & Co., Greenock (Yard No. 196) for the company. *11.1967:* Sold to D. Kalkasinas, Thessalonika, Greece and renamed PASKALIS K. *1971:* Sold to G. Siscopoulos & Co., Thessalonika, Greece. *1976:* Sold to M. Gigilinis, Thessalonika, Greece and renamed FILIPPOS G. *1981:* Broken up in Greece.

SINCERITY (1)

D. Brown

46. SINCERITY (1) (1936–1968)

O.N. 164732 634g 334n 848d 175.0 × 27.9 × 9.8 feet.
6-cyl. 2SA 'SBD' type oil engine by the Newbury Diesel Co. Ltd., Newbury.

10.1936: Completed by George Brown & Co., Greenock (Yard No. 197) for the company. *3.1968:* Sold to Van den Bosche for breaking up at Boom, Belgium.

SNOWCRETE

A. Duncan

47. SNOWCRETE (1936–1937)

O.N. 144244 351g 139n 135.0 × 23.3 × 9.7 feet.
C.2-cyl. steam engine by the shipbuilder.

3.1921: Completed by Hepples (1919) Ltd., South Shields (Yard No. 658) for Border Shipping Co. Ltd. (G.T. Gillie & Co., managers), Newcastle-upon-Tyne as LOWLAND FIRTH. *1.1929:* Sold to Cement Marketing Co. Ltd., London and renamed SNOWCRETE. *9.1936:* Acquired by the company. *6.1937:* Sold to J. Kennedy & Sons Ltd., Glasgow. *3.1947:* Sold to Challis, Stern & Co. Ltd. (Warren Shipping Co. Ltd., managers), London and renamed WARREN GROVE. *9.11.1948:* Sank off Montrose in position 56.40N, 02.05W after her coal cargo had shifted in heavy weather while on passage from Hartlepool to Buckie.

HARTFORD

National Maritime Museum

48. HARTFORD (1936–1937)

O.N. 131426 407g 156n 144.0 × 24.4 × 10.5 feet.
C.2-cyl. steam engine by the shipbuilder.

4.1912: Completed by J.P. Rennoldson & Sons Ltd., South Shields (Yard No. 275) for the Northwich Carrying Co. Ltd., Liverpool. *1925:* Sold to W.A. Wilson, Southampton. *1927:* Sold to Cement Marketing Co. Ltd., London. *1936:* Acquired by the company. *10.1937:* Sold to F. Bowles & Sons, Cardiff. *2.1939:* Converted to a sand pump dredger. *1950:* Sold to Seaborne Aggregate Co. Ltd., Southampton and renamed SEABORNE ALPHA. *1966:* Sold to Metcalf Marine Salvage Co. Ltd. for breaking up at Southampton which began *3.1966.*

SUAVITY (1)

D. Brown

49. SUAVITY (1) (1937–1940)

O.N. 165417 634g 334n 848d 175.0 × 27.9 × 9.8 feet.
6-cyl. 2SA 'SBD' type oil engine by the Newbury Diesel Co. Ltd., Newbury.

3.1937: Completed by George Brown & Co., Greenock (Yard No. 198) for the company. *27.10.1940:* Sunk by a mine off Hartlepool in position 54.44N, 01.05W while on passage from Sunderland to London with a cargo of wheat.

50. SERENITY (1) (1937–1939)

O.N. 165499 487g 244n 630d 157.8 × 27.7 × 9.5 feet.
5-cyl. 2SA 'L' type oil engine by the Newbury Diesel Co. Ltd., Newbury.

6.1937: Completed by George Brown & Co. (Marine) Ltd., Greenock (Yard No. 201) for the company. *17.12.1939:* Sunk by bombs eight miles east north east of Whitby while on passage from Methil to London with a cargo of coal.

SIGNALITY

T. Rayner

51. SIGNALITY (1937–1967)

O.N. 165568 487g 244n 630d 157.8 × 27.7 × 9.5 feet.
5-cyl. 2SA 'L' type oil engine by the Newbury Diesel Co. Ltd., Newbury.

9.1937: Completed by George Brown & Co. (Marine) Ltd., Greenock (Yard No. 202) for the company. *3.1967:* Sold to M. Gigilinis & D. Kalkasinas, Thessalonika, Greece and renamed HALKIDIKI. *1977:* Sold to G. Panagiotopoulos (M. Gigilinis, manager), Thessalonika, Greece and renamed IOANNA G. *1979:* Sold to Ch. & F. Chomata for breaking up at Thessalonika, Greece.

SEQUACITY

National Maritime Museum

52. SEQUACITY (1937–1940)

O.N. 165616   870g   455n   196.2 × 30.2 × 11.3 feet.
7-cyl. 2SA oil engine by British Auxiliaries Ltd., Glasgow.

12.1937: Completed by Goole Shipbuilding & Repairing Co. Ltd., Goole (Yard No. 329) for the company. *27.5.1940:* Sunk by gunfire from German shore batteries near Cap Gris Nez when in approximate position 52.04N, 01.39E while on passage from Greenhithe to Dunkirk in ballast.

SODALITY

T. Rayner

53. SODALITY (1938–1958)

O.N. 166564   829g   461n   1,220d   188.4 × 30.3 × 12.4 feet.
7-cyl. 2SA 'L' type oil engine by the Newbury Diesel Co. Ltd., Newbury.

1932: Laid down by R. Williamson & Son Ltd., Workington (Yard No. 244) for their own account but not completed. *4.1938:* Acquired by the company, launched and then towed to Goole for completion. *9.1938:* Completed by Goole Shipbuilding & Repairing Co. Ltd., Goole. *7.1958:* Engine removed and hull sold to T.W. Ward Ltd. for breaking up at Grays where she arrived *23.7.1958.*

FRED EVERARD (2) — *R. Griffin*

54. FRED EVERARD (2) (1938–1956)

O.N. 149743 229g 105n 250d 98.0 × 23.1 × 9.6 feet.

10.1926: Completed by Fellows & Co. Ltd., Great Yarmouth (Yard No. 316) for the company as a steel spritsail sailing barge (see S56). *12.1938:* Cut down and converted to a motor coaster and fitted with a 4-cyl. 2SA 'F' type oil engine made by the Newbury Diesel Co. Ltd., Newbury. *9.5.1956:* Sunk in collision with the motor vessel WALL BROOK 244/40 in the Princes Channel eight miles off Margate while on passage from Rochester to Totnes with a cargo of cement.

APTITY — *D. Brown*

55. APTITY (1939–1987) Tanker

O.N. 167204 434g 196n 450d 159.7 × 25.1 × 9.9 feet.
5-cyl. 2SA 'L' type oil engine by the Newbury Diesel Co. Ltd., Newbury.

3.1939: Completed by George Brown & Co. (Marine) Ltd., Greenock (Yard No. 209) for the company. *1969:* Converted for use as a steaming barge at Greenhithe. *2.1987:* Sold to R.G. Fry for breaking up at Greenhithe.

APTITY in later years with mainmast fitted.

A. Duncan

SUMMITY (1)

D. Brown

56. SUMMITY (1) (1939–1966)

O.N. 167243 554g 287n 682d 168.7 × 27.7 × 10.1 feet.
5-cyl. 2SA 'L' type oil engine by the Newbury Diesel Co. Ltd., Newbury.

5.1939: Completed by George Brown & Co. (Marine) Ltd., Greenock (Yard No. 210) for the company. *9.1966:* Sold to M. Gigilinis & D. Kalkasinas, Thessalonika, Greece and renamed PANAGIA M. *1967:* Sold to J. Deliyiannis, Thessalonika, Greece. *1968:* Sold to M. Gigilinis & D. Kalkasinas, Thessalonika, Greece. *1973:* Sold to M. Gigilinis, Thessalonika, Greece. *1981:* Broken up in Greece.

57. SUPREMITY (1) (1939–1940)

O.N. 167360 554g 287n 682d 168.6 × 27.7 × 10.1 feet.
5-cyl. 2SA 'L' type oil engine by the Newbury Diesel Co. Ltd., Newbury.

11.1939: Completed by George Brown & Co. (Marine) Ltd., Greenock (Yard No. 211) for the company. *6.12.1940:* Sunk by a mine in the River Thames near the East Oaze Buoy in position 51.28N, 01.00E while on passage from Blyth to Greenhithe with a cargo of coal.

SPIRALITY

A. Duncan

58. SPIRALITY (1939–1968)

O.N. 167364 554g 283n 692d 168.7 × 27.7 × 10.0 feet.
5-cyl. 2SA 'L' type oil engine by the Newbury Diesel Co. Ltd., Newbury.

11.1939: Completed by Goole Shipbuilding & Repairing Co. Ltd., Goole (Yard No. 346) for the company. *11.1968:* Sold to Jos. Boel et fils for breaking up at Antwerp, Belgium where she arrived *18.11.1968*.

ALACRITY (1) *T. Rayner*

59. ALACRITY (1) (1940–1963)

O.N. 167388 554g 283n 692d 168.7 × 27.7 × 10.0 feet.
5-cyl. 2SA 'L' type oil engine by the Newbury Diesel Co. Ltd., Newbury.

2.1940: Completed by Goole Shipbuilding & Repairing Co. Ltd., Goole (Yard No. 347) for the company. *13.12.1963:* Wrecked in thick fog in Portheras Cove, Cornwall while on passage from Swansea to Brussels with a cargo of coal. *16.9.1981:* Wreck finally dispersed by explosives.

ALACRITY aground in Portheras Cove. *Company archives*

SERENITY (2) *A. Duncan*

60. SERENITY (2) (1941–1967)

O.N. 168094 557g 286n 682d 168.7 × 27.7 × 9.6 feet.
5-cyl. 2SA 'O' type oil engine by the Newbury Diesel Co. Ltd., Newbury.

5.1941: Completed by George Brown & Co. (Marine) Ltd., Greenock (Yard No. 213) for the company. *5.1967:* Sold to M. Gigilinis & D. Kalkasinas, Thessalonika, Greece and renamed AGHIA MARINA. *1971:* Sold to M. Gigilinis, Thessalonika, Greece. *1981:* Broken up in Greece.

ALF EVERARD *J. Callis*

61. ALF EVERARD (1943–1953)

O.N. 148691 213g 116n 250d 98.0 × 23.1 × 9.6 feet.

10.1925: Completed by Fellows & Co. Ltd., Great Yarmouth (Yard No. 309) for the company as a steel spritsail sailing barge (See S54). *6.1943:* Cut down and converted to a motor coaster and fitted with a 4-cyl. 2SA 'F' type oil engine made by the Newbury Diesel Co. Ltd., Newbury. *24.12.1953:* Sunk in collision with the steamship CITY OF JOHANNESBURG 8,207/47 off Whitstable while on passage from Charlestown to London with a cargo of china clay.

ABILITY (2)

W.S.P.L.

62. ABILITY (2) (1943–1975)

O.N. 169603 881g 462n 1,155d 192.6 × 30.1 × 11.6 feet.
6-cyl. 2SA 'O' type oil engine by the Newbury Diesel Co. Ltd., Newbury.

9.1943: Completed by Goole Shipbuilding & Repairing Co. Ltd., Goole (Yard No. 394) for the company. *2.1975:* Sold to Annabel Shipping Co. Ltd., Panama and renamed ELENI V. *1977:* Sold to Tripolis Shipping Co. Ltd., Panama. Later renamed NAGLA STAR and registry transferred to Limassol, Cyprus. *1980:* Sold to Nagla Shipping Co. S.A., Panama. *1982:* Sold to L. Kladias, Piraeus, Greece. *1982:* Sold to Diaplem Ltd., Piraeus for breaking up at the Nikolaos Sava Shipyard, Eleusis, Greece where she arrived *11.11.1982.* *12.1982:* Work commenced.

AMENITY (2)

T. Rayner

63. AMENITY (2) (1944–1968)

O.N. 169705 881g 462n 1,155d 192.6 × 30.1 × 11.6 feet.
6-cyl. 2SA 'O' type oil engine by the Newbury Diesel Co. Ltd., Newbury.

1.1944: Completed by Goole Shipbuilding & Repairing Co. Ltd., Goole (Yard No. 395) for the company. *5.1968:* Sold to T.W. Ward Ltd. for breaking up at Inverkeithing where she arrived *16.5.1968.*

SUPREMITY (2) *J. Callis*

64. SUPREMITY (2) (1944–1964)

O.N. 169987 2,074g 1,090n 2,777d 270.2 × 40.7 × 16.3 feet.
6-cyl. 2SA 'P' type oil engine by the Newbury Diesel Co. Ltd., Newbury.

10.1944: Completed by Goole Shipbuilding & Repairing Co. Ltd., Goole (Yard No. 392) for the company. *5.1964:* Sold to Kapa Shipping Enterprises Ltd., Piraeus, Greece and renamed KAPA. *1966:* Sold to K. Karmaris Brothers Co. Ltd., Piraeus, Greece and renamed IRENE K. *10.1973:* Sold to Sidiremboriki S.A., Piraeus for breaking up at Skaramanga, Greece.

ADAPTITY (2) *A. Duncan*

65. ADAPTITY (2) (1945–1969)

O.N. 180579 945g 499n 1,190d 202.6 × 31.4 × 12.0 feet.
6-cyl. 2SA 'O' type oil engine by the Newbury Diesel Co. Ltd., Newbury.

7.1945: Completed by Goole Shipbuilding & Repairing Co. Ltd., Goole (Yard No. 425) for the company. *12.1969:* Sold to T.W. Ward Ltd. for breaking up at Inverkeithing. Work commenced *3.1.1970* and was completed by *3.1970*.

ACTUALITY (2)

W.S.P.L.

66. ACTUALITY (2) (1945–1963)

O.N. 180765 945g 499n 1,190d 202.6 × 31.4 × 12.0 feet.
6-cyl. 2SA 'O' type oil engine by the Newbury Diesel Co. Ltd., Newbury.

11.1945: Completed by Goole Shipbuilding & Repairing Co. Ltd., Goole (Yard No. 426) for the company. *27.10.1963:* Sunk in collision with the Dutch motor vessel BETTY ANNE S 499/53 in fog off Hastings while on passage from Amble to Yelland with a cargo of coal.

ANGULARITY (2)

Real Photographs

67. ANGULARITY (2) (1945–1967)

O.N. 168680 878g 460n 1,150d 203.0 × 33.2 × 11.7 feet.
8-cyl. 2SA oil engine by the shipbuilder.

6.1941: Completed by Harland & Wolff Ltd., Glasgow (Yard No. 1092G) for the Ministry of War Transport, London (W.A. Wilson, Southampton, manager) as EMPIRE SHOAL. *1942:* Managers became F.T. Everard & Sons Ltd. *11.1945:* Acquired by the company. *1946:* Renamed ANGULARITY. *12.1952:* Re-engined with a 4-cyl. 2SA 'P' type oil engine made by the Newbury Diesel Co. Ltd., Newbury. *9.1967:* Sold to G. Tzortsis & K. Sykias, Piraeus, Greece and renamed ELPIS. *22.1.1968:* Foundered between Ameland and Schiermonnikoog in position 53.35N, 05.51E after developing a leak in the engine room while on passage from London to Malta via Hamburg with a cargo of cement.

68. AUDACITY (2) (1945–1967) Tanker

O.N. 169504 656g 292n 835d 176.7 × 30.7 × 11.6 feet.
6-cyl. 2SA 'O' type oil engine by the Newbury Diesel Co. Ltd., Newbury.

6.1943: Completed by George Brown & Co. (Marine) Ltd., Greenock (Yard No. 225) for the Ministry of War Transport, London (F.T. Everard & Sons Ltd., managers) as EMPIRE AUDREY. *11.1945:* Acquired by the company and renamed AUDACITY. *8.1967:* Sold to Van den Bosche for breaking up at Boom, Belgium.

AUDACITY (2)

T. Rayner

69. ASPERITY (2) (1945–1967) Tanker

O.N. 168984 667g 311n 835d 176.7 × 30.7 × 11.6 feet.
6-cyl. 2SA 'O' type oil engine by the Newbury Diesel Co. Ltd., Newbury.

6.1942: Completed by George Brown & Co. (Marine) Ltd., Greenock (Yard No. 221) for the Ministry of War Transport, London (F.T. Everard & Sons Ltd., managers) as EMPIRE DWELLER. *11.1945:* Acquired by the company. *1946:* Renamed ASPERITY. *2.1967:* Sold to A.E. Peirce for breaking up at Canvey Island.

ASPERITY (2)

W.S.P.L.

70. FIXITY (1) (1946–1961)

O.N. 180119 411g 178n 450d 142.2 × 27.0 × 8.5 feet.
7-cyl. 4SA oil engine by Blackstone & Co. Ltd., Stamford.

7.1944: Completed by Goole Shipbuilding & Repairing Co. Ltd., Goole (Yard No. 418) for the Ministry of War Transport, London (F.T. Everard & Sons Ltd., managers) as EMPIRE FAIRHAVEN. *4.1946:* Acquired by the company and renamed FIXITY. *1950:* Re-engined with a 6-cyl. 2SA 'G' type oil engine made by the Newbury Diesel Co. Ltd., Newbury. *3.1961:* Sold to BISCO and allocated to T.W. Ward Ltd. for breaking up at Grays where she arrived *3.3.1961*.

FIXITY (1) *J. Callis*

FIRMITY

A. Duncan

71. FIRMITY (1946–1964)

O.N. 180325 411g 190n 450d 142.2 × 27.0 × 8.5 feet.
6-cyl. 2SA oil engine by British Polar Engines Ltd., Glasgow.

12.1944: Completed by Henry Scarr Ltd., Hessle (Yard No. S456) for the Ministry of War Transport, London (Hannan, Samuel & Co. Ltd., Fowey, managers) as EMPIRE FASTNESS. *4.1946:* Owner became the Ministry of Transport, London. *5.1946:* Acquired by the company and renamed FIRMITY. *10.1952:* Re-engined with a 6-cyl. 2SA 'G' type oil engine made by the Newbury Diesel Co. Ltd., Newbury. *1961:* Laid up awaiting disposal. *4.1964:* Sold to A.E. Peirce, Canvey Island. *9.1964:* Resold to Metaal Handel & Sloopwerken H.P. Heuvelman for breaking up at Krimpen aan-den-Ijssel, Holland. *12.1964:* Work completed.

FLEXITY

T. Rayner

72. FLEXITY (1946–1961)

O.N. 180308 411g 190n 450d 142.0 × 27.0 × 8.5 feet.
7-cyl. 4SA oil engine by Blackstone & Co. Ltd., Stamford.

10.1944: Completed by Henry Scarr Ltd., Hessle (Yard No. S453) for the Ministry of War Transport, London (General Steam Navigation Co. Ltd., London, managers) as EMPIRE FACILITY. *4.1946:* Owner became the Ministry of Transport, London. *7.1946:* Acquired by the company and renamed FLEXITY. *6.1950:* Re-engined with a 6-cyl. 2SA 'G' type oil engine made by the Newbury Diesel Co. Ltd., Newbury. *11.1961:* Sold to N.V. Machine & Scheepsloperij 'De Koophandel', Nieuw Lekkerland, Holland. *1962:* Resold to Metaal Handel & Sloopwerken H.P. Heuvelman for breaking up at Krimpen aan-den-Ijssel, Holland. *3.1962:* Work commenced.

73. ARDUITY (2) (1946–1969) Tanker.

O.N. 180905 959g 406n 1,044d 193.0 × 34.1 × 14.7 feet.
4-cyl. 2SA oil engine by British Polar Engines Ltd., Glasgow.

7.1946: Completed by Grangemouth Dockyard Co. Ltd., Grangemouth (Yard No. 474) for the Ministry of Transport, London as EMPIRE TEDSON. *7.1946:* Acquired by the company and renamed ARDUITY. *1956:* Lengthened to 234.0 feet and tonnages became 1,115g, 526n and 1,260d. *9.1969:* Sold to Filisberto Valente da Almeida, Lisbon, Portugal for use as a non-propelled barge and deleted from Lloyds Register.

ARDUITY (2) after lengthening. *J. Callis*

74. FLUIDITY (1946–1960)

O.N. 180123 410g 190n 450d 142.2 × 27.0 × 8.5 feet.
7-cyl. 4SA oil engine by Blackstone & Co. Ltd., Stamford.

9.1944: Completed by Goole Shipbuilding & Repairing Co. Ltd., Goole (Yard No. 421) for the Ministry of War Transport, London (General Steam Navigation Co. Ltd., London, managers) as EMPIRE FANE. *4.1946:* Owner became the Ministry of Transport, London. *7.1946:* Acquired by the company and renamed FLUIDITY. *5.1956:* Re-engined with a 6-cyl. 2SA 'G' type oil engine made by the Newbury Diesel Co. Ltd., Newbury. *12.1960:* Engine removed and hull sold to Gaselee & Son Ltd., London for use as a mooring barge. Renamed APAR and deleted from Lloyds Register.

FLUIDITY *A. Duncan*

FRIVOLITY (1) *A. Duncan*

75. FRIVOLITY (1) (1946–1961)

O.N. 180122 410g 190n 450d 142.2 × 27.0 × 8.5 feet.
7-cyl. 4SA oil engine by Blackstone & Co. Ltd., Stamford.

8.1944: Completed by Goole Shipbuilding & Repairing Co. Ltd., Goole (Yard No. 420) for the Ministry of War Transport, London (J. Fisher & Sons Ltd., Barrow-in-Furness, managers) as EMPIRE FASHION. *4.1946:* Owner became the Ministry of Transport, London. *7.1946:* Acquired by the company and renamed FRIVOLITY. *7.1961:* Sold to BISCO and allocated to T.W. Ward Ltd. for breaking up at Grays.

FESTIVITY (1) *A. Duncan*

76. FESTIVITY (1) (1946–1961)

O.N. 180299 411g 190n 450d 142.2 × 27.0 × 8.5 feet.
7-cyl. 4SA oil engine by Blackstone & Co. Ltd., Stamford.

10.1944: Completed By Henry Scarr Ltd., Hessle (Yard No. S452) for the Ministry of War Transport, London (T.E. Evans & Co. Ltd., London, managers) as EMPIRE FANFARE. *4.1946:* Owner became the Ministry of Transport, London. *7.1946:* Acquired by the company and renamed FESTIVITY. *5.1949:* Re-engined with a 6-cyl. 2SA 'G' type oil engine made by the Newbury Diesel Co. Ltd., Newbury. *7.1961:* Sold to N.V. Machine & Scheepsloperij 'De Koophandel' for breaking up at Nieuw Lekkerland, Holland where work was completed by *9.1961*.

FUTURITY (1)

T. Rayner

77. FUTURITY (1) (1946–1960)

O.N. 180319 411g 190n 450d 142.2 × 27.0 × 8.5 feet.
7-cyl. 4SA oil engine by Blackstone & Co. Ltd., Stamford.

11.1944: Completed by Henry Scarr Ltd., Hessle (Yard No. S455) for the Ministry of War Transport, London (Wm. Robertson, Glasgow, manager) as EMPIRE FANAL. *4.1946:* Owner became the Ministry of Transport, London. *8.1946:* Acquired by the company and renamed FUTURITY. *3.1954:* Re-engined with a 6-cyl. 2SA 'G' type oil engine made by the Newbury Diesel Co. Ltd., Newbury. *7.1960:* Sold to BISCO and allocated to T.W. Ward Ltd. for breaking up at Grays where work commenced *21.7.1960*.

FORMALITY (1)

A. Duncan

78. FORMALITY (1) (1946–1962)

O.N. 180120 410g 189n 450d 142.2 × 27.0 × 8.5 feet.
7-cyl. 4SA oil engine by Blackstone & Co. Ltd., Stamford.

7.1944: Completed by Goole Shipbuilding & Repairing Co. Ltd., Goole (Yard No. 419) for the Ministry of War Transport, London (R. Rix & Sons, Hull, managers) as EMPIRE FAVOURITE. *4.1946:* Owner became the Ministry of Transport, London. *8.1946:* Acquired by the company and renamed FORMALITY. *1950:* Re-engined with a 6-cyl. 2SA 'G' type oil engine made by the Newbury Diesel Co. Ltd., Newbury. *1961:* Laid up awaiting disposal. *3.1962:* Sold to T.W. Ward Ltd., Grays. *8.1962:* Re-sold to Metaal Handel & Sloopwerken H.P. Heuvelman for breaking up at Krimpen aan-den-Ijssel, Holland where work commenced *13.8.1962.*

GRIT (4)

C. Hill

79. GRIT (4) (1946–1957)

O.N. 169102 2,066g 1,073n 2,875d 272.0 × 40.0 × 17.2 feet.
T.3-cyl. steam engine by North Eastern Marine Engineering Co. (1938) Ltd., Wallsend.

11.1943: Completed by Grangemouth Dockyard Co. Ltd., Grangemouth (Yard No. 451) for the Ministry of War Transport, London (S. Marshall & Co. Ltd., Sunderland, managers) as EMPIRE VILLAGER. *4.1946:* Owner became the Ministry of Transport, London. *10.1946:* Acquired by the company and renamed GRIT. *5.1957:* Sold to Bankstone Shipping Co. Ltd. (Thomas Stone (Shipping) Ltd., managers), Llanelli and renamed BANKSTONE. *1959:* Sold to Virtu Steamship Co. Ltd., Malta and renamed SAVER. *1965:* Sold to Marespuma Cia. Nav. S.A., Piraeus, Greece and renamed CHRISTOYANNIS. *1967:* Sold to A. Poulos, Piraeus, Greece. *7.1967:* Broken up at Piraeus, Greece.

GRIT (4)

J. Laird

SAGACITY (2)

A. Duncan

80. SAGACITY (2) (1946–1972)

O.N. 181501 943g 498n 1,190d 204.5 × 31.4 × 11.7 feet.
6-cyl. 2SA 'O' type oil engine by the Newbury Diesel Co. Ltd., Newbury.

11.1946: Completed by Grangemouth Dockyard Co. Ltd., Grangemouth (Yard No. 469) for the company.

2.1972: Sold to Van den Bosche for breaking up at Boom, Belgium where she arrived *19.2.1972*.

SUAVITY (2)

J. Laird

81. SUAVITY (2) (1946–1970)

O.N. 181552 943g 498n 1,190d 204.5 × 31.4 × 11.7 feet.
6-cyl. 2SA 'O' type oil engine by the Newbury Diesel Co. Ltd., Newbury.

12.1946: Completed by Grangemouth Dockyard Co. Ltd., Grangemouth (Yard No. 470) for the company.

4.1970: Sold to Scrappingco S.A. for breaking up at Willebroek, Belgium.

AQUEITY (2) *W.S.P.L.*

82. AQUEITY (2) (1947) Tanker

O.N. 169440 891g 381n 900d 193.0 × 32.0 × 14.5 feet.
4-cyl. 2SA oil engine by British Polar Engines Ltd., Glasgow.

6.1945: Completed by A. & J. Inglis Ltd., Glasgow (Yard No. 1299) for the Ministry of War Transport, London (Anglo-Saxon Petroleum Co. Ltd., London, managers) as EMPIRE BELGRAVE. *4.1946:* Owner became the Ministry of Transport, London. *3.1947:* Acquired by the company and renamed AQUEITY. *11.11.1947:* Sunk by a mine off Terschelling in position 53.32N, 05.02E while on passage from Bremen to Bromborough in ballast.

ANONITY (2) *W.S.P.L.*

83. ANONITY (2) (1947–1966) Tanker

O.N. 169447 890g 379n 900d 193.0 × 32.0 × 14.5 feet.
4-cyl. 2SA oil engine by British Polar Engines Ltd., Glasgow.

8.1945: Completed by A. & J. Inglis Ltd., Glasgow (Yard No. 1300) for the Ministry of War Transport, London (Anglo-Saxon Petroleum Co. Ltd., London, managers) as EMPIRE CAMPDEN. *4.1946:* Owner became the Ministry of Transport, London. *5.1947:* Acquired by the company and renamed ANONITY. *6.1966:* Sold to S.J. & J.S. Latsis, Piraeus, Greece and renamed PETROLA II. *1969:* Sold to P. Chryssochoides & M. Chalkiopoulos, Piraeus, Greece and renamed KALYMNOS. *12.4.1970:* Wrecked on the east coast of Rhodes while on passage from Eleusis to Rhodes. Later salved and towed to Piraeus. *27.5.1970:* Sold to D. Vittiotis & Salmina for breaking up at Piraeus, Greece.

ALLURITY (1)

A. Duncan

84. ALLURITY (1) (1947–1964) Tanker

O.N. 169415 813g 334n 850d 193.0 × 30.7 × 13.8 feet.
T.3-cyl. steam engine by Aitchison, Blair Ltd., Clydebank.

6.1944: Completed by A. & J. Inglis Ltd., Glasgow (Yard No. 1227) for the Ministry of War Transport, London (F.T. Everard & Sons Ltd., managers) as EMPIRE DOMBEY. *1945:* Managers became Anglo-Saxon Petroleum Co. Ltd., London. *1946:* Managers became F.T. Everard & Sons Ltd. *4.1946:* Owner became the Ministry of Transport, London. *8.1947:* Acquired by the company and renamed ALLURITY. *9.1964:* Sold to A.E. Peirce, Canvey Island. *3.1965:* Resold to Brugse Scheepsloperij for breaking up at Bruges, Belgium where work commenced during *4.1965.*

AUSTERITY

J. Laird

85. AUSTERITY (1947–1967)

O.N. 181761 592g 305n 750d 177.1 × 27.6 × 9.4 feet.
5-cyl. 2SA 'O' type oil engine by the Newbury Diesel Co. Ltd., Newbury.

10.1947: Completed by Grangemouth Dockyard Co. Ltd., Grangemouth (Yard No. 472) for the company. *5.1967:* Sold to M. Gigilinis & D. Kalkasinas, Thessalonika, Greece and renamed KAPETAN KOSTANTIS. *1971:* Sold to Prodomos Varvakis & Co., Thessalonika, Greece. *1977:* Sold to Andreas Myrianthous, Limassol, Cyprus and renamed SANESTO. Still in service (1990).

86. SUPERIORITY (1) (1947–1969)

O.N. 181797 2,145g 1,134n 2,960d 270.3 × 40.7 × 17.3 feet.
6-cyl. 2SA 'P' type oil engine by the Newbury Diesel Co. Ltd., Newbury.

12.1947: Completed by Goole Shipbuilding & Repairing Co. Ltd., Goole (Yard No. 393) for the company.
9.1969: Transferred by J. Hay & Sons Ltd., Glasgow.
12.1969: Sold to T.W. Ward Ltd. for breaking up at Preston where work commenced *27.4.1970*.

SUPERIORITY (1) *C. Hill*

87. ATOMICITY (1947–1966)

O.N. 181800 592g 305n 750d 177.1 × 27.6 × 9.4 feet.
5-cyl. 2SA 'O' type oil engine by the Newbury Diesel Co. Ltd., Newbury.

12.1947: Completed by Grangemouth Dockyard Co. Ltd., Grangemouth (Yard No. 473) for the company.
3.1966: Sold to A.C. Doucas & T.A. Vianellis, Piraeus, Greece and renamed EOLOS. *1970:* Owner became Mrs. A.C. Doucas, Piraeus, Greece. *21.6.1973:* Sunk by a mine 13 miles off Tripoli while on passage from Kavalla to Tripoli, Libya with a cargo of limestone.

ATOMICITY

W.S.P.L.

SCARCITY

A. Duncan

88. SCARCITY (1948–1972)

O.N. 181976 586g 300n 750d 177.5 × 27.7 × 9.4 feet.
5-cyl. 2SA 'O' type oil engine by the Newbury Diesel Co. Ltd., Newbury.

8.1948: Completed by Goole Shipbuilding & Repairing Co. Ltd., Goole (Yard No. 470) for the company. *1955:* Re-engined with a 5-cyl. 2SA 'O' type oil engine made by the Newbury Diesel Co. Ltd., Newbury. *5.1972:* Sold to T.W. Ward Ltd. for breaking up at Grays where she arrived *17.5.1972.*

ASHBEL HUBBARD
alongside the Plaster Products Jetty, Greenhithe.

R. Griffin

89. ASHBEL HUBBARD/SOLIDARITY (1949–1951)

O.N. 169556 1,793g 995n 2,400d 250.4 × 42.1 × 18.4 feet.
C.6-cyl. steam engine by Ajax Uniflow Co., Corry, Pennsylvania, U.S.A.

5.1943: Completed by Leathem D. Smith Shipbuilding Co., Sturgeon Bay, Wisconsin, U.S.A. (Yard No. 276) for the United States Maritime Commission, New York, U.S.A. as ASHBEL HUBBARD (type N3-S-A1). Bareboat chartered by the War Shipping Administration, Washington, D.C., U.S.A. to the Ministry of War Transport, London (G. Heyn & Sons Ltd., Belfast, managers). *4.1946:* Charterer became the Ministry of Transport, London. *1.1949:* Acquired by the company and later renamed SOLIDARITY. *4.3.1951:* Foundered in heavy weather off Aalesund in position 63.02N, 06.19E while on passage from Hommelvik to London with a cargo of wood pulp.

Note: SOLIDARITY was converted to oil burning and was re-boilered with the boiler removed from the Flower class corvette HMS HONEYSUCKLE (K27) purchased in 1948 with such a purpose in mind. Other items were also removed including the steam whistle later fitted to the steam tanker ALLURITY before the corvette was sold to T.W. Ward Ltd. for breaking up at Grays in 1950.

90. SENIORITY (1) (1949–1950)

O.N. 168945 2,895g 1,706n 4,700d 315.4 × 46.5 × 23.0 feet.
T.3-cyl. steam engine by the Central Marine Engine Works, West Hartlepool.

9.1942: Completed by Wm. Gray & Co. Ltd., West Hartlepool (Yard No. 1135) for the Ministry of War Transport, London (Currie Line Ltd., Leith, managers) as EMPIRE BOSWELL. *1945:* Managers became British India Steam Navigation Co. Ltd., London. *4.1946:* Owner became the Ministry of Transport, London. *1.1947:* Sold to Aviation & Shipping Co. Ltd. (N.W. Purvis, manager), London and renamed AVISWELL. *2.1949:* Acquired by the company and renamed SENIORITY. *7.11.1950:* Stranded 12 miles north east of Barra Head, Outer Hebrides while on passage from Ellesmere Port to Risor, Norway in ballast. *9.11.1950:* Sank in position 56.57N, 07.25W.

SENIORITY (1)

J. Laird

91. ETHEL EVERARD (2) (1949–1954)

O.N. 180076 3,539g 2,257n 4,310d 315.5 × 46.5 × 22.1 feet.
T.3-cyl. steam engine by the Central Marine Engine Works, West Hartlepool.

9.1944: Completed by Wm. Gray & Co. Ltd., West Hartlepool (Yard No. 1169) for the Ministry of War Transport, London (H. Hogarth & Sons, Glasgow, managers) as EMPIRE NEWFOUNDLAND. *4.1946:* Owner became the Ministry of Transport, London. *8.1946:* Managers became H.P. Lenaghan & Sons Ltd., Belfast. *1949:* Sold to Irish Bay Lines Ltd. (H.P. Lenaghan & Sons Ltd., managers), Belfast. *9.1949:* Acquired by the company and renamed ETHEL EVERARD. *7.1954:* Sold to Indo-China Steam Navigation Co. Ltd., Hong Kong and renamed HOP SANG. *1962:* Renamed HANG SANG. *1968:* Sold to Fui Nam Co. Ltd., Hong Kong and renamed HOI SOON. *1969:* Sold to Chan Cheung Man (Fui Nam Co. Ltd., managers), Somalia. *3.1970:* Sold to Yuen Hing Godown Co. Ltd. for breaking up at Hong Kong where work began *15.3.1970.*

ETHEL EVERARD (2)

G. Osbon

AQUEITY (3) *J. Callis*

92. AQUEITY (3) (1949–1964) Tanker

O.N. 169471 891g 381n 900d 193.0 × 32.0 × 14.5 feet.
4-cyl. 2SA oil engine by British Polar Engines Ltd., Glasgow.

5.1946: Completed by A. & J. Inglis Ltd., Glasgow (Yard No. 1313) for the Ministry of Transport, London (Anglo-Saxon Petroleum Co. (Eastern) Ltd., London, managers) as EMPIRE TEDMUIR. *12.1946:* Sold to Anglo-Saxon Petroleum Co. Ltd., London and renamed FUSINUS. *7.1949:* Acquired by the company and renamed AQUEITY. *8.1961:* Re-engined with a 5-cyl. 2SA oil engine made by the Newbury Diesel Co. Ltd., Newbury. *12.1964:* Sold to Jos. de Smedt, Boom, Belgium. Resold to Brugse Scheepsloperij for breaking up at Bruges, Belgium where she arrived *1.1965.*

ALCHYMIST (2) *A. Duncan*

93. ALCHYMIST (2) (1949–1969) Tanker

O.N. 169433 813g 334n 845d 193.0 × 30.7 × 13.8 feet.
T.3-cyl. steam engine by Aitchison, Blair Ltd., Clydebank.

3.1945: Completed by A. & J. Inglis Ltd., Glasgow (Yard No. 1288) for the Ministry of War Transport, London (C. Rowbotham & Sons, London, managers) as EMPIRE ORKNEY. *4.1946:* Owner became the Ministry of Transport, London. *8.1946:* Chartered to Tankers Transit & Shipping Co. Ltd., London. *10.1949:* Acquired by the company and renamed ALCHYMIST. *5.1969:* Sold to Brugse Scheepsloperij for breaking up at Bruges, Belgium where she arrived *3.5.1969.*

T: A small ship
g way from
e. King On,
erly the Everard
ter Stability,
completed by
Goole
building and
air Co in 1949.
was sold out of
British register
973 and moved
e Far East by
new owners,
eo Timber. She
ctured at anchor
Singapore
975.

Italian text. A breathtaking book on a magnificent liner. There are 117 colour, plus 385 duo-tone photographs. Produced in a manner suggesting that cost was not a great factor, this is the 'must-have' book of 2003 for all lovers of the world's great liners. The [illegible]tory is charted; from the shipyard, through 1933 when the REX was awarded the 'nastro azzurro' (Blue Riband); and finally to 1944 and the well-documented air bombing assalt that brought the REX to its sad end. *(October 2004). 312pp. 117 colour, 385 sepia photographs. HBK. 310x250mm.*

SHIPS OF THE ROYAL NAVY **[17754]**

Colledge, J.J. & Warlow, Lt.Cdr. Ben (Comp.)

£25.00

Essentially a reference book for those intereste[illegible] maritime history. It is a complete re[illegible] of a[illegible] fighting ships of the Royal Navy [illegible]nth century to the present day [illegible] vessel is given key data, plu[illegible]f its build and ultimate fate. Th[illegible] a labour of love for J.J. Colledge when it was first published and it has now been brought up-to-date by Ben Warlow. *(2003). 368pp. HBK. 235x155mm.*

[illegible] Personal Reflections by Duncan Francis, Coaster of the Past by Dave Hocquard, Farewell to the Thomas M by Volker van Bargen, Channel Island News, Coasters and Cargos by Roy Cressey, Arctic Sea to Esbjerg: Elbe to Breast by Ian Wilson, and The Story of the Lindholm by Volker von Bargen.

(October 2003). 36pp. 7 colour, 29 b&w photographs. LBK. 147x210mm.

Back numbers are available:

No. 49.	February 2003.	£2.40.	**[17583]**
No. 50.	April 2003.	£2.40.	**[17584]**
No. 51.	June 2003.	£2.40.	**[17585]**
No. 52.	August 2003.	£2.40.	**[17586]**

[illegible] everybody else. *(2002). 176pp. 100s photographs, some colour. HBK. 215x280mm.*

STEAMERS OF THE CLYDE **[17736]**

Deayton, Alistair £12.99

Takes the reader on a nostalgic trip back to the days when steam was King of the Clyde, and when you could actually travel from Arran to Glasgow in just two hours! *(September 2003). 160pp. 100s b&w photographs. LBK. 235x165mm.*

Carmania Press

Liners & Cruise Ships - 1 (Cooke) £12.95.
Liners & Cruise Ships - 2 (Cooke) £13.95.
Liners & Cruise Ships - 3: (Cooke) £18.[illegible]
Seven Seas Navigator (Eliseo) £32.50.
Passenger Liners French Style (Mille[illegible]) [illegible]
The Sitmar Liners & V Ships, 1928-1[illegible] ([illegible]eo) £17.50.
Mediterranean Shipping (Dunn) £15.95.
Ocean Liner Chronicles (Miller) £16.95.
The Saxonia Sisters (Harvey) £13.95.
Thames Shipping (Dunn) 3rd Reprint £13.95.
Passenger Liners American Style (Miller) £15.95.
Merchant Ships of a[illegible] **post-war years** (Mille[illegible]
New York Shipping [illegible]
Ocean Liner Odysse[illegible] (Scull) £10.95.
Liners To The Sun ([illegible] Graham) £19.95.
The Nurse Family of [illegible] **Ships** (Nurse) £5.95.

94. STABILITY (1) (1949–1973)

O.N. 183136 1,490g 845n 1,740d 230.2 × 36.2 × 14.0 feet.
4-cyl. 2SA 'P' type oil engine by the Newbury Diesel Co. Ltd., Newbury.

11.1949: Completed by Goole Shipbuilding & Repairing Co. Ltd., Goole (Yard No. 463) for the company. *1964:* Transferred to Scottish Navigation Co. Ltd., Glasgow. *10.1973:* Sold to Borneo Timber Ltda. S.A., Panama and renamed KING ON. *1978:* Renamed PRAJOGO I. *1978:* Sold to P.T. Maskapai Pelayaran Sumatera, Surabaya, Indonesia and renamed VANDARATANA. *1986:* Broken up at Cigading, Indonesia.

STABILITY (1) with original black hull. *T. Rayner*

95. AMITY (1) (1950–1966) Tanker

O.N. 181117 947g 392n 1,040d 193.0 × 34.1 × 14.7 feet.
4-cyl. 2SA oil engine by British Polar Engines Ltd., Glasgow.

12.1945: Completed by Sir J. Laing & Sons Ltd., Sunderland (Yard No. 772) for the Ministry of War Transport, London (Anglo-Saxon Petroleum Co. Ltd., London, managers) as EMPIRE TEDASSA. *4.1946:* Owner became the Ministry of Transport, London. *3.1947:* Sold to Anglo-Saxon Petroleum Co. Ltd., London and renamed FOSSARINA. *2.1950:* Acquired by the company and renamed AMITY. *1.1966:* Sold to A. King & Sons Ltd. for breaking up in dry dock at Great Yarmouth.

AMITY (1)

T. Rayner

ATONALITY

J. Callis

96. ATONALITY (1950–1967) Tanker

O.N. 183200 1,221g 548n 1,374d 218.0 × 36.0 × 14.9 feet.
4-cyl. 2SA 'P' type oil engine by J.I. Thornycroft & Co. Ltd., Southampton.

3.1950: Completed by George Brown & Co. (Marine) Ltd., Greenock (Yard No. 249) for the company. *8.1967:* Sold to Marine Water Supply Co. Ltd., Athens, Greece and renamed ATHENA. *1975:* Renamed AGIOS GEORGIOS. *1982:* Broken up in Greece.

SECURITY (2) with later yellow hull.

C. Hill

97. SECURITY (1) (1950–1964)

O.N. 183257 1,490g 845n 1,740d 230.2 × 36.2 × 14.0 feet.
4-cyl. 2SA 'P' type oil engine by J.I. Thornycroft & Co. Ltd., Southampton.

6.1950: Completed by Goole Shipbuilding & Repairing Co. Ltd., Goole (Yard No. 464) for the company. *2.2.1964:* Run down and sunk when at anchor in the River Elbe during thick fog by the German motor vessel CARPATHIA 1,342/57 while on passage from Arklow to Hamburg with a cargo of stone. Raised on *16.3.1964* and sold by auction to Eckhardt & Co. G.m.b.H. for breaking up in Hamburg, West Germany where work was completed *5.7.1965*.

lowing the publication of the 'Voyage Report' 'The Night the South Goodwin Light Vessel s Lost' by D.H. James-Green in the April issue, 'SM' reader Charles Traill of Ashford, Kent, t in this photograph of the Everard motor coaster *Celebrity* at Whitstable in September 2. The *Celebrity* was formerly the *Watersmeet*, the subject of the published article. The tograph clearly shows the new steel bulwarks which replaced the rails on the ship's foc's'le l the single mast amidships which replaced the goal post masts originally in place. Mr. Traill nders if the old ship is still in service somewhere?

ned AKINITY. *29.2.1964:* Damaged in collision the Norwegian motor vessel SKRIM 8,937/57 in fog off South Goodwin Sands. Sold to A.E. e, Canvey Island. Re-sold to Metaal Handel & pwerken H.P. Heuvelman, Krimpen aan-den-Ijssel, nd. Resold to Brugse Scheepsloperij for breaking t Bruges, Belgium where she arrived *3.4.1965*.

AKINITY

T. Rayner

99. WATERSMEET/CELEBRITY (1) (1950–1966)

O.N. 180183 310g 144n 415d 138.7 × 24.6 × 9.6 feet.
6-cyl. 4SA oil engine by the shipbuilder.

2.1947: Completed by S.A. Ansaldo, Genoa-Sestri, Italy (Yard No. 858) for A/B Glucksmann, Gothenburg, Sweden as BRITTA. *1947:* Sold to Martin's Coastal Steamships Ltd. (W.D. Tamlyn & Co. Ltd., managers), Plymouth and renamed WATERSMEET. *12.1950:* Company acquired and name changed to Everard Shipping Co. Ltd. *1955:* Renamed CELEBRITY. *1961:* Re-engined with a 6-cyl. 2SA 'G/A' type oil engine made by the Newbury Diesel Co. Ltd., Newbury. *8.1966:* Sold to M. Gigilinis & D. Kalkasinas, Thessalonika, Greece and renamed AEGEON. *1968:* Sold to J. Mamas & Co., Piraeus, Greece. *1972:* Sold to M. Cladias, Thessalonika, Greece. *1979:* Sold to A. Saade, Lebanon and renamed LITSA. *1979:* Renamed VASSOS and registered in Panama. Still in service (1990).

CELEBRITY (1)

A. Duncan

CAPACITY (1)

T. Rayner

100. DALESMEET/CAPACITY (1) (1950–1961)

O.N. 180186 310g 143n 415d 138.7 × 24.6 × 9.6 feet.
6-cyl. 4SA oil engine by the shipbuilder.

2.1947: Completed by S.A. Ansaldo, Genoa-Sestri, Italy (Yard No. 857) for A/B Glucksmann, Gothenburg, Sweden as KERSTIN. *1948:* Sold to Martin's Coastal Steamships Ltd. (W.D. Tamlyn & Co. Ltd., managers), Plymouth and renamed DALESMEET. *12.1950:* Company acquired and name changed to Everard Shipping Co. Ltd. *1951:* Renamed CAPACITY. *1960:* Re-engined with a 6-cyl. 2SA 'G/A' type oil engine made by the Newbury Diesel Co. Ltd., Newbury. *12.1961:* Sold to N.V. Machine & Scheepsloperij 'De Koophandel' for breaking up at Nieuw Lekkerland, Holland where she arrived *17.12.1961*. Engine removed and hull used as a barge on inland waters.

ACUITY

A. Duncan

101. ACUITY (1951–1967) Tanker

O.N. 169460 890g 381n 900d 193.0 × 32.0 × 14.5 feet.
4-cyl. 2SA oil engine by British Polar Engines Ltd., Glasgow.

2.1946: Completed by A. & J. Inglis Ltd., Glasgow (Yard No. 1311) for the Ministry of War Transport, London (Anglo-Saxon Petroleum Co. Ltd., London, managers) as EMPIRE TEDSHIP. *4.1946:* Owner became the Ministry of Transport, London. *1.1947:* Sold to Anglo-Saxon Petroleum Co. Ltd., London and renamed FISCHERIA. *1948:* Sold to Sheikh of Kuwait (Kuwait Oil Co. Ltd., managers), Kuwait. *3.1951:* Transferred to Kuwait Oil Co. Ltd., London. *3.1951:* Acquired by Everard Shipping Co. Ltd. and renamed ACUITY. *10.1967:* Sold to Bettamar Carriers Ltd., Mogadishu, Somalia and renamed VITTORIOSA. *1969:* Sold to 'Campania'di Davide Russo & Compagnia S.a.S., Castellammare di Stabia, Italy and renamed NEPTUNIA TERZA. *4.1975:* Sold to S. Ricardi for breaking up at Vado Ligure, Italy where work began *21.4.1975*.

AUSTILITY

T. Rayner

102. AUSTILITY (1951–1969) Tanker

O.N. 181134 933g 382n 1,040d 193.0 × 34.1 × 14.7 feet.
4-cyl. 2SA oil engine by British Polar Engines Ltd., Glasgow.

5.1946: Completed by Short Brothers Ltd., Sunderland (Yard No. 490) for the Ministry of Transport, London (Anglo-Saxon Petroleum Co. Ltd., London, managers) as EMPIRE TEDLORA. *1.1947:* Sold to Anglo-Saxon Petroleum Co. Ltd., London and renamed FORRERIA. *1948:* Sold to Sheikh of Kuwait (Kuwait Oil Co. Ltd., managers), Kuwait. *3.1951:* Transferred to Kuwait Oil Co. Ltd., London. *3.1951:* Acquired by Everard Shipping Co. Ltd. and renamed AUSTILITY. *1.1969:* Sold to G. Kalogeratos, Piraeus, Greece and renamed PIRAEUS IV. *1971:* Sold to Naftiliaki E.P.E., Piraeus, Greece and renamed ASPROPYRGOS. *1983:* Sold to G. Lyberis, Piraeus, Greece. *1985:* Derated to a non-propelled oil barge and deleted from Lloyds Register.

AUREITY

T. Rayner

103. AUREITY (1951–1968) Tanker

O.N. 168795 813g 334n 825d 193.0 × 30.7 × 13.8 feet.
T.3-cyl. steam engine by Aitchison, Blair Ltd., Clydebank.

2.1942: Completed by the Grangemouth Dockyard Co. Ltd., Grangemouth (Yard No. 436) for the Ministry of War Transport, London (Bulk Oil Steamship Co. Ltd., London, managers) as EMPIRE CADET. *12.1945:* Sold to the French Government (Ministère de la Marine Marchande) (SOFLUMAR [Société d'Armement Fluvial & Maritime] managers), Paris, France and renamed MASCARA. *1948:* Sold to SOFLUMAR (Société d'Armement Fluvial & Maritime), Oran, Algeria (French flag). *4.1951:* Acquired by the company and renamed AUREITY. *6.1968:* Sold to A.E. Peirce, Canvey Island and resold to Scrappingco S.A. for breaking up at Antwerp, Belgium where work was completed during *6.1968.*

SPECIALITY (1)

T. Rayner

104. SPECIALITY (1) (1951–1972)

O.N. 184485 1,557g 702n 1,805d 230.6 × 38.0 × 14.0 feet.
4-cyl. 2SA 'P' type oil engine by the Newbury Diesel Co. Ltd., Newbury.

8.1951: Completed by the Grangemouth Dockyard Co. Ltd., Grangemouth (Yard No. 495) for the company.
28.6.1972: Damaged in collision with the Argentinian motor vessel RIO TERCERO 5,036/47 in the River Thames off Greenhithe while on passage from Deptford to Rotterdam in ballast. Beached off Stone Ness Point and subsequently sold to T.W. Ward Ltd. for breaking up at Grays where she arrived *28.7.1972.*

SPECIALITY (1) on trials at Grangemouth. *J. Laird*

ALLEGRITY

A. Duncan

105. ALLEGRITY (1951–1961) Tanker

O.N. 180363 798g 380n 850d 193.0 × 30.7 × 14.1 feet.
T.3-cyl. steam engine by Aitchison, Blair Ltd., Clydebank.

3.1945: Completed by the Grangemouth Dockyard Co. Ltd., Grangemouth (Yard No. 463) for the Ministry of War Transport, London (F.T. Everard & Sons Ltd., managers) as EMPIRE TAVISTOCK. *1945:* Managers became Anglo-Saxon Petroleum Co. (Eastern) Ltd., London. *2.1946:* Sold to Van Castricum Co. Ltd., London and renamed SOBAT. *1947:* Sold to Saki Tanker Co. Ltd. (E. Gray & Co., managers), London. *1950:* Sold to Berkeley Shipping Co. Ltd. (same managers), London. *8.1951:* Acquired by the company and renamed ALLEGRITY. *13.12.1961:* Stranded on Greeb Point while on passage from Le Havre to Stanlow with a cargo of oil. Drifted off but subsequently grounded again and on *22.12.1961* capsized in Veryan Bay during a gale and became a total loss.

ADHERITY

T. Rayner

106. ADHERITY (1951–1962) Tanker

O.N. 168798 780g 363n 850d 193.0 × 30.7 × 14.1 feet.
T.3-cyl. steam engine by D. Rowan & Co. Ltd., Glasgow.

5.1942: Completed by the Grangemouth Dockyard Co. Ltd., Grangemouth (Yard No. 439) for the Ministry of War Transport, London (Bulk Oil Steamship Co. Ltd., London, managers) as EMPIRE ARTHUR. *22.11.1943:* Capsized and sank at Kissy Jetty, Freetown. Removed, beached, later refloated and repaired. *1949:* Sold to 'Ape' Azionaria Petroliere, Genoa, Italy and renamed MERULA. *11.1951:* Acquired by the company and renamed ADHERITY. *1.1962:* Sold to N.V. Machine & Scheepsloperij 'De Koophandel' for breaking up at Nieuw Lekkerland, Holland.

107. SIMILARITY (1951–1975)

O.N. 184531 1,575g 714n 1,850d 230.6 × 38.0 × 14.0 feet.
4-cyl. 2SA 'P' type oil engine by J.I. Thornycroft & Co. Ltd., Southampton.

11.1951: Completed by the Grangemouth Dockyard Co. Ltd., Grangemouth (Yard No. 496) for the company. *4.1975:* Sold to Kalifornia Primera Cia. Nav. S.A., Piraeus, Greece and renamed DESPINA T. *1977:* Sold to Taf Shipping Co. S.A., Piraeus, Greece. *1980:* Sold to Crystal Island Shipping Co. S.A., Panama and renamed CRYSTAL ISLAND. *8.1980:* Towed to an anchorage in Dakar Roads after an engine failure. *5.7.1981:* Sank during a storm.

SIMILARITY *T. Rayner*

108. SENIORITY (2) (1951–1971)

O.N. 184538 1,566g 715n 1,850d 231.1 × 38.2 × 14.0 feet.
4-cyl. 2SA 'P' type oil engine by J.I. Thornycroft & Co. Ltd., Southampton.

12.1951: Completed by Goole Shipbuilding & Repairing Co. Ltd., Goole (Yard No. 480) for the company. *10.1971:* Sold to Salefterios Ltd., Limassol, Cyprus and renamed SALEFTERIOS. *5.1972:* Sold to Don Bernadino Sanchez for breaking up at Aviles, Spain where she arrived on *21.5.1972*. Work was completed by *2.1973*.

SENIORITY (2) *T. Rayner*

SERIALITY

T. Rayner

109. SERIALITY (1952–1971)

O.N. 184558 1,575g 714n 1,870d 230.6 × 38.0 × 14.0 feet.
4-cyl. 2SA 'P' type oil engine by the Newbury Diesel Co. Ltd., Newbury.

1.1952: Completed by the Grangemouth Dockyard Co. Ltd., Grangemouth (Yard No. 501) for the company. *7.1971:* Sold to T.W. Ward Ltd. for breaking up at Grays where she arrived *13.7.1971*.

SINGULARITY (1) at the 1953 Spithead Review with the motor launch **HILARITY** alongside. *T. Rayner*

110. SINGULARITY (1) (1952–1971)

O.N. 184635 1,566g 715n 1,850d 231.1 × 38.2 × 14.0 feet.
4-cyl. 2SA 'P' type oil engine by J.I. Thornycroft & Co. Ltd., Southampton.

1.1952: Completed by Goole Shipbuilding & Repairing Co. Ltd., Goole (Yard No. 481) for the company. *10.1971:* Sold to Safanourios Ltd., Limassol, Cyprus and renamed SAFANOURIOS. *1972:* Sold to Gulf Coast Navigation Ltd., Limassol, Cyprus and renamed MARIANNE K. *29.10.1972:* Beached near Canakkale after an engine room fire when entering the Dardanelles while on a voyage from the Mediterranean to a Russian Black Sea port. Subsequently declared a constructive total loss although later repaired and returned to service. *1982:* Owners became Gulf Coast Navigation Ltd., Istanbul, Turkey and renamed KALKAVANLAR. *1984:* Owner became Kalkavan Denizcilik ve Ticaret A.S., Istanbul, Turkey. *1987:* Owner became Kalkavanlar Deniz Nakilyat A.S., Istanbul, Turkey. Still in service (1990).

111. SONORITY (1952–1975)

O.N. 184654 589g 304n 725d 176.7 × 27.6 × 9.4 feet.
5-cyl. 2SA 'O' type oil engine by the Newbury Diesel Co. Ltd., Newbury.

6.1952: Completed by Fellows & Co. Ltd., Great Yarmouth (Yard No. 356) for the company. *6.1975:* Sold to G. Dupenois Shipping Co. Ltd., Ashburton. *1976:* Renamed ROWANCRAIG. *1976:* Sold to Eviport Maritime S.A., Panama and renamed SCANDIA III. *1977:* Sold to G. Katrakis, G. Tzortzopoulos & St. Tzortzopoulos, Piraeus, Greece and renamed ALMY. *1982:* Sold to G. Lisikatos, K. Soulanis & Ef. Stavrakis, Piraeus, Greece. *1986:* Broken up in Greece.

SONORITY

J.K. Byass

112. ACCLIVITY (2) (1952–1966) Tanker

O.N. 161116 1,179g 568n 1,300d 221.8 × 36.3 × 14.0 feet.
T.3-cyl. steam engine by the shipbuilder.

9.1929: Completed by Cammell Laird & Co. Ltd., Birkenhead (Yard No. 958) for the United Molasses Co. Ltd., London as ATHELTARN. *12.1939:* Owners restyled Athel Line Ltd., London. *6.1952:* Acquired by Everard Shipping Co. Ltd. and renamed ACCLIVITY. *5.1966:* Sold to Van den Bosche & Co. for breaking up at Boom, Belgium where she arrived *4.5.1966.*

ACCLIVITY (2)

A. Duncan

SELECTIVITY (1) *J. Clarkson*

113. SELECTIVITY (1) (1952–1975)

O.N. 184672 1,575g 714n 1,850d 230.6 × 38.0 × 14.0 feet.
4-cyl. 2SA 'P' type oil engine by the Newbury Diesel Co. Ltd., Newbury.

7.1952: Completed by the Grangemouth Dockyard Co. Ltd., Grangemouth (Yard No. 502) for the company. *5.1975:* Sold to Four Friends Shipping Co. Ltd., Limassol, Cyprus and renamed IOANNIS. *17.1.1985:* Went aground and abandoned in position 05.46N, 00.29E while on passage from Tema to Apapa with general cargo.

ALIGNITY *T. Rayner*

114. ALIGNITY (1952–1971) Tanker

O.N. 169450 890g 379n 900d 193.0 × 32.0 × 14.5 feet.
4-cyl. 2SA oil engine by British Polar Engines Ltd., Glasgow.

10.1945: Completed by A. & J. Inglis Ltd., Glasgow (Yard No. 1301) for the Ministry of War Transport, London (Anglo-Saxon Petroleum Co. Ltd., London, managers) as EMPIRE FITZROY. *1946:* Managers became British Tanker Co. Ltd., London. *4.1946:* Owner became the Ministry of Transport, London. *12.1946:* Managers became Anglo-Saxon Petroleum Co. Ltd., London. *1949:* Managers became Coastal Tankers Ltd., London. *9.1952:* Acquired by Everard Shipping Co. Ltd. and renamed ALIGNITY. *11.1971:* Sold to Hughes Bolckow Ltd. for breaking up at Blyth where she arrived *10.11.1971*.

APEXITY

Author's collection

115. APEXITY (1952–1964) Tanker

O.N. 185895 136g 49n 180d 100.0 × 19.7 × 7.2 feet.
C.2-cyl. steam engine by A. Hall & Co. Ltd., Aberdeen.

1945: Completed by the Shipbuilding Corporation Ltd. (Tyne Branch, Walker Yard) (Yard No. 22) for the Admiralty, London as the military oil barge MOB. 8. *1951:* Sold to Pounds Shipowners & Shipbreakers Ltd., Portsmouth. *11.1952:* Acquired by the company and renamed APEXITY. *1.1959:* Transferred to Everard Shipping Co. Ltd. *4.1964:* Sold to W.G.S. Crouch & Sons Ltd., Greenhithe. *1965:* Renamed WILLIAM SPEARING. *1969:* Re-engined with a 6-cyl. 2SA 'D' type oil engine made by the Newbury Diesel Co. Ltd., Newbury. *1974:* Sold to C. Crawley Ltd., Gravesend and renamed AQUASEAL. *1975:* Engine removed and hull sold to Liguria Maritime Ltd. for breaking up at Sittingbourne.

ATTUNITY

L. Sawyer

116. ATTUNITY (1952–1966) Tanker

O.N. 185896 136g 49n 180d 100.0 × 19.7 × 7.2 feet.
C.2-cyl. steam engine by A. Hall & Co. Ltd., Aberdeen.

1945: Completed by the Shipbuilding Corporation Ltd. (Tyne Branch, Walker Yard) (Yard No. 23) for the Admiralty, London as the military oil barge MOB. 9. *1951:* Sold to Pounds Shipowners & Shipbreakers Ltd., Portsmouth. *11.1952:* Acquired by the company and renamed ATTUNITY. *1.1959:* Transferred to Everard Shipping Co. Ltd. *5.1966:* Sold to W.G.S. Crouch & Sons Ltd., Greenhithe. *1967:* Renamed ERNIE SPEARING. *1969:* Re-engined with a 6-cyl. 2SA 'D' type oil engine made by the Newbury Diesel Co. Ltd., Newbury. *1974:* Sold to Dundee Harbour Trust, Dundee and renamed ABERCRAIG. *1985:* Sold to G. Beazley (Maritime Services) Ltd., Stockton-on-Tees. *1985:* Sold to N. Keedy & Sons Ltd., Cleadon, Sunderland. *1987:* Sold to Tyne Water Boats Ltd., Cleadon, Sunderland. Still in service (1990).

ADROITY *A. Duncan*

117. ADROITY (1953–1969) Tanker

O.N. 184759 457g 179n 569d 144.3 × 25.1 × 10.4 feet.
6-cyl. 4SA oil engine by Werkspoor N.V., Amsterdam, Holland.

10.1947: Completed by N.V. Scheepswerf Gebroeder van der Werf, Deest, Holland (Yard No. 221) for A/B Finland Syd Amerika Linjen O/Y (B. Krogius, manager), Helsingfors, Finland as T.3. *1949:* Owners became A/B Oceanfart, Helsingfors, Finland. *2.1953:* Acquired by the company and renamed ADROITY. *6.1962:* Re-engined with a 6-cyl. 2SA 'G' type oil engine made by the Newbury Diesel Co. Ltd., Newbury. *5.1969:* Sold to T. Hubbard & Co. Ltd., Colchester for breaking up at Hythe Quay.

AZURITY *A. Duncan*

118. AZURITY (1953–1965) Tanker

O.N. 185868 347g 157n 399d 143.6 × 24.5 × 10.0 feet.
3-cyl. 2SA oil engine by Appingedammer Bronsmotorenfabriek N.V., Appingedam, Holland.

1949: Completed by Scheepswerf De Haan & Oerleman's N.V., Heusden, Holland (Yard No. 253) for Gebroeder Broere N.V., Dordrecht, Holland as ELIZABETH B. *2.1953:* Acquired by the company and renamed AZURITY. *1964:* Laid up awaiting sale. *3.1965:* Sold to Metaalhandel & Sloopwerken H.P. Heuvelman for breaking up at Krimpen aan-den-Ijssel, Holland.

AFFIRMITY

J. Callis

119. AFFIRMITY (1953–1964) Tanker

O.N. 185983 249g 109n 280d 128.2 × 21.9 × 7.7 feet.
4-cyl. 4SA oil engine by Motorenfabrik Deutz A.G., Koln-Deutz, Germany.

1928: Completed by J. Koster Hzn. 'De Gideon', Groningen, Holland (Yard No. 115) for N.V. Scheepvaart Maatschappij 'Palmlijn', Rotterdam, Holland as PALMA. *1932:* Sold to Algemeen Vrachtkantoor N.V., Rotterdam, Holland. *1933:* Lengthened from 112.3 to 128.2 feet. *10.1953:* Acquired by the company and renamed AFFIRMITY. *3.1958:* Re-engined with a 4-cyl. 2SA 'G' type oil engine made by the Newbury Diesel Co. Ltd., Newbury. *8.1964:* Sold to A.E. Peirce, Canvey Island but resold to Metaalhandel & Sloopwerken H.P. Heuvelman for breaking up at Krimpen-aan-den-Ijssel, Holland where work had commenced by *12.1964.*

SOCIALITY (1)

A. Duncan

120. SOCIALITY (1) (1953–1973)

O.N. 167949 500g 337n 800d 178.8 × 29.3 × 9.8 feet.
8-cyl. 4SA oil engine by Appingedammer Bronsmotorenfabriek N.V., Appingedam, Holland.

9.1953: Completed by N.V. Scheepswerf "Westerbroek", Westerbroek, Holland (Yard No. 143) for Bosscher & Zoon, Groningen, Holland as JUNE B. *11.1953:* Acquired by the company and renamed SOCIALITY. *6.1973:* Sold to N. Barbas (V. Barbas, manager), Salonika, Greece and renamed CAPTANIKOLAS. *1976:* Manager became M. Gigilinis, Thessalonika, Greece. *1979:* Renamed VASILIS D. *1981:* Sold to Skordalakis Brothers Shipping Enterprises, Thessalonika, Greece. *1985:* Renamed STRATOS. *1987:* Renamed DESPINA. *1990:* Sold to S. Papademetriou and N. Kafiris and renamed FOURNOI III. Still in service (1990).

121. FORTUNITY (1953–1961)

O.N. 180312 411g 190n 450d 142.0 × 27.0 × 8.5 feet.
7-cyl. 4SA oil engine by Blackstone & Co. Ltd., Stamford.

11.1944: Completed by Henry Scarr Ltd., Hessle (Yard No. S454) for the Ministry of War Transport, London (Walford Lines Ltd., London, managers) as EMPIRE FARAWAY. *1945:* Managers became W.G. James & Sons, Cardigan. *1946:* Managers became T. Mills & Co. (Export) Ltd., London. *1947:* Sold to Seaway Coasters Ltd., London and renamed SEABROOK. *1951:* Managers became James Fisher & Sons Ltd., Barrow-in-Furness. *12.1953:* Acquired by the company and renamed FORTUNITY. *1955:* Re-engined with a 6-cyl. 2SA 'G' type oil engine made by the Newbury Diesel Co. Ltd., Newbury. *10.1961:* Sold to N.V. Machine & Scheepsloperij 'De Koophandel' for breaking up at Nieuw Lekkerland, Holland where work commenced during *3.1962.*

FORTUNITY

T. Rayner

122. SPONTANEITY (1954–1968)

O.N. 186018 500g 259n 735d 163.3 × 28.3 × 9.7 feet
6-cyl. 2SA oil engine by N.V. Werkspoor, Amsterdam, Holland.

6.1949: Completed by Gebroeder Van Diepen, Waterhuizen, Holland (Yard No. 908) for K.P. Bosma, Groningen, Holland as REMMERT. *1.1954:* Acquired by the company and renamed SPONTANEITY. *11.1968:* Sold to D. Kalkasinas, Thessalonika, Greece and renamed KALKAS. *1969:* Renamed GEORGAKIS. *1971:* Sold to Achilleas Farmakis Co., Piraeus, Greece. *1973:* Sold to D. Valoglou, Piraeus, Greece. *1979:* Sold to K. Valahis & N. Vekris, Piraeus, Greece and renamed AGHIA VARVARA. *1982:* Sold to Brodospas Poduzece Z.A. for breaking up at Split, Yugoslavia where she arrived *5.9.1982.*

SPONTANEITY

J. Callis

ANTERIORITY (1) on charter to Esso with original black hull. *T. Rayner*

123. ANTERIORITY (1) (1954–1968) Tanker

O.N. 186057 2,003g 889n 2,350d 265.7 × 41.6 × 17.6 feet.
6-cyl. 2SA 'P' type oil engine by the Newbury Diesel Co. Ltd., Newbury.

5.1954: Completed by Goole Shipbuilding & Repairing Co. Ltd., Goole (Yard No. 493) for the company. *10.1968:* Sold to Greek Tankershipping Co. Ltd., Piraeus, Greece and renamed VARI. *4.2.1982:* Stranded on the north coast of Crete and abandoned while on passage from Eleusis to Iraklion with a cargo of heavy fuel oil. Later refloated and towed to Kynosoura where she arrived on *1.3.1982.* Subsequently declared a constructive total loss and laid up. *8.3.1989:* Left under tow for breaking up at Aliaga, Turkey where she arrived two days later.

ANTERIORITY (1) on charter to Esso and with later grey hull colour. *C. Hill*

SIMULTANEITY

T. Rayner

124. SIMULTANEITY/GLEN URQUHART (1954–1968)

O.N. 186078 500g 248n 740d 157.4 × 28.4 × 9.7 feet.
8-cyl. 4SA oil engine by Appingedammer Bronsmotorenfabriek N.V., Appingedam, Holland.

7.1949: Completed by Scheepswerf 'Vooruitgang', Gebroeder Suurmeyer N.V., Foxhol, for N.V. Reederij Maatschappij 'Nelly' (Kamps Scheepvaart & Handelmaatschappij N.V., managers), Hoogezand, Holland as NELLY. *1953:* Owners became N.V. Reederij Maatschappij 'Wenda' (same managers), Hoogezand, Holland. *5.1954:* Acquired by the company and renamed SIMULTANEITY. *8.1965:* Sold to Glen Scheepvaart Maatschappij N.V. (N.V. Trias, managers), Rotterdam, Holland and renamed GLEN URQUHART. *9.1968:* Sold to Dimitrios Ventouris, Piraeus, Greece and renamed AGHIOS FANOURIOS. *1981:* Sold to Coronation Shipping Co. Ltd., Piraeus, Greece. *1983:* Sold to Christos Paraschis, Piraeus, Greece. *1985:* Sold to Kladias Scrap for breaking up at Eleusis, Greece where work commenced *9.1985*.

AUTHENTICITY (1)

J. Clarkson

125. AUTHENTICITY (1) (1954–1966) Tanker

O.N. 168779 871g 362n 890d 188.7 × 31.3 × 14.0 feet.
T.3-cyl. steam engine by Amos and Smith Ltd., Hull.

3.1942: Completed by Goole Shipbuilding & Repairing Co. Ltd., Goole (Yard No. 371) for the Ministry of War Transport, London (Coastal Tankers Ltd., London, managers) as EMPIRE HARP. *1942:* Managers became Anglo-Saxon Petroleum Co. Ltd., London. *4.1946:* Owner became the Ministry of Transport, London. *1946:* Managers became Coastal Tankers Ltd., London. *11.1947:* Sold to Kuwait Oil Co. Ltd., London and renamed ANIS. *5.1954:* Acquired by the company and renamed AUTHENTICITY. *1956:* Lengthened to 213.8 feet and tonnages became 983g, 466n and 1,057d. *5.1966:* Sold to S.J. & J.S. Latsis, Athens, Greece and renamed PETROLA I. *1967:* Sold to Margarita Shipping & Trading Corp. (J.S. Latsis, manager), Piraeus, Greece. *1970:* Owner became S.J. Latsis, Piraeus, Greece. *1977:* Sold to Maritime & Commercial Co. Argonaftis S.A. (same managers), Piraeus, Greece. *1984:* Sold for breaking up by Chalivdemboriki E.P.E. at Aspropyrgos, Greece where she arrived *8.9.1984*.

126. ASTRALITY (1) (1954) Tanker

O.N. 161218 2,231g 1,117n 3,227d 275.4 × 44.2 × 19.9 feet.
3-cyl. 2SA oil engine by Richardsons, Westgarth & Co. Ltd., Hartlepool.

4.1929: Completed by Blythswood Shipbuilding Co. Ltd., Glasgow (Yard No. 21) for Iranian Tanker Co. Ltd., London as IRANIA. *1936:* Sold to Skibs A/S Irania (H. Hannevig, manager), Oslo, Norway. *1948:* Renamed ELIZABETH MARY and manager became E.C. Hannevig. *1954:* Sold to Borre D/S A/S, Oslo, Norway. *1954:* Acquired by the company and renamed ASTRALITY. *1954:* Sold to Société Frêt-Maroc (Cie. d'Armement de Navires-Citernes, managers), Casablanca, Morocco and renamed FRIMAU. *1957:* Sold to Gem Shipping Co., Puerto Cortes, Honduras, and renamed MONT KETO. *1957:* Sold to Cie. d'Armement Maritime, Djibouti, French Somaliland and renamed OBOCK. *1958:* Sold to C. Diamantis, Piraeus, Greece and renamed THESSALONIKA. *1961:* Sold to Greek Tankershipping Co. Ltd., Piraeus, Greece. *22.11.1963:* Wrecked on Euboea Island in position 38.41N, 24.03E while on passage from Thessalonika to Piraeus in ballast.

SEVERITY

J. Callis

127. SEVERITY (1954–1975)

O.N. 186118 590g 304n 750d 176.5 × 27.6 × 9.4 feet.
5-cyl. 2SA 'O' type oil engine by the Newbury Diesel Co. Ltd., Newbury.

8.1954: Completed by Fellows & Co. Ltd., Great Yarmouth (Yard No. 357) for the company. *9.1975:* Sold to E. Naughton, Cayman Islands and renamed ADINA. *1979:* Owners became P.M. International Shipping Co. & E. Naughton, Cayman Islands. Still in service (1990).

SEVERITY

M. Cassar

FREDERICK T. EVERARD

T. Rayner

128. FREDERICK T. EVERARD (1954–1972)

O.N. 186131 2,535g 1,215n 3,297d 93.38 × 12.96 × 5.47 metres.
6-cyl. 2SA 'P' type oil engine by the Newbury Diesel Co. Ltd., Newbury.

9.1954: Completed by Goole Shipbuilding & Repairing Co. Ltd., Goole (Yard No. 488) for the company. *3.1972:* Sold to Nautilus IV Compania Naviera S.A. (M. Gigilinis, manager), Thessalonika, Greece and renamed EMILIA G. *1975:* Renamed ALEXIS G. *1981:* Sold to Athens Luck Compania Naviera S.A. (Jetwave Shipping S.A., managers), Piraeus, Greece and renamed ATHENS LUCK. *1982:* Sold to Marcomiso S.A. (Kassos Maritime Shipping Co. S.A., managers), Panama and renamed ANNA KASSIANI. *7.1982:* Sold to Baptista y Irmaos Ltda. for breaking up at Moita, Portugal where she arrived *30.7.1982*.

FREDERICK T. EVERARD

Company archives

AVERITY (1)

A. Duncan

129. AVERITY (1) (1954–1972) Tanker

O.N. 169128 401g 212n 450d 45.11 × 8.32 × 3.08 metres.
4-cyl. 2SA oil engine by Crossley Brothers Ltd., Manchester.

2.1944: Completed by Furness Shipbuilding Co. Ltd., Haverton Hill (Yard No. 366) for the Ministry of War Transport, London (Coastal Tankers Ltd., London, managers) as CHANT 53. *1946:* Sold to Royal Netherlands Government (N.V. Teerbedrijf Uithoorn, managers), Uithoorn, Holland and renamed THEODORA. *1950:* Sold to N.V. Rederij Theodora, Uithoorn, Holland. *11.1954:* Acquired by the company and renamed AVERITY. *1964:* Re-engined with a 6-cyl. 2SA 'G' type oil engine made by the Newbury Diesel Co. Ltd., Newbury. *6.1972:* Sold to West of Scotland Shipbreaking Co. Ltd. for breaking up at Troon where work commenced *23.6.1972.*

AUSPICITY

A. Duncan

130. AUSPICITY (1954–1972)

O.N. 180112 402g 215n 450d 45.11 × 8.32 × 3.08 metres.
4-cyl. 2SA oil engine by Crossley Brothers Ltd., Manchester.

5.1944: Completed by Goole Shipbuilding & Repairing Co. Ltd., Goole (Yard No. 415) for the Ministry of War Transport, London (C. Rowbotham & Sons, London, managers) as CHANT 27. *4.1946:* Owner became the Ministry of Transport. *1947:* Sold to Sociedad de Navegacion Comagre S.A., Panama and renamed COMAGRE. *1947:* Sold to N.V. Teerbedrijf Uithoorn, Uithoorn, Holland and renamed FRANS. *1954:* Sold to N.V. Rederij 'Frans', Uithoorn, Holland. *12.1954:* Acquired by the company and renamed AUSPICITY. *1969:* Re-engined with a 6-cyl. 2SA 'G' type oil engine made by the Newbury Diesel Co. Ltd., Newbury. *8.1972:* Sold to Panagiotis Vourdahas, Piraeus, Greece and renamed THEKLI. *1974:* Sold for breaking up at Perama, Greece.

ASTRALITY (2) *T. Rayner*

131. ASTRALITY (2) (1955–1965) Tanker

O.N. 180147 3,744g 1,998n 5,127d 109.0 × 14.74 × 6.69 metres.
3-cyl. 2SA oil engine by W. Doxford & Sons Ltd., Sunderland.

12.1944: Completed by J.L. Thompson & Sons Ltd., Sunderland (Yard No. 636) for the Ministry of War Transport, London (F.T. Everard & Sons Ltd., managers) as EMPIRE GANGES. *1946:* Sold to Anglo-Saxon Petroleum Co. Ltd., London and renamed BOLMA. *3.1955:* Acquired by the company and renamed ASTRALITY. *12.1965:* Sold to Oriana S.p.A. di Navigazione, Venice (V. Bollerino, Genoa, manager), Italy and renamed MONTE BERICO. *1966:* Sold to Marittima Fluviale Meridionale, Palermo, Sicily. *1967:* Sold to Venezia Tankers S.a.S., Venice, Italy. *1975:* Sold to Misano di Navigazione S.p.A., Venice, Italy. *1975:* Sold to 'Oriana' Societa di Navigazione per Azione, Venice, Italy. *1977:* Sold to Maralba S.p.A., Venice, Italy. *1978:* Sold to De Co Mar for breaking up at La Spezia, Italy where work commenced during *11.1978.*

CONTINUITY

A. Duncan

132. CONTINUITY (1955–1977)

O.N. 186250 655g 329n 785d 58.37 × 8.64 × 3.58 metres.
5-cyl. 2SA 'O' type oil engine by the Newbury Diesel Co. Ltd., Newbury.

6.1955: Completed by Clelands (Successors) Ltd., Wallsend (Yard No. 203) for the company. *1.1977:* Sold to Erika Shipping Co. S.A., Panama and renamed SALOME. *1986:* Sold to Lotus Shipping Ltd., Colon, Panama. Still in service (1990).

GEORGINA V. EVERARD *J. Clarkson*

133. GEORGINA V. EVERARD (1955–1978)

O.N. 186267 2,535g 1,218n 3,297d 93.38 × 12.96 × 5.47 metres.
6-cyl. 2SA 'P' type oil engine by the Newbury Diesel Co. Ltd., Newbury.

7.1955: Completed by Goole Shipbuilding & Repairing Co. Ltd., Goole (Yard No. 489) for the company. *12.1971:* Transferred to Clydesdale Shipowners Co. Ltd. *7.1978:* Sold to Mohamed Ali Mohamed Dib Sawalhi, Lebanon and renamed MYASSA. *1979:* Renamed MYASSAR. *1979:* Sold to Al Saad Shipping Co., Tripoli, Lebanon. *1985:* Sold for breaking up.

134. CENTRICITY (1955–1977)

O.N. 186294 655g 329n 785d 58.37 × 8.64 × 3.58 metres.
5-cyl. 2SA 'O' type oil engine by the Newbury Diesel Co. Ltd., Newbury.

9.1955: Completed by Clelands (Successors) Ltd., Wallsend (Yard No. 202) for the company. *2.1977:* Sold to Internavo Co. Ltd., Limassol, Cyprus and renamed DEMI. *1978:* Sold to Magda Shipping & Commercial Enterprises of Honduras, Puerto Cortes, Honduras and renamed MAGDALENA. *11.1979:* Sold to Sloop en Bergingsbedrijf van der Varelat for breaking up at Vianen, Holland.

CENTRICITY *A. Duncan*

ARGOSITY after being lengthened. *A. Duncan*

135. ARGOSITY (1956–1969) Tanker

O.N. 168794 813g 333n 850d 61.72 × 9.29 × 3.92 metres.
T.3-cyl. steam engine by Aitchison, Blair Ltd., Clydebank.

12.1941: Completed by the Grangemouth Dockyard Co. Ltd., Grangemouth (Yard No. 435) for the Ministry of War Transport, London (C. Rowbotham & Sons, London, managers) as EMPIRE LASS. *2.1944:* Managers became Anglo-Saxon Petroleum Co. Ltd., London. *4.1946:* Owner became the Ministry of Transport, London. *8.1946:* Sold to Anglo-American Oil Co. Ltd., London and renamed ESSO JUNIATA. *1951:* Owners became Esso Petroleum Co. Ltd., London. *1.1956:* Acquired by the company and renamed ARGOSITY. *1957:* Lengthened to 69.95 metres and tonnages became 877g, 416n and 1,018d. *5.1969:* Sold to Brugse Scheepsloperij for breaking up at Bruges, Belgium.

ASSURITY (2) *M. Cassar*

136. ASSURITY (2) (1956–1969) Tanker

O.N. 187373 2,228g 1,062n 2,600d 85.93 × 12.73 × 5.21 metres.
6-cyl. 2SA 'P' type oil engine by the Newbury Diesel Co. Ltd., Newbury.

4.1956: Completed by Goole Shipbuilding & Repairing Co. Ltd., Goole (Yard No. 500) for the company. *5.1969:* Sold to Heracles Shipping Co. S.A. (General Cement Co., managers), Piraeus, Greece and renamed PETROCLIS. *1982:* Sold to United Brothers Co. S.A., Panama and renamed TAMIN II. *1989:* Sold to unknown owner in the United Arab Emirates and renamed MARWAN IV. *1989:* Sold to Malvi Shipbuilding Co. for breaking up at Port Alang, India where she arrived *11.10.1989*.

CONFORMITY (1)

J. Clarkson

137. CONFORMITY (1) (1956–1970) Tanker

O.N. 168043 344g 148n 361d 40.54 × 7.47 × 3.19 metres.
T.3-cyl. steam engine by the shipbuilder.

11.1940: Completed by W.J. Yarwood & Sons Ltd., Northwich (Yard No. 648) for the Admiralty, London as the coaling lighter C.85. *5.1956:* Acquired by the company and renamed CONFORMITY. *1959:* Rebuilt as a tanker, tonnages and dimensions became 484g, 227n, 600d and 52.27 × 8.61 × 3.19 metres. *10.1970:* Sold to Arie Rijsdijk, Boss & Zonen for breaking up at Hendrik Ido Ambacht, Holland and passed Dordrecht *24.10.1970*.

COMMODITY (1)

A. Duncan

138. COMMODITY (1) (1956–1969) Tanker

O.N. 168464 346g 140n 361d 40.54 × 7.52 × 3.19 metres.
T.3-cyl. steam engine by shipbuilder.

7.1943: Completed by W.J. Yarwood & Sons Ltd., Northwich (Yard No. 713) for the Admiralty, London as the coaling lighter C.614. *5.1956:* Acquired by the company and renamed COMMODITY. *1957:* Rebuilt as a tanker, tonnages and dimensions became 470g, 225n, 570d and 50.67 × 8.61 × 3.19 metres. *5.1969:* Sold to Belcon Shipping & Trading Co. for breaking up and arrived at Bruges *28.5.1969*. Resold to Jacques Bakker & Zonen for breaking up. Work commenced at Bruges in *8.1969*.

CITY (1) before conversion. *J. Callis*

139. CITY (1) (1956–1969) Tanker

O.N. 180582 352g 148n 361d 40.54 × 7.53 × 3.19 metres.
T.3-cyl. steam engine by the shipbuilder.

8.1945: Completed by W.J. Yarwood & Sons Ltd., Northwich (Yard No. 768) for the Admiralty, London as the coaling lighter C.633. *5.1956:* Acquired by the company and renamed CITY. *1960:* Rebuilt as a tanker, tonnages and dimensions became 500g, 228n, 600d and 52.30 × 8.61 × 3.19 metres. *7.1969:* Sold to Shell Mex & B.P. Ltd., London. *7.1969:* Sold to J. Cashmore & Sons Ltd. for breaking up at Newport where work was completed by *31.7.1969.*

CITY (1) after conversion with charterer's funnel colours. *M. Cassar*

CANDOURITY (1) and **COMMODITY (1)** awaiting commissioning at Goole. *C. Hill*

140. CANDOURITY (1) (1956–1969) Tanker

O.N. 180837 352g 148n 361d 40.54 × 7.53 × 3.10 metres.
T.3-cyl. steam engine by the shipbuilder.

3.1946: Completed by W.J. Yarwood & Sons Ltd., Northwich (Yard No. 773) for the Admiralty, London as the coaling lighter C.641. *5.1956:* Acquired by the company and renamed CANDOURITY. *1958:* Rebuilt as a tanker, tonnages and dimensions became 474g, 225n, 570d and 50.67 × 8.61 × 3.19 metres. *6.1969:* Sold to Van den Bosche & Co. for breaking up at Antwerp, Belgium where she arrived *19.6.1969.*

CANDOURITY (1) after conversion. *J. Clarkson*

CLANITY before conversion. *C. Hill*

141. CLANITY (1956–1969) Tanker

O.N. 181548 352g 148n 361d 40.54 × 7.53 × 3.19 metres.
T.3-cyl. steam engine by the shipbuilder.

12.1946: Completed by W.J. Yarwood & Sons Ltd., Northwich (Yard No. 774) for the Admiralty, London as the coaling lighter C.642. *5.1956:* Acquired by the company and renamed CLANITY. *1958:* Rebuilt as a tanker, tonnages and dimensions became 495g, 224n, 600d and 52.27 × 8.61 × 3.19 metres. *9.1969:* Sold to Scrappingco S.A. for breaking up at Antwerp, Belgium where work commenced *11.9.1969*.

CLANITY after conversion and with charterer's funnel colours. *J.K. Byass*

AWARDITY *C. Hill*

142. AWARDITY (1956–1965) Tanker

O.N. 187436 479g 233n 625d 51.17 × 7.88 × 3.39 metres.
6-cyl. 2SA oil engine by Sulzer Brothers, Winterthur, Switzerland.

4.1937: Completed by Jos. L. Meyer, Papenburg, Germany (Yard No. 407) for Algemeen Vrachtkantoor N.V., Rotterdam, Holland as INGEBORG. *7.1956:* Acquired by the company and renamed AWARDITY. *11.1960:* Re-engined with a 6-cyl. 2SA 'G/A' type oil engine made by the Newbury Diesel Co. Ltd., Newbury. *12.1965:* Sold to N. Thanapoulos & M. Koutlakis, Piraeus, Greece and renamed AGIA TRIAS. *1970:* Sold to J. Emmanouelides, Piraeus, Greece and renamed KOPANOS. *1973:* Sold to N. Thanapoulos & M. Koutlakis, Piraeus, Greece and renamed AGIA TRIAS. *1974:* Renamed PROPROMAKI. *1974:* Sold for breaking up in Greece.

SANGUITY (1) *A. Duncan*

143. SANGUITY (1) (1956–1978)

O.N. 187467 1,577g 712n 1,850d 73.44 × 11.64 × 4.79 metres.
4-cyl. 2SA 'P' type oil engine by the Newbury Diesel Co. Ltd., Newbury.

10.1956: Completed by the Grangemouth Dockyard Co. Ltd., Grangemouth (Yard No. 511) for the company. *2.1978:* Sold to Lisca Shipping Co. S.A., Panama and renamed RAMONA. *1986:* Sold to Lotus Shipping Ltd., St. Vincent. Still in service (1990).

144. CENTURITY (1956–1975)

O.N. 187499 780g 391n 885d 62.18 × 9.22 × 3.62 metres.
6-cyl. 2SA 'O' type oil engine by the Newbury Diesel Co. Ltd., Newbury.

11.1956: Completed by Goole Shipbuilding & Repairing Co. Ltd., Goole (Yard No. 502) for the company. *11.1975:* Sold to Sangri-La Shipping Enterprises Co. Ltd., Limassol, Cyprus and renamed TEMPESTA. *1987:* Deleted from Lloyds Register as continued existence in doubt.

CENTURITY with later black hull.

W.S.P.L.

THE DUKE

Skyfotos

145. THE DUKE (1956–1961)

O.N. 148937 820g 387n 1,100d 57.97 × 9.17 × 3.69 metres.
T.3-cyl. steam engine by the shipbuilder.

7.1927: Completed by Ailsa Shipbuilding Co. Ltd., Troon (Yard No. 400) for J. Hay & Sons Ltd., Glasgow. *2.1961:* Sold to BISCO and allocated to T.W. Ward Ltd. for breaking up at Grays where she arrived *8.2.1961*.

THE BARON

W.S.P.L.

146. THE BARON (1956–1960)

O.N. 148940 820g 388n 1,100d 57.97 × 9.17 × 3.69 metres.
T.3-cyl. steam engine by the shipbuilder.

8.1927: Completed by Ailsa Shipbuilding Co. Ltd., Troon (Yard No. 401) for J. Hay & Sons Ltd., Glasgow. *4.1960:* Sold to BISCO and allocated to C.W. Dorkin & Co. Ltd. for breaking up at Gateshead where she arrived *27.4.1960*.

THE COUNTESS

W.S.P.L.

147. THE COUNTESS (1956–1960)

O.N. 160226 824g 405n 1,100d 59.47 × 9.23 × 3.69 metres.
T.3-cyl. steam engine by the shipbuilder.

10.1928: Completed by Ailsa Shipbuilding Co. Ltd., Troon (Yard No. 406) for J. Hay & Sons Ltd., Glasgow. *5.1960:* Sold to BISCO and allocated to Clayton & Davie Ltd., for breaking up at Dunston where she arrived *24.5.1960*.

THE PRESIDENT J. Callis

148. THE PRESIDENT (1956–1962)

O.N. 164074 926g 481n 1,230d 63.79 × 9.81 × 3.69 metres.
T.3-cyl. steam engine by the shipbuilder.

5.1936: Completed by Ailsa Shipbuilding Co. Ltd., Troon (Yard No. 421) for J. Hay & Sons Ltd., Glasgow. *12.1962:* Sold to BISCO and allocated to W.H. Arnott, Young & Co. Ltd. for breaking up at Troon where she arrived *13.12.1962*.

THE EARL J. Clarkson

149. THE EARL (1956–1961)

O.N. 164081 926g 481n 1,230 63.79 × 9.81 × 3.69 metres.
T.3-cyl. steam engine by the shipbuilder.

6.1936: Completed by Ailsa Shipbuilding Co. Ltd., Troon (Yard No. 422) for J. Hay & Sons Ltd., Glasgow. *4.1961:* Sold to N.V. Machine & Scheepsloperij 'De Koophandel' for breaking up at Nieuw Lekkerland, Holland where she arrived *17.5.1961*.

THE MONARCH

W.S.P.L.

150. THE MONARCH (1956–1962)

O.N. 169529 1,059g 585n 1,1430d 64.86 × 9.94 × 4.63 metres.
T.3-cyl. steam engine by D. Rowan & Co. Ltd., Glasgow.

2.1946: Completed by George Brown & Co. (Marine) Ltd., Greenock (Yard No. 234) for the Ministry of War Transport, London (J. Hay & Sons Ltd., Glasgow, managers) as EMPIRE LEWISHAM. *1946:* Acquired by J. Hay & Sons Ltd., Glasgow and renamed THE MONARCH. *5.1962:* Sold to P. Vrangos, (Mediterranean Shipping Co. Ltd., managers), Piraeus, Greece and renamed SILVER CLOUD. *1968:* Sold to P. Pavlidis, Athens, Greece and renamed CHRYSANTHI. *1968:* Sold to Nikos Tzorsis for breaking up at Eleusis, Greece where work commenced *6.9.1968*.

THE EMPEROR *J. Callis*

151. THE EMPEROR (1956–1963)

O.N. 169482 1,058g 584n 1,430d 64.86 × 9.94 × 4.63 metres.
T.3-cyl. steam engine by Rankin & Blackmore Ltd., Greenock.

9.1946: Completed by George Brown & Co. (Marine) Ltd., Greenock (Yard No. 235) for J. Hay & Sons Ltd., Glasgow. (Originally laid down for the Ministry of War Transport as EMPIRE KINGSWAY but purchased and renamed before launching in *5.1946*). *1.1963:* Sold to Van den Bosche for breaking up at Boom, Belgium where work commenced *25.2.1963*.

152. CLARITY (1957–1978)

O.N. 187548 764g 386n 890d 62.18 × 9.22 × 3.62 metres.
6-cyl. 2SA 'O' type oil engine by the Newbury Diesel Co. Ltd., Newbury.

3.1957: Completed by Goole Shipbuilding & Repairing Co. Ltd., Goole (Yard No. 501) for the company. *11.1957:* Transferred to Cattedown Wharves Ltd., Plymouth. *7.1967:* Transferred to Everard Shipping Co. Ltd. *1969:* Re-engined with a 6-cyl. 2SA 'O' type oil engine made by the Newbury Diesel Co. Ltd., Newbury. *12.1971:* Transferred to F.T. Everard & Sons Ltd. *2.1978:* Sold to Olympios Shipping Co. Ltd. (Olympios Zeus Shipping Co. Ltd., managers), Panama and renamed AGIOS THOMAS. *1984:* Managers became Sonia Shipping Co. *1984:* Sold to Tringali Attilio Shipyard for breaking up at Augusta, Sicily.

CLARITY with later black hull.

W.S.P.L.

153. TANKITY (1957–1967) Tanker

O.N. 187698 145g 48n 180d 31.69 × 5.99 × 2.17 metres.
C.2-cyl. steam engine by White's Marine Engine Co., Hebburn.

1945: Completed by the Shipbuilding Corporation Ltd. (Tyne Branch, Walker Yard) (Yard No. 20) for the Admiralty, London as the military oil barge MOB. 7. *2.1957:* Sold to Pounds Shipowners & Shipbreakers Ltd., Portsmouth. *4.1957:* Acquired by the company and renamed TANKITY. *10.1967:* Sold to Northern Slipway Ltd., Dublin and resold to W.H. Arnott, Young & Co. (Shipbreakers) Ltd. for breaking up at Dalmuir where work commenced *10.5.1968*.

TANKITY

C. Hill

154. TOTALITY (1957–1970) Tanker

O.N. 307942 145g 48n 180d 31.69 × 5.99 × 2.17 metres.
C.2-cyl. steam engine by White's Marine Engine Co., Hebburn.

1945: Completed by the Shipbuilding Corporation Ltd. (Wear Branch, Southwick Yard) (Yard No. 12) for the Admiralty, London as the military oil barge MOB. 13. *2.1957:* Sold to Pounds Shipowners & Shipbreakers Ltd., Portsmouth. *4.1957:* Acquired by the company and renamed TOTALITY. *8.1970:* Sold to A.E. Peirce for breaking up at Canvey Island where she arrived *17.8.1970*.

ALFRED EVERARD with Hay funnel colours. *Company archives*

155. ALFRED EVERARD (1957–1978)

O.N. 300172 1,543g 678n 1,893d 73.44 × 11.64 × 4.78 metres.
4-cyl. 2SA 'P' type oil engine by the Newbury Diesel Co. Ltd., Newbury.

5.1957: Completed by the Grangemouth Dockyard Co. Ltd., Grangemouth (Yard No. 512) for J. Hay & Sons Ltd., Glasgow. *2.1978:* Sold to Rapid Transit Shipping Co. Ltd., Georgetown, Cayman Islands and renamed MARYS KETCH. *1982:* Sold to Cia. Linea Caribe Pacifico S. de R.L., San Lorenzo, Honduras and renamed ALDEBARAN. Still in service (1990).

ALFRED EVERARD in later years.

M. Cassar

ETHEL EVERARD (3)

C. Hill

156. ETHEL EVERARD (3)/GUARDIAN CARRIER (1957–1967)

O.N. 187688 1,542g 674n 1,883d 73.44 × 11.64 × 4.78 metres.
6-cyl. 2SA oil engine by Nydqvist & Holm A/B, Trollhattan, Sweden.

12.1957: Completed by the Grangemouth Dockyard Co. Ltd., Grangemouth (Yard No. 513) for the company. *7.1963:* Transferred to West River Shipping Co. Ltd., London (jointly owned with Tunnel Portland Cement Co. Ltd.), converted to a self discharging cement carrier and renamed GUARDIAN CARRIER. *3.1967:* Sold to New Zealand Cement Holdings Ltd., Dunedin, New Zealand. *1977:* Sold to St. Lawrence Cement Co., Toronto, Canada and renamed ROBERT KOCH. *1982:* Owners restyled St. Lawrence Cement Inc., Toronto, Canada. *1984:* Reclassified as a non-propelled barge. *19.12.1985:* Went aground one mile south east of Oswego port breakwater, New York, U.S.A. and sustained considerable damage. *1987:* Broken up.

GUARDIAN CARRIER

Company archives

GRIT (5) with later black hull. *J.K. Byass*

157. GRIT (5) (1958–1968) Tanker

O.N. 187729 2,739g 1,350n 3,350d 94.52 × 13.80 × 5.75 metres.
6-cyl. 2SA 'P' type oil engine by the Newbury Diesel Co. Ltd., Newbury.

2.1958: Completed by Goole Shipbuilding & Repairing Co. Ltd., Goole (Yard No. 506) for the company. *6.1968:* Sold to Evinos Compania Naviera S.A., Piraeus, Greece and renamed ELENI. *1973:* Sold to Ortansia Shipping Co. S.A., Piraeus, Greece and renamed KATERINA V. *1983:* Sold to Katerina V Shipping Co. Ltd., Piraeus, Greece. *1985:* Sold to E.E.C. Consortium Inc. (Sultan Shipping Co. Ltd., managers), Athens, Greece and renamed ALNOUR. *3.1986:* Sold to Halivdemboriki E.P.E. for breaking up at Eleusis, Greece.

FRED EVERARD (3)

C. Hill

158. FRED EVERARD (3) (1958–1965)

O.N. 187792 1,542g 673n 1,890d 73.44 × 11.64 × 4.78 metres.
6-cyl. 2SA oil engine by Nydqvist & Holm A/B, Trollhattan, Sweden.

6.1958: Completed by the Grangemouth Dockyard Co. Ltd., Grangemouth (Yard No. 514) for the company. *27.11.1965:* Grounded off Ravenscar in bad weather while on passage from Lervik to Ridham Dock with a cargo of paper pulp. *1.12.1965:* Sank in position 54.24N, 00.28W.

COMITY (1) as C648.

Author's collection

159. COMITY (1) (1958–1964)

O.N. 182906 198g 81n 230d 32.16 × 6.58 × 2.60 metres.
6-cyl. 2SA oil engine by H. Widdop & Co. Ltd., Keighley.

5.1949: Completed by J. Pollock, Sons & Co. Ltd., Faversham (Yard No. 1848) for the Admiralty, London as the lubricating oil lighter C.648. She had been launched in 1946. *8.1958:* Acquired by the company and renamed COMITY. *1960:* Re-engined with a 4-cyl. 2SA 'G' type oil engine made by the Newbury Diesel Co. Ltd., Newbury. *2.1964:* Sold to Marine Salvage & Survey Service Ltd. (W.J. Sutton, manager), Croydon and renamed CONSTELLATION. *1966:* Sold to Overseas & General Brokerage & Finance Co. Ltd., London. *1968:* Sold to Southwold Marine Aggregates Ltd., Southwold and renamed CAREYNA. *1972:* Sold to Carter & Ward of Wickford Ltd., Wickford. *1.1977:* Sold to Metal Recoveries Ltd. for breaking up at Newhaven.

AGILITY (2) with original grey hull.

C. Hill

160. AGILITY (2) (1959–1976) Tanker

O.N. 301012 1,016g 448n 1,270d 65.33 × 10.83 × 4.48 metres.
6-cyl. 2SA oil engine by British Polar Engines Ltd., Glasgow.

11.1959: Completed by Goole Shipbuilding & Repairing Co. Ltd., Goole (Yard No. 514) for the company. *2.1976:* Sold to Maldives Shipping Ltd., Male, Maldive Islands and renamed MALDIVE ENTERPRISE. *1977:* Sold to Elhawi Shipping Co. Ltd., Jeddah, Saudi Arabia and renamed GHAZI-B. *1987:* Renamed MUBARAK II. *1987:* Sold to S.Z. Enterprises Ltd. for breaking up at Gadani Beach, Pakistan where she arrived *10.3.1987*.

THE MARCHIONESS *J. Clarkson*

161. THE MARCHIONESS (1960–1966)

O.N. 163567 324g 151n 420d 41.60 × 7.65 × 2.98 metres.
3-cyl. 4SA oil engine by W.H. Allen, Sons & Co. Ltd., Bedford.

1935: Completed by J. Pollock, Sons & Co. Ltd., Faversham (Yard No. 1466) for Newcastle Coal & Shipping Co. Ltd., London as CAMROUX II. *1937:* Re-engined with a 6-cyl. 4SA oil engine made by Humboldt-Deutz Motoren A.G., Koln-Deutz, Germany. *1946:* Re-engined with a 6-cyl. 4SA oil engine made by Humboldt-Deutz Motoren A.G., Koln-Deutz, West Germany. *7.1960:* Acquired by J. Hay & Sons Ltd., Glasgow and renamed THE MARCHIONESS. *3.1966:* Sold to Tay Sand Co. Ltd., Dundee and renamed MIDDLEBANK. *3.1974:* Sold to T.W. Ward Ltd. for breaking up at Inverkeithing where work commenced *22.3.1974*.

THE MARQUIS *D. Hocquard*

162. THE MARQUIS (1960–1966)

O.N. 163555 324g 151n 427d 41.60 × 7.65 × 2.98 metres.
3-cyl. 4SA oil engine by W.H. Allen, Sons & Co. Ltd., Bedford.

12.1934: Completed by J. Pollock, Sons & Co. Ltd., Faversham (Yard No. 1465) for Newcastle Coal & Shipping Co. Ltd., London as CAMROUX I. *1937:* Re-engined with a 6-cyl. 2SA oil engine made by Humboldt-Deutz Motoren A.G., Koln-Deutz, Germany. *10.1941:* Re-engined with a 6-cyl. 2SA oil engine made by H. Widdop & Co. Ltd., Keighley. *5.1945:* Re-engined with a 4-cyl. 2SA oil engine made by British Polar Engines Ltd., Glasgow. *8.1960:* Acquired by J. Hay & Sons Ltd., Glasgow and renamed THE MARQUIS. *2.1966:* Sold to M. Gigilinis & D. Kalkasinas, Thessalonika, Greece and renamed ANGELIKA. *1968:* Sold to I. Kabanaros, Piraeus, Greece and renamed AGIOS IOANNIS THEOLOGOS. *1971:* Sold to P. Konidaris & T. Soukas, Piraeus, Greece and renamed STAMATA II. *1974:* Sold to Papaioanou Brothers, Piraeus, Greece. Still in service (1990).

WESTPORT

Company archives

163. WESTPORT (1960–1967)

O.N. 302546 948g 473n 900d 73.12 × 9.35 × 4.16 metres.
9-cyl. 2SA oil engine by Ateliers & Chantiers de la Loire, St. Nazaire, France.

1948: Completed by Jos. Boel & Fils, Tamise, Belgium (Yard No. 1152) for Worms & Cie., Le Havre, France as FRONSAC. Original tonnages 835g, 372n, 850d and length 64.86 metres. *1955:* Lengthened, tonnages and dimensions becoming those shown in line 1. *11.1960:* Acquired by West River Shipping Co. Ltd., London (jointly owned with Tunnel Portland Cement Co. Ltd.) and renamed WESTPORT. *3.1967:* Sold to New Zealand Cement Holdings Ltd., Dunedin, New Zealand. *7.1973:* Sold to Pacific Steel Ltd. for breaking up at Auckland, New Zealand where she arrived *26.7.1973.*

THE SULTAN

W.S.P.L.

164. THE SULTAN (1960–1969)

O.N. 302574 524g 260n 725d 53.00 × 8.59 × 4.42 metres.
8-cyl. 4SA oil engine by Gebroeder Stork & Co. N.V., Hengelo, Holland.

2.1950: Completed by Scheepswerf 'Waterhuizen' N.V. J. Pattje, Waterhuizen, Holland (Yard No. 207) for N.V. Europeesche Kustvaart (N.V. Gebroeder van Uden's Scheepvaart & Agentuur Maatschappij, managers), Rotterdam, Holland as NIEUWHAVEN. *12.1960:* Acquired by J. Hay & Sons Ltd., Glasgow and renamed THE SULTAN. *1963:* Re-engined with a 5-cyl. 2SA 'O' type oil engine made by the Newbury Diesel Co. Ltd., Newbury. *3.1969:* Sold to T. Hubbard & Co. Ltd. for breaking up at Rowhedge.

165. ANNUITY (2) (1961–1983) Tanker

O.N. 302591 1,599g 754n 2,388d 81.16 × 12.27 × 4.83 metres.
4-cyl. 2SA type oil engine by the Newbury Diesel Co. Ltd., Newbury.

2.1961: Completed by Goole Shipbuilding & Repairing Co. Ltd., Goole (Yard No. 515) for the company. *2.1975:* Re-engined with two 8-cyl. 4SA oil engines made by Mirrlees Blackstone Ltd., Stamford. *4.1983:* Sold to Hyma Shipping Co. (Therapiotis Shipping Co. Ltd., managers), Piraeus, Greece and renamed THITA TRIENNA. *1986:* Sold to Blue Eyes Shipping Co. (same managers), Piraeus, Greece and renamed BLUE EYES. *1987:* Sold to Jet Tank Maritime Co., Piraeus, Greece and renamed JET VI. *1988:* Sold to N.E. Promethus, Piraeus, Greece and renamed PROMETHUS. Still in service (1990).

ANNUITY (2) with later black hull and yellow funnel. *C. Hill*

Note: Glen & Co. Ltd., of Glasgow, together with the managed fleets of Clydesdale Shipowners Co. Ltd. and Scottish Navigation Co. Ltd., were acquired in December 1961. The six vessels (166 to 171 inclusive) although remaining under the registered ownership of their original companies were integrated into the fleet of F.T. Everard & Sons Ltd.

166. META (1961–1962)

O.N. 161932 1,575g 924n 2,632d 76.90 × 12.19 × 5.03 metres.
T.3-cyl. steam engine by the North Eastern Marine Engineering Co. Ltd., Wallsend.

4.1931: Completed by the Burntisland Shipbuilding Co. Ltd., Burntisland (Yard No. 166) for Scandinavian Shipping Co. Ltd. (Glen & Co., managers), Glasgow. *1937:* Transferred to Clydesdale Shipowners Co. Ltd. (same managers), Glasgow. *1939:* Managers became Glen & Co. Ltd., Glasgow. *2.1962:* Sold to Christiania Portland Cement Fabrik A/S, Oslo, Norway. Engine removed and hull used as an unregistered lighter.

META *J. Clarkson*

THELMA

W.S.P.L.

167. THELMA (1961–1964)

O.N. 164053 1,593g 933n 2,774d 80.77 × 12.34 × 4.97 metres.
T.3-cyl. steam engine by D. Rowan & Co. Ltd., Glasgow.

6.1935: Completed by the Burntisland Shipbuilding Co. Ltd., Burntisland (Yard No. 185) for Scandinavian Shipping Co. Ltd. (Glen & Co. managers), Glasgow. *1938:* Transferred to Clydesdale Shipowners Co. Ltd. (same managers), Glasgow. *1939:* Managers became Glen & Co. Ltd., Glasgow. *3.1964:* Sold to Fairport Compania Naviera S.A., Panama and renamed FAIRPORT. *1965:* Sold to Compania Maritima Dover S.A., Panama and renamed AUGUST. *1972:* Sold to Officine Ionio for breaking up at Catania, Sicily, Italy.

RUNA

Company archives

168. RUNA (1961–1964)

O.N. 180848 1,942g 964n 3,200d 91.81 × 13.50 × 4.83 metres.
C.4-cyl. steam engine by Verschure & Co.'s Scheepswerf & Machinefabriek, Amsterdam, Holland.

1944: Completed by C. Van der Giessen & Zonen's Scheepswerven N.V., Krimpen aan-den-Ijssel, Holland (Yard No. 727) for August Bolton, Wm. Miller's Nachfolger, Hamburg, Germany as EICHBERG. *5.1945:* Taken as a prize by Allied Forces at Bremerhaven. *7.1945:* Taken over by the Ministry of War Transport, London (Witherington & Everett Ltd., Newcastle, managers) and renamed EMPIRE CONSENT. *4.1946:* Owner became the Ministry of Transport, London. *3.1949:* Acquired by Clydesdale Shipowners Co. Ltd. (Glen & Co. Ltd., managers), Glasgow and renamed RUNA. *3.1964:* Sold to Globus Shipping Corp., Panama and renamed KARYATIS. *4.1968:* Sold to Lee Sing & Co. for breaking up at Hong Kong where she arrived *13.4.1968.*

WINGA J. Clarkson

169. WINGA (1961–1967)

O.N. 300168 2,234g 1,006n 2,670d 90.25 × 13.53 × 6.00 metres.
C.4-cyl. steam engine by Christiansen & Meyer, Hamburg, West Germany.

4.1957: Completed by A. Hall & Co. Ltd., Aberdeen (Yard No. 750) for Clydesdale Shipowners Co. Ltd. (Glen & Co. Ltd., managers), Glasgow. *3.1967:* Sold to Ambassador Steamships Pvt. Ltd., Cochin, India and renamed RADIANT. *1969:* Sold to Collis Line Pvt. Ltd., Cochin, India. *20.2.1978:* Sank in Bombay Harbour in position 18.56N, 72.52E following a collision with the Greek motor vessel ALTONA 8,497/59 when outward bound for Cochin, India.

SHUNA T. Rayner

170. SHUNA (1961–1963)

O.N. 164116 1,652g 787n 2,298d 80.77 × 12.34 × 4.97 metres.
T.3-cyl. steam engine by D. Rowan & Co. Ltd., Glasgow.

4.1937: Completed by Burntisland Shipbuilding Co. Ltd., Burntisland (Yard No. 208) for Scandinavian Shipping Co. Ltd. (Glen & Co. managers), Glasgow. *1938:* Transferred to Scottish Navigation Co. Ltd., Glasgow. *1939:* Managers became Glen & Co. Ltd., Glasgow. *11.1963:* Sold to Tamis S.A., Panama and renamed JULIE. *1964:* Sold to Praba Compania Naviera S.A. (Union Commercial Steamship Co., managers), Piraeus, Greece and renamed PANTARALI. *21.12.1969:* Stranded south of Susa in heavy weather while on passage from Bejaia to Susa, Tunisia in ballast.

171. ZENA (1961–1964)

O.N. 185036 1,685g 759n 2,315d 71.17 × 11.70 × 6.40 metres.
C.4-cyl. steam engine by the shipbuilder.

1951: Completed by Amsterdamsche Droogdok Maatschappij, Amsterdam, Holland (Yard No. 88) for Société Navale Caennaise, Caen, France as ENEE. *1956:* Acquired by Scottish Navigation Co. Ltd. (Glen & Co. Ltd., managers), Glasgow and renamed ZENA. *6.1964:* Sold to Trisagi Corp., Panama and renamed STASSA. *15.8.1966:* Went aground in calm weather on Renish Point, Harris. Refloated and towed into Rodel Bay where she sank on *17.8.1966* in position 57.42N, 06.56W. She was on passage from Archangel to Limerick with a cargo of timber.

ZENA *J. Clarkson*

WILLIAM J. EVERARD *Company archives*

172. WILLIAM J. EVERARD (1963–1982)

O.N. 304481 1,589g 993n 2,450d 81.01 × 11.97 × 5.16 metres.
8-cyl. 2SA oil engine by Nydqvist & Holm A/B, Trollhattan, Sweden.

3.1963: Completed by Goole Shipbuilding & Repairing Co. Ltd., Goole (Yard No. 536) for the company. *5.1974:* Re-engined with a 8-cyl. 4SA 'V' oil engine made by British Polar Engines Ltd., Glasgow. *1.1982:* Sold to Wimpey Marine Ltd., London, converted to a drillship and renamed WIMPEY GEOCORE. *1984:* Owners became Wimpey Laboratories Ltd., London. *1988:* Sold to Olympia Shipping Ltd., Gibraltar, rebuilt as a dry cargo vessel and renamed SEABURN GIRL. *1990:* Sold to Leighton Shipping Ltd., Gibraltar and renamed HUSUM. Still in service (1990).

PENELOPE EVERARD *C. Hill*

173. PENELOPE EVERARD (1963–1984)

O.N. 304487 1,583g 969n 2,545d 80.70 × 11.97 × 5.18 metres.
5-cyl. 2SA 'P' type oil engine by the Newbury Diesel Co. Ltd., Newbury.

3.1963: Completed by Clelands Shipbuilding Co. Ltd., Wallsend (Yard No. 257) for the company. *3.1974:* Re-engined with a 8-cyl. 4SA 'V' oil engine made by British Polar Engines Ltd., Glasgow. *5.1984:* Sold to Galatia Shipping Co. Ltd. (Interuniversal Chartering S.A., managers), Valletta, Malta and renamed PANAYIOTIS G. *1985:* Sold to Sykeon Shipping Co. Ltd., Valletta, Malta and renamed PANAGIOTIS G. *1986:* Sold to Saini Shipping Co. Ltd., Piraeus, Greece and renamed ELPIDA. Still in service (1990).

THE DUCHESS *C. Hill*

174. THE DUCHESS (1963–1981)

O.N. 304496 461g 213n 610d 51.95 × 8.64 × 3.16 metres.
6-cyl. 2SA 'G' type oil engine by the Newbury Diesel Co. Ltd., Newbury.

3.1963: Completed by J. Pollock, Sons & Co. Ltd., Faversham (Yard No. 2128) for J. Hay & Sons Ltd., Glasgow. *8.1972:* Re-engined with a 6-cyl. 4SA oil engine made by Mirrlees Blackstone Ltd., Stamford. *1.1981:* Sold to R.W. Fielding, Liverpool. *1981:* Sold to Gardscreen Shipping Ltd., Rainham and renamed THEO. *1986:* Sold to Pewterdag Ltd., London. *1989:* Sold to Archimedes Shipping Ltd., Ridderkerk, Holland and renamed MARJAN. Still in service (1990).

FRIVOLITY (2) *Company archives*

175. FRIVOLITY (2) (1963–1976)

O.N. 304573 199g 98n 287d 33.46 × 7.73 × 2.83 metres.
4-cyl. 4SA oil engine by Lister Blackstone Marine Ltd., Dursley.

5.1963: Completed by Fellows & Co. Ltd., Great Yarmouth (Yard No. 373) for the company. *5.1976:* Sold to Conrad Shipping Ltd., London and renamed VOL. *1977:* Sold to Ocean Liner Services Ltd., London. *14.9.1978:* Foundered in heavy weather in the North Sea in position 52.05N, 02.27E while on passage from Stein to Colchester with a cargo of coal.

FESTIVITY (2) *C. Hill*

176. FESTIVITY (2) (1963–1974)

O.N. 304695 199g 99n 287d 33.46 × 7.73 × 2.83 metres.
4-cyl. 4SA oil engine by Lister Blackstone Marine Ltd., Dursley.

9.1963: Completed by Fellows & Co. Ltd., Great Yarmouth (Yard No. 374) for the company. *7.1974:* Sold to Kennedy Marine Freights, Rochester and renamed GYRINUS. *1977:* Sold to Sully Freight, London and renamed SUBRO VICTOR. *1979:* Sold to Wm. Dennison Shipping Ltd., Kirkwall and renamed NORTH SOUND. *1985:* Sold to T. & D. Murrell & T. Wood, London. *1986:* Renamed SWIFTWOOD. Still in service (1990).

GILLIAN EVERARD *Company archives*

177. GILLIAN EVERARD (1963–1984)

O.N. 304694 1,598g 990n 2,635d 81.23 × 11.97 × 5.16 metres.
8-cyl. 2SA oil engine by Nydqvist & Holm A/B, Trollhattan, Sweden.

9.1963: Completed by Clelands Shipbuilding Co. Ltd., Wallsend (Yard No. 259) for Cattedown Wharves Ltd., Plymouth. *7.1967:* Transferred to Clydesdale Shipowners Co. Ltd., Glasgow. *9.1974:* Re-engined with a 8-cyl. 4SA oil engine made by British Polar Engines Ltd., Glasgow. *1.1975:* Transferred to F.T. Everard & Sons Ltd. *6.1984:* Sold to Dimita Shipping Co. Ltd. (Interuniversal Chartering S.A., managers), Valletta, Malta and renamed CAPTAIN CHRISTOS G. *1987:* Sold to Hippocrates Nikoretzis, Honduras and renamed GEORGIOS. *1988:* Sold to Galatia Shipping Co. S.A., San Lorenzo, Honduras. Still in service (1990).

GILLIAN EVERARD, ROSEMARY EVERARD and **PENELOPE EVERARD** awaiting disposal at Greenhithe in 1984.

E. Coker

CAPACITY (2)

C. Hill

× 3.16 metres.
Co. Ltd., Newbury.

.td.,
Co.
ngine
71:

Transferred to F.T. Everard & Sons Ltd., *1.1981:* Sold to R.W. Fielding, Liverpool. *5.1981:* Sold to Shipbreaking (Queenborough) Ltd. for breaking up at Queenborough.

ASSIDUITY (2)

C. Hill

179. ASSIDUITY (2) (1964–1983)

O.N. 306015 1,249g 497n 1,488d 71.48 × 11.05 × 4.47 metres.
4-cyl. 2SA 'P' type oil engine by the Newbury Diesel Co. Ltd., Newbury.

5.1964: Completed by Goole Shipbuilding & Repairing Co. Ltd., Goole (Yard No. 537) for the company. *5.1973:* Re-engined with a 8-cyl. 4SA oil engine made by Mirrlees Blackstone Ltd., Stamford. *4.1983:* Sold to M. Koutlakis, C. Leonardos & P. Leonardos, Piraeus, Greece and renamed VASILIKI V. *1984:* Owners became Vasiliki V Shipping Co., Piraeus, Greece. Still in service (1990).

ROSEMARY EVERARD *A. Duncan*

180. ROSEMARY EVERARD (1964–1984)

O.N. 306192 1,599g 985n 2,593d 81.08 × 11.97 × 5.16 metres.
5-cyl. 2SA 'P' type oil engine by the Newbury Diesel Co. Ltd., Newbury.

11.1964: Completed by Clelands Shipbuilding Co. Ltd., Wallsend (Yard No. 260) for the company. *10.1975:* Re-engined with a 12-cyl 4SA oil engine made by Mirrlees Blackstone Ltd., Stamford. *5.1984:* Sold to Sikeon Shipping Co. Ltd. (Interuniversal Chartering S.A., managers), Valletta, Malta and renamed THEODOROS G. *1988:* Sold to Galatia Shipping Co. S.A., San Lorenzo, Honduras. Still in service (1990).

FIXITY (2) *P. White*

181. FIXITY (2) (1966–1976)

O.N. 308013 199g 125n 324d 35.82 × 7.70 × 2.83 metres.
4-cyl. 4SA oil engine by Lister Blackstone Marine Ltd., Dursley.

1.1966: Completed by Fellows & Co. Ltd., Great Yarmouth (Yard No. 375) for the company. *5.1976:* Sold to Howard Doris Ltd., London and renamed KIRSTIE OF KISHORN. *1979:* Sold to Johnson Combined Enterprises Ltd., St. Johns, Newfoundland, Canada and renamed BACALAC TRANSPORT. *1988:* Sold to Claymorr Shipping Ltd., St. Johns, Newfoundland, Canada. Still in service (1990).

ETHEL EVERARD (4) *Company archives*

182. ETHEL EVERARD (4) (1966–1984)

O.N. 308116 1,599g 919n 2,601d 85.10 × 12.50 × 5.10 metres.
5-cyl. 2SA 'P' type oil engine by the Newbury Diesel Co. Ltd., Newbury.

4.1966: Completed by Clelands Shipbuilding Co. Ltd., Wallsend (Yard No. 287) for the company. *7.1975:* Re-engined with a 12-cyl. 4SA oil engine made by Mirrlees Blackstone Ltd., Stamford. *6.1984:* Sold to Mortek Shipping Co. Ltd., Piraeus, Greece and renamed ANGIE. *15.8.1985:* Ran aground off the north coast of Crete while on passage from Bar to Tripoli in ballast. *2.9.1985:* Sank in position 35.28N, 25.14E.

ALACRITY (2) *C. Hill*

183. ALACRITY (2) (1966–1986) Tanker

O.N. 309733 943g 428n 1,337d 65.99 × 10.75 × 4.36 metres.
5-cyl. 2SA 'P' type oil engine by the Newbury Diesel Co. Ltd., Newbury.

9.1966: Completed by Goole Shipbuilding & Repairing Co. Ltd., Goole (Yard No. 553) for the company. *11.1977:* Re-engined with a 8-cyl. 4SA oil engine made by Mirrlees Blackstone Ltd., Stamford. *3.1986:* Sold to Aminata Shipping Lines Ltd., Monrovia, Liberia and renamed ABRAHAM. *24.3.1989:* Damaged by fire and explosion while berthed for repairs at the Old Iron Ore Jetty, Monrovia. *7.1989:* Beached for breaking up by the owners at Monrovia, Liberia.

ACTUALITY (3) after modifications. *A. Duncan*

184. ACTUALITY (3) (1966–1982)

O.N. 309771 698g 488n 1,154d 68.23 × 10.60 × 3.72 metres.
6-cyl. 2SA 'O' type oil engine by the Newbury Diesel Co. Ltd., Newbury.

11.1966: Completed by Clelands Shipbuilding Co. Ltd., Wallsend (Yard No. 289) for the company. *2.1974:* Re-engined with a 8-cyl. 4SA oil engine made by Mirrlees Blackstone Ltd., Stamford. *9.1982:* Sold to Allsworth Shipping Ltd., Queenborough and renamed HUGHINA. *6.1983:* Sold to Carisbrooke Shipping Ltd., Cowes and renamed GRETA C. *7.1988:* Sold to Runwave Ltd., Avonmouth and renamed DEVONIA. Still in service (1990).

AUTHORITY (2) *W.S.P.L.*

185. AUTHORITY (2) (1967–1985) Tanker

O.N. 309796 500g 298n 1,100d 65.41 × 9.91 × 3.54 metres.
6-cyl. 4SA oil engine by Klockner-Humboldt-Deutz A.G., Koln-Deutz, West Germany.

1.1967: Completed by Nieuwe Noord Nederlandse Scheepswerven N.V., Groningen, Holland (Yard No. 351) for the company. *4.1970:* Re-engined with a 6-cyl. 4SA oil engine made by Klockner-Humboldt-Deutz A.G., Koln-Deutz, West Germany. *11.1975:* Transferred to Thames Tankers Ltd., London. *1.1984:* Transferred to F.T. Everard & Sons Ltd. *1.1985:* Sold to Sosco Shipping Co., Piraeus, Greece and renamed SOSCO I. *1987:* Renamed GEORGIOS S and registered at San Lorenzo, Honduras. *1989:* Sold to Karmel Shipping Co., Piraeus, Greece and renamed GEORGIOS. Still in service (1990).

APRICITY (2) as completed. *J. Callis*

186. APRICITY (2) (1967–1982)

O.N. 334510 692g 496n 1,164d 68.23 × 10.60 × 3.72 metres.
6-cyl. 2SA 'O' type oil engine by the Newbury Diesel Co. Ltd., Newbury.

6.1967: Completed by Clelands Shipbuilding Co. Ltd., Wallsend (Yard No. 292) for the company. *2.1974:* Re-engined with a 8-cyl. 4SA oil engine made by Mirrlees Blackstone Ltd., Stamford. *12.1982:* Sold to Carisbrooke Shipping Ltd., Cowes and renamed HELEEN C. *9.1988:* Sold to S.E. Taylor, Lyndhurst. *1.1989:* Renamed ERNEST T. *7.1989:* Sold to Denver Shipping Ltd. (Seawaves Shipping Co., managers), Gibraltar and renamed ERNEST 1. Still in service (1990).

APRICITY (2) after modifications. *C. Hill*

ASPERITY (3) on trials, and still flying the Dutch ensign. *Company archives*

187. ASPERITY (3) (1967–1989) Tanker

O.N. 334607 698g 402n 1,326d 71.86 × 9.91 × 3.84 metres.
6-cyl. 4SA oil engine by Klockner-Humboldt-Deutz A.G., Koln-Deutz, West Germany.

8.1967: Completed by Nieuwe Noord Nederlandse Scheepswerven N.V., Groningen, Holland (Yard No. 354) for the company. *1.1973:* Transferred to Clydesdale Shipowners Co. Ltd., Glasgow. *1.1984:* Transferred to Thames Tankers Ltd., London. *3.1958:* Transferred to F.T. Everard & Sons Ltd. *12.1989:* Sold to Transpet Maritime Co., Piraeus, Greece and renamed KASTOR. Still in service (1990).

ACCLIVITY (3) *W.S.P.L.*

188. ACCLIVITY (3) (1968–1981) Tanker

O.N. 317567 299g 187n 633d 51.06 × 8.62 × 3.21 metres.
5-cyl. 2SA 'O' type oil engine by the Newbury Diesel Co. Ltd., Newbury.

5.1968: Completed by Goole Shipbuilding & Repairing Co. Ltd., Goole (Yard No. 563) for the company. *7.1972:* Re-engined with a 8-cyl. 4SA oil engine made by Mirrlees Blackstone Ltd., Stamford. *8.1981:* Sold to Société Marocaine des Petroles Mory, Casablanca, Morocco and renamed ASNI. Still in service (1990).

FUTURITY (2) *P. White*

189. FUTURITY (2) (1968–1983)

O.N. 335785 199g 158n 432d 41.89 × 7.73 × 2.70 metres.
4-cyl. 4SA oil engine by Lister Blackstone Marine Ltd., Dursley.

6.1968: Completed by Clelands Shipbuilding Co. Ltd., Wallsend (Yard No. 300) for the company. *1.1973:* Transferred to J. Hay & Sons Ltd., Glasgow. *9.1983:* Sold to B.F. & R.J. Sully, T.J., A.H. & G.J. Palmer, London and renamed SUBRO VICTOR. *1984:* Owners became Sully Freight, London. *1985:* Sold to G. Palmer, Gravesend. *1986:* Owners became G., T. & A. Palmer, Gravesend. *1987:* Renamed KATIE W. *7.1987:* Sold to Lima Services S.A., Kingstown, St. Vincent and renamed KATIE. Still in service (1990).

FORMALITY (2) *C. Hill*

190. FORMALITY (2) (1968–1987)

O.N. 335826 199g 159n 412d 41.89 × 7.73 × 2.70 metres.
4-cyl. 4SA oil engine by Lister Blackstone Marine Ltd., Dursley.

7.1968: Completed by Clelands Shipbuilding Co. Ltd., Wallsend (Yard No. 304) for the company. *9.1987:* Sold to Panther Trading Ltd. (A.J. & A. Pratt, managers), Douglas, Isle of Man and renamed EAU DE VIE. *1988:* Sold to T. &. D. Murrell & T. Wood, London and renamed THAMESWOOD. Still in service (1990).

AUDACITY (3) *A. Duncan*

191. AUDACITY (3) (1968–1990) Tanker

O.N. 336965 699g 460n 1,605d 72.60 × 11.10 × 4.40 metres.
5-cyl. 2SA 'P' type oil engine by the Newbury Diesel Co. Ltd., Newbury.

11.1968: Completed by Goole Shipbuilding & Repairing Co. Ltd., Goole (Yard No. 564) for the company. *8.1972:* Re-engined with a 6-cyl. 4SA oil engine made by Klockner-Humboldt-Deutz A.G., Koln, West Germany. *12.1981:* Transferred to Gowan Shipping Co. Ltd., London. *1.1984:* Transferred to County Ships Ltd., London. *3.1985:* Transferred to F.T. Everard & Sons Ltd. *6.1990:* Sold to Dole S.A., Monrovia, Liberia and renamed HAWK. Still in service (1990).

ACTIVITY (2) *W.S.P.L.*

192. ACTIVITY (2) (1969–1989) Tanker

O.N. 337127 698g 395n 1,335d 73.97 × 10.42 × 3.97 metres.
6-cyl. 4SA oil engine by Klockner-Humboldt-Deutz A.G., Koln, West Germany.

4.1969: Completed by Nieuwe Noord Nederlandse Scheepswerven N.V., Groningen, Holland (Yard No. 461) for the company. *11.1989:* Sold to M. Koutlakis & P. Leonardos, Piraeus, Greece and renamed VASILIOS XIV. Still in service (1990).

ALLURITY (2) *W.S.P.L.*

193. ALLURITY (2) (1969–1989) Tanker

O.N. 337901 698g 395n 1,335d 73.97 × 10.42 × 3.97 metres.
6-cyl. 4SA oil engine by Klockner-Humboldt-Deutz A.G., Koln, West Germany.

8.1969: Completed by Nieuwe Noord Nederlandse Scheepswerven N.V., Groningen, Holland (Yard No. 362) for the company. *1.1984:* Transferred to Comben Longstaff & Co. Ltd., London. *3.1985:* Transferred to F.T. Everard & Sons Ltd. *5.1989:* Sold to Elmeca Maritime Co., Piraeus, Greece and renamed MARIA. Still in service (1990).

GRIT (6) *C. Hill*

194. GRIT (6) (1970–1974)

O.N. 339272 498g 328n 1,208d 67.09 × 10.44 × 3.91 metres.
8-cyl. 4SA oil engine by Klockner-Humboldt-Deutz A.G., Koln, West Germany.

11.1966: Completed by Husumer Schiffswerft, Husum at Tyskland, West Germany (Yard No. 1234) for Stenhoj Shipping I/S, Barrit, Denmark as DAGMAR STENHOJ. *7.1970:* Acquired by Clydesdale Shipowners Co. Ltd., Glasgow and renamed GRIT. *12.1974:* Sold to Rederiet Dancoast 5 I/S (R. Staerke Kristensen, manager), Marstal, Denmark and renamed KATHE DANCOAST. *1981:* Managers became H. Folmer & Co., Marstal, Denmark. *1988:* Sold to Lemnos II Shipping Co., Piraeus, Greece and renamed ATHINA S. Still in service (1990).

Launch of **SUPREMITY (3)** at Groningen.

Company archives

195. SUPREMITY (3) (1970–1980)

O.N. 339360 698g 504n 1,704d 80.73 × 13.63 × 4.14 metres.
2 × 8-cyl. 2SA oil engines by British Polar Engines Ltd., Glasgow.

10.1970: Completed by Nieuwe Noord Nederlandse Scheepswerven N.V., Groningen, Holland (Yard No. 364) for Scottish Navigation Co. Ltd., Glasgow. *8.1980:* Sold to Charles M. Willie & Co. (Shipping) Ltd., Cardiff and renamed CELTIC CRUSADER. *1983:* Sold to Blackwood Investments Ltd. (Bernuth Agencies Inc., managers), Cayman Islands and renamed KORIMU. Still in service (1990).

Note: A sister vessel was ordered from the same shipbuilders (Yard No. 365), but was cancelled before launching. No name had been allocated.

SUPREMITY (3)

C. Hill

SECURITY (2)
the author's first command.

C. Hill

196. SECURITY (2) (1971–1986)

O.N. 341352 1,596g 1,014n 2,778d 85.02 × 12.78 × 5.07 metres.
2 × 6-cyl. 4SA oil engines by British Polar Engines Ltd., Glasgow.

5.1971: Completed by R. Dunston (Hessle) Ltd., Hessle (Yard No. S877) for the company. *3.1986:* Sold to Carisbrooke Shipping Ltd., Cowes, renamed MARK and later MARK C. Still in service (1990).

SINCERITY (2)

C. Hill

197. SINCERITY (2) (1971–1986)

O.N. 342914 1,596g 1,014n 2,779d 85.02 × 12.78 × 5.07 metres.
2 × 6-cyl. 4SA oil engines by British Polar Engines Ltd., Glasgow.

10.1971: Completed by R. Dunston (Hessle) Ltd., Hessle (Yard No. S878) for the company. *11.1986:* Sold to Ocean Hope Shipping Ltd., Nicosia, Cyprus and renamed WILLEM W. Owner later restyled Oceanhope Navigation Ltd. Still in service (1990).

AMITY (2) *W.S.P.L.*

198. AMITY (2) (1971–1977) Tanker

O.N. 337352 2,901g 1,681n 5,013d 98.30 × 14.41 × 6.55 metres.
12-cyl. 4SA 'V' oil engine by English Electric Diesels Ltd., Lincoln.

2.1970: Completed by Goole Shipbuilding & Repairing Co. Ltd., Goole (Yard No. 566) for Thun Tankers Ltd., Newcastle as THUNTANK 5. *11.1971:* Company acquired and name changed to Thames Tankers Ltd., London. Ship renamed AMITY. *1975:* Bareboat chartered to Société Bretonne d'Armement Maritime (BRETAM), Brest, France and renamed POINTE DU TOULINGUET. *1976:* Reverted to owners and renamed AMITY. *5.1977:* Sold to Hans Yngve Johnsson (Rederi A/B Ektank, managers), Donso, Sweden and renamed EKFJORD. *10.1987:* Re-engined with a 6-cyl. 4SA oil engine made by Ruston Diesels Ltd., Newton-le-Willows. *1.1989:* Sold to Rederi A/B Veritas Tankers, Donso, Sweden and renamed AVIOR. Still in service (1990).

ANTERIORITY (2) *J. Clarkson*

199. ANTERIORITY (2) (1971–1975) Tanker

O.N. 337356 2,901g 1,679n 5,013d 98.30 × 14.41 × 6.55 metres.
12-cyl. 4SA 'V' oil engine by English Electric Diesels Ltd., Lincoln.

4.1970: Completed by Clelands Shipbuilding Co. Ltd., Wallsend (Yard No. 309) for Thun Tankers Ltd., Newcastle as THUNTANK 6. *11.1971:* Company acquired and name changed to Thames Tankers Ltd., London. Ship renamed ANTERIORITY. *1.1975:* Sold to Texaco Canada Ltd., Toronto, Canada and renamed TEXACO WARRIOR. *1984:* Sold to Waterose Marine Ltd. (Thenamaris [Ships Managers] Inc., managers), Limassol, Cyprus and renamed TRADER. *1985:* Renamed SEA CORAL. *1985:* Sold to Brenda Shipping Ltd. (Gulf Oceanic Shipmanagement Pte Ltd., managers), Kingstown, St. Vincent and renamed TALIA II. Still in service (1990).

SERENITY (3)

J.K. Byass

200. SERENITY (3) (1971–1986)

O.N. 342948 1,597g 1,060n 2,805d 86.72 × 12.88 × 5.14 metres.
2 × 6-cyl. 4SA oil engines by British Polar Engines Ltd., Glasgow.

11.1971: Completed by Goole Shipbuilding & Repairing Co. Ltd., Goole (Yard No. 570) for the company. *11.1986:* Sold to Venisol Shipping Corp. (Silver River Shipping Inc., managers), Panama and renamed SERENIA. *1988:* Sold to Izrada S.A. & Onesimus (Shipowners) Ltd., Nassau, Bahamas (Alexanders Partners [Shipbroking] Ltd., London, managers) and renamed SERENE. *5.1990:* Sold to Donnington Shipping Ltd. (Havelet Marine Services, managers), Valletta, Malta and renamed EMMA. Still in service (1990).

SUPERIORITY (2)

C. Hill

201. SUPERIORITY (2) (1972–1986)

O.N. 343076 1,597g 1,060n 2,805d 86.72 × 12.88 × 5.14 metres.
2 × 6-cyl. 4SA oil engines by British Polar Engines Ltd., Glasgow.

2.1972: Completed by Goole Shipbuilding & Repairing Co. Ltd., Goole (Yard No. 571) for the company. *10.1986:* Sold to West Frakt, Kyrkesund, Sweden and renamed ALVA. *1988:* Sold to Universal Industri & Invest A/S (Louis Ormestad A/S, manager), Sandefjord, Norway and renamed LOBO. Still in service (1990).

FRED EVERARD (4) *Company archives*

202. FRED EVERARD (4) (1972–1985)

O.N. 358502 1,595g 1,162n 3,272d 91.14 × 13.34 × 5.14 metres.
16-cyl. 4SA 'V' oil engine by British Polar Engines Ltd., Glasgow.

7.1972: Completed by Goole Shipbuilding & Repairing Co. Ltd., Goole (Yard No. 573) for the company. *6.1985:* Sold to Speed Bulk II Co. Ltd. (Speed Bulk Shipping, managers), Valletta, Malta and renamed TARA BULK. *4.1987:* Sold to Mira Bulk Co. Ltd., Valletta, Malta (R.G. Hagland Shipping A/S, Haugesund, Norway, managers) and renamed MIRA BULK. Still in service (1990).

SUAVITY (3) *C. Hill*

203. SUAVITY (3) (1972–1984)

O.N. 358680 1,595g 1,162n 3,272d 91.14 × 13.34 × 5.14 metres.
16-cyl. 4SA 'V' oil engine by British Polar Engines Ltd., Glasgow.

11.1972: Completed by Clelands Shipbuilding Co. Ltd., Wallsend (Yard No. 321) for the company. *5.1984:* Sold to K/S A/S Speedbulk (Speed Bulk Shipping, managers), Haugesund, Norway and renamed SPEEDBULK. *9.1986:* Sold to Spartacus Navigation Ltd., Valletta, Malta (HVA Coasting N.V., Antwerp, Belgium, managers) and renamed CORONA. *1987:* Managers became Paal Wilson & Co. A/S, Hop, Norway. *1988:* Renamed BIRONA. *1989:* Sold to Barco Transport Ltd., Valletta, Malta (Paal Wilson Management A/S, Hop, Norway, manager) and renamed BARCO. Still in service (1990).

SUMMITY (2) *A. Duncan*

204. SUMMITY (2) (1972–1987)

O.N. 358722 1,595g 1,162n 3,272d 91.14 × 13.34 × 5.14 metres.
16-cyl. 4SA 'V' oil engine by British Polar Engines Ltd., Glasgow.

11.1972: Completed by Goole Shipbuilding & Repairing Co. Ltd., Goole (Yard No. 574) for the company. *9.1987:* Sold to Izrada S.A., Panama (Alexanders Partners [Shipbroking] Ltd., London, managers) and renamed SUMNIA. *16.10.1987:* Capsized and sank after engine breakdown 100 metres from Dover Western Entrance in very heavy weather while on passage from Barking to Shoreham in ballast. Wreck recovered in two sections; the fore part was towed to Flushing, Holland for breaking up by Vliemeta B.V. and arrived *7.11.1987* and the after part was taken on a pontoon to s'Gravendeel, Holland for breaking up by Heuvelman Staal B.V. and arrived *23.11.1987.*

SAGACITY (3) *A. Duncan*

205. SAGACITY (3) (1973–)

O.N. 358935 1,595g 1,162n 3,272d 91.14 × 13.34 × 5.14 metres.
16-cyl. 4SA 'V' oil engine by British Polar Engines Ltd., Glasgow.

4.1973: Completed by Goole Shipbuilding & Repairing Co. Ltd., Goole (Yard No. 575) for the company. *5.1990:* Re-registered at Nassau, Bahamas. In present fleet (1990).

MAIRI EVERARD

Company archives

206. MAIRI EVERARD (1974–1990)

O.N. 363354 1,599g 1,027n 2,652d 77.78 × 13.19 × 4.97 metres.
16-cyl. 4SA oil engine by Mirrlees Blackstone Ltd., Stamford.

6.1974: Completed by Clelands Shipbuilding Co. Ltd., Wallsend (Yard No. 328) for the company. *3.1990:* Sold to Carisbrooke Shipping Ltd., Cowes and renamed GRETA C. Still in service (1990).

MAIRI EVERARD
inward bound for Gunness with a cargo of timber.

C. Hill

COMMODITY (2) *C. Hill*

207. COMMODITY (2) (1975–)

O.N. 365946 582g 366n 946d 57.61 × 10.01 × 3.35 metres.
6-cyl. 4SA oil engine by Mirrlees Blackstone Ltd., Stamford.

9.1975: Completed by J.W. Cook & Co. (Wivenhoe) Ltd., Wivenhoe (Yard No. 1447) for the company. In present fleet (1990).

CONFORMITY (2) *C. Hill*

208. CONFORMITY (2) (1975–)

O.N. 365981 499g 330n 880d 56.11 × 9.89 × 3.25 metres.
6-cyl. 4SA oil engine by Mirrlees Blackstone Ltd., Stamford.

11.1975: Completed by N.V. Scheepswerf Ferus Smit, Foxhol, Holland (Yard No. 213) for the company. In present fleet (1990).

CANDOURITY (2)

C. Hill

209. CANDOURITY (2) (1975–)

O.N. 365982 499g 330n 880d 56.11 × 9.89 × 3.25 metres.
6-cyl. 4SA oil engine by Mirrlees Blackstone Ltd., Stamford.

11.1975: Completed by Scheepswerf Bijlholt B.V., Foxhol, Holland (Yard No. 599) for the company. In present fleet (1990).

CELEBRITY (2)

J.K. Byass

210. CELEBRITY (2) (1976–)

O.N. 366030 582g 366n 946d 57.61 × 10.01 × 3.35 metres.
6-cyl. 4SA oil engine by Mirrlees Blackstone Ltd., Stamford.

1.1976: Completed by J.W. Cook & Co. (Wivenhoe) Ltd., Wivenhoe (Yard No. 1448) for the company. In present fleet (1990).

CITY (2) *C. Hill*

211. CITY (2) (1976–)

O.N. 366082 499g 330n 880d 56.11 × 9.89 × 3.25 metres.
6-cyl. 4SA oil engine by Mirrlees Blackstone Ltd., Stamford.

3.1976: Completed by Scheepswerf Bijlholt B.V., Foxhol, Holland (Yard No. 600) for the company. In present fleet (1990).

GRIT (7) *C. Hill*

212. GRIT (7) (1976–1988)

O.N. 366114 499g 330n 880d 56.11 × 9.89 × 3.25 metres.
6-cyl. 4SA oil engine by Mirrlees Blackstone Ltd., Stamford.

4.1976: Completed by N.V. Scheepswerf Ferus Smit, Foxhol, Holland (Yard No. 214) for the company.
25.1.1988: Sank in Hull Roads after a collision with the anchored motor dredger BOWPRINCE 1,485/64 while on passage from Rotterdam to Gunness with a cargo of scrap furnace materials. Forepart raised *31.3.1988* and after part on *2.4.1988* and both taken to New Holland for breaking up by D. Cook Ltd.

SINGULARITY (2) *C. Hill*

213. SINGULARITY (2) (1977–1987)

O.N. 377323 1,597g 1,056n 4,156d 89.72 × 14.28 × 6.04 metres.
18-cyl. 4SA 'V' oil engine by Alpha Diesel A/S, Frederikshavn, Denmark.

6.1977: Completed by Swan Hunter Shipbuilders Ltd. (Readhead Shipyard), South Shields (Yard No. 594) for the company. *3.1987:* Sold to Alba S.a.S. di Michele Mazella, Pozzuoli, Italy and renamed SINGOLARITA. *1990:* Sold to Montemare di Navigazione S.a.S., Naples, Italy. Still in service (1990).

SPECIALITY (2)

Company archives

214. SPECIALITY (2) (1977–)

O.N. 377430 1,597g 1,053n 4,245d 89.72 × 14.28 × 6.04 metres.
18-cyl. 4SA 'V' oil engine by Alpha Diesel A/S, Frederikshavn, Denmark.

10.1977: Completed by Goole Shipbuilding & Repairing Co. Ltd., Goole (Yard No. 592) for the company. *7.1990:* Re-registered at Nassau, Bahamas. In present fleet (1990).

JACK WHARTON

C. Hill

215. JACK WHARTON (1977–1987)

O.N. 364572 1,597g 1,052n 4,161d 89.72 × 14.28 × 6.04 metres.
18-cyl. 4SA 'V' oil engine by Alpha Diesel A/S, Frederikshavn, Denmark.

11.1977: Completed by Richards (Shipbuilders) Ltd., Lowestoft (Yard No. 532) for J. Wharton (Shipping) Ltd., Gunness and bareboat chartered to F.T. Everard & Sons Ltd. *6.1986:* Acquired by F.T. Everard Shipping Ltd. *2.1987:* Sold to Charles M. Willie & Co. (Shipping) Ltd., Cardiff and renamed CELTIC AMBASSADOR. *5.1990:* Sold to Oceanlaser Shipping Ltd., Limassol, Cyprus (George Roussos Sons, Piraeus, Greece, managers) and renamed SMARO. Still in service (1990).

STABILITY (2)

C. Hill

216. STABILITY (2) (1978–)

O.N. 377599 1,597g 1,053n 4,245d 89.72 × 14.28 × 6.04 metres.
18-cyl. 4SA 'V' oil engine by Alpha Diesel A/S, Frederikshavn, Denmark.

4.1978: Completed by Goole Shipbuilding & Repairing Co. Ltd., Goole (Yard No. 593) for the company.
11.1989: Re-registered at Nassau, Bahamas. In present fleet (1990).

ABILITY (3) C. Hill

217. ABILITY (3) (1979–) Tanker

O.N. 379868 1,409g 860n 2,550d 79.25 × 13.10 × 4.95 metres.
12-cyl. 4SA 'V' oil engine by Ruston Diesels Ltd., Newton-le-Willows.

3.1979: Completed by Goole Shipbuilding & Repairing Co. Ltd., Goole (Yard No. 595) for the company. In present fleet (1990).

AUTHENTICITY (2) C. Hill

218. AUTHENTICITY (2) (1979–) Tanker

O.N. 388171 1,409g 860n 2,550d 79.25 × 13.10 × 4.95 metres.
12-cyl. 4SA 'V' oil engine by Ruston Diesels Ltd., Newton-le-Willows.

10.1979: Completed by Goole Shipbuilding & Repairing Co. Ltd., Goole (Yard No. 596) for the company. In present fleet (1990).

SOLENTBROOK
with a deck cargo of timber.

J.K. Byass

223. SOLENTBROOK (1980–1982)

O.N. 358547 1,597g 1,131n 2.982d 86.34 × 12.93 × 5.10 metres.
8-cyl. 4SA oil engine by Ruston Paxman Diesels Ltd., Lincoln.

7.1972: Completed by Drypool Engineering & Dry Dock Co. Ltd., Hull (Cochrane Yard, Selby) (Yard No. 1541) for County Ships Ltd. (Comben Longstaff & Co. Ltd., managers), London. *11.1982:* Sold to Kemp Navigation Co. Ltd., Limassol, Cyprus and renamed STAVROS H. Still in service (1990).

LONDONBROOK *C. Hill*

224. LONDONBROOK (1980–1986)

O.N. 365882 1,599g 1,067n 3,700d 93.60 × 13.67 × 5.64 metres.
7-cyl. 2SA oil engine by Smit & Bolnes N.V., Zierikzee, Holland.

7.1975: Completed by Handel & Scheepsbouw Maatschappij Kramer & Booy B.V., Kootstertille, Holland (Yard No. 189) for Consolidated Gold Fields Ltd. (Comben Longstaff & Co. Ltd., managers), London. *11.1976:* Renamed TOWERSTREAM and managers became Gowan Shipping Co. Ltd., London. *8.1979:* Transferred to County Ships Ltd. (same managers), Hove. *1.1980:* Renamed LONDONBROOK and managers became Comben Longstaff & Co. Ltd. *4.1980:* Transferred to Consolidated Gold Fields Ltd. (same managers), London. *4.1980:* Sold to Midland Montague Leasing Ltd., London and leased to F.T. Everard & Sons Ltd. *10.1986:* Acquired by the company. *10.1986:* Sold to K.E. Nordgren, Ornskoldsvik, Sweden and renamed JOKER. Still in service (1990).

LANCASTERBROOK

C. Hill

225. LANCASTERBROOK (1980–1990)

O.N. 365987 1,599g 1,067n 3,700d 93.60 × 13.67 × 5.64 metres.
7-cyl. 2SA oil engine by Smit & Bolnes N.V., Zierikzee, Holland.

11.1975: Completed by Handel & Scheepsbouw Maatschappij Kramer & Booy B.V., Kootstertille, Holland (Yard No. 190) for Consolidated Gold Fields Ltd. (Comben Longstaff & Co. Ltd., managers), London. *11.1976:* Renamed CHELSEASTREAM and managers became Gowan Shipping Co. Ltd., London. *8.1979:* Transferred to County Ships Ltd. (same managers), Hove. *12.1979:* Renamed LANCASTERBROOK and managers became Comben Longstaff & Co. Ltd. *4.1980:* Sold to Midland Montague Leasing Ltd., London and leased to F.T. Everard & Sons Ltd. *6.1990:* Acquired by the company. *6.1990:* Sold to Prime Shipping Inc. Three (Hellenic Seaways Overseas Corp., managers), Piraeus, Greece and renamed PRIME VISION. Still in service (1990).

LINCOLNBROOK

C. Hill

226. LINCOLNBROOK (1980–1986)

O.N. 366278 1,599g 1,118n 3,700d 93.60 × 13.67 × 5.64 metres.
18-cyl. 4SA 'V' oil engine by Alpha Diesel A/S, Frederikshavn, Denmark.

9.1976: Completed by Tille Scheepsbouw B.V., Kootstertille, Holland (Yard No. 201) for Mining & Industrial Holdings Ltd. (Comben Longstaff & Co. Ltd., managers), London. *8.1979:* Transferred to County Ships Ltd. (same managers), Hove. *4.1980:* Transferred to Mining & Industrial Holdings Ltd. (same managers), London. *4.1980:* Sold to Midland Montague Leasing Ltd., London and leased to F.T. Everard & Sons Ltd. *10.1986:* Acquired by the company. *10.1986:* Sold to Franco de Paolis S.p.A., Genoa, Italy and renamed DEPA SECONDA. *1989:* Sold to Prime Shipping Inc. Two (Hellenic Seaways Overseas Corp., managers), Piraeus, Greece and renamed PRIME VICTORY. Still in service (1990).

LEICESTERBROOK C. Hill

227. LEICESTERBROOK (1980–)

O.N. 377164 1,599g 2,228n 3,619d 93.60 × 13.67 × 5.60 metres.
18-cyl. 4SA 'V' oil engine by Alpha Diesel A/S, Frederikshavn, Denmark.

1.1977: Completed by Tille Scheepsbouw B.V., Kootstertille, Holland (Yard No. 202) for Consolidated Gold Fields Ltd. (Comben Longstaff & Co. Ltd., managers), London. *8.1979:* Transferred to County Ships Ltd. (same managers), Hove. *4.1980:* Transferred to Consolidated Gold Fields Ltd. (same managers), London. *4.1980:* Sold to Midland Montague Leasing Ltd., London and leased to F.T. Everard & Sons Ltd. In present fleet (1990).

AMENITY (3) J.K. Byass

228. AMENITY (3) (1980–) Tanker

O.N. 390692 1,453g 883n 2,528d 79.23 × 13.19 × 4.97 metres.
12-cyl. 4SA 'V' oil engine by Ruston Diesels Ltd., Newton-le-Willows.

12.1980: Completed by Goole Shipbuilding & Repairing Co. Ltd., Goole (Yard No. 598) for Finance for Shipping Ltd., London and leased to F.T. Everard & Sons Ltd. *1984:* Owners restyled Investors in Industry p.l.c., London. In present fleet (1990).

SELECTIVITY (2) *C. Hill*

229. SELECTIVITY (2) (1984–)

O.N. 705631 799g 585n 2,415d 79.02 × 12.68 × 4.55 metres.
6-cyl. 4SA oil engine by Krupp M.a.K. Maschinenbau G.m.b.H., Kiel, West Germany.

5.1984: Completed by Cochrane Shipbuilders Ltd., Selby (Yard No. 126) for Investors in Industry p.l.c., London and leased to F.T. Everard & Sons Ltd. In present fleet (1990).

PAMELA EVERARD *C. Hill*

230. PAMELA EVERARD (1984–)

O.N. 705699 799g 585n 2,415d 79.02 × 12.68 × 4.56 metres.
6-cyl. 4SA oil engine by Krupp M.a.K. Maschinenbau G.m.b.H., Kiel, West Germany.

7.1984: Completed by Richards (Shipbuilders) Ltd., Lowestoft (Yard No. 558) for Investors in Industry p.l.c., London and leased to F.T. Everard & Sons Ltd. In present fleet (1990).

CAPACITY (3). Note that the bow is modified to bring overall length below 60 metres. *C. Hill*

231. LIZZONIA/CAPACITY (3) (1986–)

O.N. 364574 798g 554n 1,315d 60.30 × 11.28 × 3.90 metres.
8-cyl. 4SA oil engine by Mirrlees Blackstone (Stockport) Ltd., Stockport.

2.1980: Completed by Cochrane Shipbuilders Ltd., Selby (Yard No. 109) for J. Wharton (Shipping) Ltd., Gunness as LIZZONIA. *4.1986:* Managers became F.T. Everard & Sons Management Ltd. *6.1986:* Transferred to F.T. Everard Shipping Ltd. *2.1989:* Renamed CAPACITY. In present fleet (1990).

COMITY (2) *C. Hill*

232. ANGELONIA/COMITY (2) (1986–)

O.N. 364575 798g 554n 1,315d 60.30 × 11.28 × 3.90 metres.
8-cyl. 4SA oil engine by Mirrlees Blackstone (Stockport) Ltd., Stockport.

4.1980: Completed by Cochrane Shipbuilders Ltd., Selby (Yard No. 110) for J. Wharton (Shipping) Ltd., Gunness as ANGELONIA. *4.1986:* Managers became F.T. Everard & Sons Management Ltd. *6.1986:* Transferred to F.T. Everard Shipping Ltd. *6.1988:* Renamed COMITY. In present fleet (1990).

SANGUITY (2) *C. Hill*

233. WILLONIA/SANGUITY (2) (1986–)

O.N. 364589 799g 585n 2,415d 79.00 × 12.68 × 4.55 metres.
6-cyl. 4SA oil engine by Krupp M.a.K. Maschinenbau G.m.b.H., Kiel, West Germany.

2.1984: Completed by Cochrane Shipbuilders Ltd., Selby (Yard No. 125) for J. Wharton (Shipping) Ltd., Gunness (F.T. Everard & Sons Management Ltd., managers) as WILLONIA. *6.1986:* Transferred to F.T. Everard Shipping Ltd. *5.1988:* Renamed SANGUITY. In present fleet (1990).

SOCIALITY (2) *C. Hill*

234. STEVONIA/SOCIALITY (2) (1986–)

O.N. 364590 799g 585n 2,415d 79.00 × 12.68 × 4.55 metres.
6-cyl. 4SA oil engine by Krupp M.a.K. Maschinenbau G.m.b.H., Kiel, West Germany.

3.1986: Completed by Cochrane Shipbuilders Ltd., Selby (Yard No. 127) for J. Wharton (Shipping) Ltd., Gunness (F.T. Everard & Sons Management Ltd., managers) as STEVONIA. *6.1986:* Transferred to F.T. Everard Shipping Ltd. *2.1987:* Renamed SOCIALITY. In present fleet (1990).

AVERITY (2)

C. Hill

235. AVERITY (2) (1988–) Tanker

O.N. 715254 1,114g 613n 1,770d 69.53 × 11.82 × 4.31 metres.
6-cyl. 4SA oil engine by Yanmar Diesel Engine Co. Ltd., Amagasaki, Japan.

4.1981: Completed by Fukuoka Zosen K.K., Fukuoka, Japan (Yard No. 1087) for First Maritime K.K., Tokyo, Japan (Hull Gates Shipping Management Ltd., Hull, managers) as NATALIE. *10.1982:* Managers became Rowbotham Tankships Ltd., London. *9.1983:* Managers became Maritime Ship Management Ltd., Hull. *5.1985:* Sold to Gemmar Tank Ship S.A., Panama (Nihon Fleet Co. Ltd., Tokyo, Japan, managers). *6.1988:* Acquired by F.T. Everard Shipping Ltd., and renamed AVERITY. Registered in Nassau, Bahamas. In present fleet (1990).

AMITY (3)

Company archives

236. AMITY (3) (1988–) Tanker

O.N. 399840 1,099g 679n 1,767d 69.53 × 11.82 × 4.31 metres.
6-cyl. 4SA oil engine by Yanmar Diesel Engine Co. Ltd., Amagasaki, Japan.

10.1980: Completed by Fukuoka Zosen K.K., Fukuoka, Japan (Yard No. 1081) for K.K. Nippo Unyo Shokai, Tokyo, Japan (Hull Gates Shipping Management Ltd., Hull, managers) as CHRISTIAN. *10.1982:* Managers became Rowbotham Tankships Ltd., London. *9.1983:* Managers became Maritime Ship Management Ltd., Hull. *2.1985:* Sold to Jewel Tank Ship S.A., Panama and registered in Nassau, Bahamas (same managers). *8.1988:* Acquired by F.T. Everard Shipping Ltd., and renamed AMITY. In present fleet (1990).

AGILITY (3) *Company archives*

237. AGILITY (3) (1990–) Tanker

O.N. 718681 1,930g 927n 3,145d 79.95 × 14.50 × 5.10 metres.
6-cyl. 4SA oil engine by Ruston Diesels Ltd., Newton-le-Willows.

6.1990: Completed by Richards (Shipbuilders) Ltd., Lowestoft (Yard No. 581) for F.T. Everard Shipping Ltd. In present fleet (1990).

ALACRITY (3) at Newcastle for British Shipping Day 1990. *J. Urquhart*

238. ALACRITY (3) (1990–) Tanker

O.N. 718902 1,930g 927n 3,145d 79.95 × 14.50 × 5.10 metres.
6-cyl. 4SA oil engine by Ruston Diesels Ltd., Newton-le-Willows.

10.1990: Completed by Richards (Shipbuilders) Ltd., Lowestoft (Yard No. 582) for F.T. Everard Shipping Ltd. In present fleet (1990).

239. SUPERIORITY (3)

3,100d 99.99 × 12.60 × 4.20 metres.
8-cyl. 4SA oil engine by Alpha Diesel A/S, Frederikshavn, Denmark.

1.1990: Ordered from Cochrane Shipbuilders Ltd., Selby (Yard No. 167) by Scottish Navigation Co. Ltd. for delivery in 4.1991.

240. SENIORITY (3)

4,940d 99.99 × 18.50 × 5.20 metres.
8-cyl. 4SA oil engine by Ruston Diesels Ltd., Newton-le-Willows.

4.1990: Ordered from Appledore Shipbuilders Ltd., Appledore (Yard No. AS150) by Scottish Navigation Co. Ltd. for delivery in 4.1991.

Launch of **SUPERIORITY (3)** at Selby. *N. Burnitt*

MANAGED VESSELS

M1. ELIN (1940–1943) Wooden auxiliary

O.N. 167515 317g 265n 120.5 × 28.2 × 13.7 feet.

1919: Completed by N.A. Nielsen, Thuro, Svendborg, Denmark for A/S Seilskibsselskabet Else (R.S. Hansen, manager), Thuro, Svendborg, Denmark as the three masted schooner ELSE. *1933:* Fitted with a 2-cyl. 2SA auxiliary oil engine made by A/S Volund, Copenhagen, Denmark and renamed FORTUNA. *1933:* Sold to Rederi A/S Elin (A.E. Sorensen, manager), Svendborg, Denmark and renamed ELIN. *1940:* Taken over at Methil by the Ministry of Shipping, London (F.T. Everard & Sons Ltd., managers). *1941:* The Ministry of Shipping became the Ministry of War Transport. *1943:* Managers became Imperial Chemical Industries Ltd., London. *1944:* Managers became Coppack Brothers & Co., Connahs Quay. *1945:* Returned to pre-war owners. *1946:* Sold to P/F 'Norlysid' A/S (N.J.F. Arge, manager), Thorshavn, Faroes and renamed GLYVURSNES. *1948:* Renamed GRONLANDSFARID. *1949:* Sold to P/F Holmur A/S (K. Hansen, manager), Sorvag, Faroes. *1.8.1953:* Sank after striking an underwater object in approximate position 62.56N, 50.36W while on passage from Tassiussarssuak River, Greenland to Faeringehavn with a cargo of salt.

ELIN *S. Thorsoe collection*

RUTH II as **RUTH** *S. Thorsoe collection*

M2. RUTH II (1940–1943) Wooden auxiliary

O.N. 167530 321g 255n 125.7 × 28.7 × 12.8 feet.

1920: Completed by T. Ph. Jorgensen, Thuro, Svendborg, Denmark for Rederiaktieselskabet Ruth (A.E. Sorensen, manager), Svendborg, Denmark as the four masted schooner RUTH. *1928:* Sold to Sjelskibs A/S, Svendborg, Denmark (same manager). *1930:* Fitted with a 2-cyl. 2SA oil engine made by A/S Volund, Copenhagen, Denmark. *1939:* Re-engined with a 2-cyl. 2SA auxiliary oil engine made by A/S Volund, Copenhagen, Denmark. *1940:* Taken over by the Ministry of Shipping, London (F.T. Everard & Sons Ltd., managers) and renamed RUTH II. *1941:* The Ministry of Shipping became the Ministry of War Transport. *10.1.1943:* Stranded at Ballyvester, about 1.5 miles south of Donaghadee, while on passage from Workington to Londonderry with a cargo of coal. *29.1.1943:* Back broken and abandoned as a total loss.

THYRA III as THYRA

C. Hill

M3. THYRA III (1940–1944)

O.N. 168007 828g 488n 211.6 × 31.5 × 13.2 feet.
T.3-cyl. steam engine by the shipbuilder.

7.1912: Completed by A/S Kjobenhavns Flydedok & Skibsvaerft, Copenhagen, Denmark (Yard No. 97) for D/S A/S Vesterhavet (J. Lauritzen, manager), Esbjerg, Denmark as THYRA. *7.1918:* Sold to A/S Dampskibsselskabet Progress (Marius Nielsen & Son, managers), Copenhagen, Denmark. *1940:* Taken over by the Ministry of Shipping, London but registered under the management of Transport Maritime, Paris, France. Later that year transferred to British registry for the Ministry of Shipping (F.T. Everard & Sons Ltd., managers) and renamed THYRA III. *1941:* The Ministry of Shipping became the Ministry of War Transport. *1944:* Managers became A.F. Henry & Macgregor Ltd., Leith. *1945:* Returned to pre-war owners and renamed THYRA. *10.2.1955:* Arrived at Bremerhaven, West Germany to be broken up by Eisen & Metall K.G. Lehr & Co.

EMPIRE CLIFF as MARNA.

T. Rayner

M4. EMPIRE CLIFF (1940–1942)

O.N. 164908 873g 459n 1,124d 197.7 × 30.2 × 11.6 feet.
7-cyl. 2SA oil engine by British Auxiliaries Ltd., Glasgow.

12.1940: Completed by Goole Shipbuilding & Repairing Co. Ltd., Goole (Yard No. 357) for the Ministry of Shipping, London (F.T. Everard & Sons Ltd., managers). *1941:* The Ministry of Shipping became the Ministry of War Transport. *1942:* Managers became Capper, Alexander & Co., London. *8.1942:* Managers became Christian Salvesen & Co., Leith. *9.1945:* Sold to the South Georgia Co. (Christian Salvesen & Co., managers), Leith and renamed MARNA. *1960:* Sold to Hargreaves Coal & Shipping Ltd. (Comben Longstaff & Co. Ltd., managers), London and renamed HARCLIFF. *1963:* Sold to Componave Companhia Portuguesa de Navegacao Ltda., Panama and renamed RICARDO MANUEL. *4.9.1971:* Sank off Casablanca after a collision with the Moroccan motor vessel ZAGORA 1,437/56 while on passage from Lisbon to Casablanca in ballast.

M5. EMPIRE FORELAND (1941–1942)

O.N. 164909 873g 459n 1,137d 197.7 × 30.2 × 11.6 feet.
7-cyl. 2SA oil engine by British Auxiliaries Ltd., Glasgow.

3.1941: Completed by Goole Shipbuilding & Repairing Co. Ltd., Goole (Yard No. 358) for the Ministry of Shipping, London (F.T. Everard & Sons Ltd., managers). Later in 1941 owners became the Ministry of War Transport. *8.1942:* Managers became Comben Longstaff & Co. Ltd., London. *10.1945:* Sold to Woodtown Shipping Co. Ltd. (Comben Longstaff & Co. Ltd., managers), London and renamed NORFOLKBROOK. *2.1946:* Sold to Williamstown Shipping Co. Ltd. (same managers), London. *2.1950:* Sold to William Robertson Shipowners Ltd., Glasgow and renamed AGATE. *1958:* Owners became Gem Line Ltd. (William Robertson Shipowners Ltd., managers), Glasgow. *1961:* Sold to Pio Tomei, Viaregio, Italy and renamed SILVANA TOMEI. *1970:* Owner became Paolo Tomei, Viaregio, Italy. *1971:* Sold to Navalprotector, Rome, Italy and renamed SABBIATORE PRIMO. *1984:* Deleted from Lloyds Register as no longer sea-going.

EMPIRE FORELAND as **NORFOLKBROOK**. *J. Clarkson*

M6. EMPIRE BOY (1941–1942) Tanker

O.N. 168776 859g 362n 1,180d 188.7 × 31.3 × 14.0 feet.
T.3-cyl. steam engine by Amos & Smith Ltd., Hull.

12.1941: Completed by Goole Shipbuilding & Repairing Co. Ltd., Goole (Yard No. 361) for the Ministry of War Transport, London (F.T. Everard & Sons Ltd., managers). *1942:* Transferred to Royal Netherlands Government (Netherlands Shipping & Trading Committee Ltd., London, managers) and renamed DOORMAN (Dutch flag). *1945:* Managers became N.V. Hollandsche Stoomboot Maatschappij, Amsterdam, Holland. *1946:* Managers became N.V. Phs. van Ommeren's Scheepvaartbedrijf, Rotterdam, Holland. *1947:* Sold to N.V. Maatschappij 'Flandria' (same managers), Rotterdam, Holland and renamed FLANDRIA. *1948:* Sold to Vereenigde Tankkustvaart, Rotterdam, Holland. *1951:* Sold to Ulrick Thomas (S. Stein K.G., managers), Hamburg, West Germany and renamed ALICE. *1952:* Sold to Bauermann & Metzendorf G.m.b.H., Hamburg, West Germany, renamed HAMMONIA and lengthened to 215.2 feet. *1954:* Sold to Regia Reederei & Handels G.m.b.H. (Olea Tankschiffs, managers), Hamburg, West Germany, renamed PETRA and re-engined with a 6-cyl. 4SA oil engine made by Maschinenfabrik Augsburg Nurnberg A.G., Augsburg, West Germany. *1962:* Sold to Umberto Foresi, Livorno, Italy and renamed ANNY. *1963:* Sold to Vittorio Rossetti, Leghorn, Italy. *1971:* Renamed TOSCO. *16.6.1975:* Sold to De Co Mar for breaking up at La Spezia, Italy.

M7. EMPIRE SHOAL (1942–1945)

For details see under ship No. 67 **ANGULARITY (2)**.

M8. EMPIRE DWELLER (1942–1945) Tanker

For details see under ship No. 69 **ASPERITY (2)**.

Note: EMPIRE RUBY, an earlier sister vessel to EMPIRE DWELLER and EMPIRE AUDREY by the same shipbuilder (Yard No. 217), was originally allocated to F.T. Everard & Sons Ltd. for management but was transferred to Elder Dempster Lines Ltd. before completion for work on the African coast. The yard number had originally been allocated to a dry cargo coaster ordered by F.T. Everard & Sons Ltd.

EMPIRE DWELLER *D. Brown*

M9. EMPIRE HARBOUR (1943–1946) Tanker

O.N. 169098 797g 380n 830d 193.0 × 30.7 × 14.1 feet.
T.3-cyl. steam engine by D. Rowan & Co. Ltd., Glasgow.

4.1943: Completed by the Grangemouth Dockyard Co. Ltd., Grangemouth (Yard No. 446) for the Ministry of War Transport, London (F.T. Everard & Sons Ltd., managers). *1946:* Sold to Anglo-American Oil Co. Ltd., London and renamed ESSO GENESEE. *1950:* Owners became Esso Petroleum Co. Ltd., London. *21.3.1961:* Sold to Jos. Boel et fils S.A. for breaking up at Tamise, Belgium which was completed by *6.1961*.

EMPIRE HARBOUR as **ESSO GENESEE**. *W.S.P.L.*

M10. EMPIRE AUDREY (1943–1946) Tanker

For details see under ship No. 68 **AUDACITY (2)**.

M11. JENNINGS (1943–1945) Tanker

O.N. 169598 1,148g 732n 1,600d 209.7 × 37.0 × 13.2 feet.
5-cyl. 2SA oil engine by Fairbanks Morse & Co., Beloit, Wisconsin, U.S.A.

6.1943: Completed by Barnes-Duluth Shipbuilding Co., Duluth, Minnesota, U.S.A. (Yard No. 6) for the United States Maritime Commission, New York, U.S.A. (type T1-M-A1) and bareboat chartered by the War Shipping Administration, Washington, D.C., U.S.A. to the Ministry of War Transport, London (F.T. Everard & Sons Ltd., managers). *1945:* Managers became Anglo-Saxon Petroleum Co. (Eastern) Ltd., London. *4.1946:* Charterer became the Ministry of Transport, London. *8.1946:* Returned to United States Maritime Commission and sold to China Tanker Co. Ltd., Shanghai, China and renamed YUNG LOO (Oil Number 130). *24.5.1949:* Scuttled in the Whangpoo River during the Chinese hostilities.

EMPIRE WRESTLER as **ESSO TIOGA**. *W.S.P.L.*

M12. EMPIRE WRESTLER (1943–1944) Tanker

O.N. 169100 797g 380n 830d 193.0 × 30.7 × 14.1 feet.
T.3-cyl. steam engine by Aitchison, Blair Ltd., Clydebank.

7.1943: Completed by the Grangemouth Dockyard Co. Ltd., Grangemouth (Yard No. 447) for the Ministry of War Transport, London (F.T. Everard & Sons Ltd., managers). *1944:* Managers became Elder Dempster Lines Ltd., Liverpool. *1946:* Sold to Anglo-American Oil Co. Ltd., London and renamed ESSO TIOGA. *1950:* Owners became Esso Petroleum Co. Ltd., London. *12.1963:* Sold to T.W. Ward Ltd. for breaking up at Inverkeithing where work commenced *7.1.1964*.

M13. RIO BRAVO (1943–1944) Tanker

O.N. 169645 1,141g 718n 1,600d 209.7 × 37.0 × 13.2 feet.
5-cyl. 2SA oil engine by Fairbanks Morse & Co., Beloit, Wisconsin, U.S.A.

8.1943: Completed by Barnes-Duluth Shipbuilding Co., Duluth, Minnesota, U.S.A. (Yard No. 10) for the United States Maritime Commission, New York, U.S.A. (type T1-M-A1) and bareboat chartered by the War Shipping Administration, Washington, D.C., U.S.A. to the Ministry of War Transport, London (F.T. Everard & Sons Ltd., managers). *2.11.1944:* Capsized and sank after being torpedoed by a German E-boat while at anchor in Ostend Roads in position 51.16N, 02.54E during a voyage from Ostend to Southend in ballast.

M14. COTTON VALLEY (1943–1944) Tanker

O.N. 169647 1,179g 554n 1,528d 213.7 × 37.1 × 14.3 feet.
8-cyl. 4SA oil engine by Union Diesel Engine Co., Oakland, California, U.S.A.

9.1943: Completed by Lancaster Ironworks Inc., Perryville, Maryland, U.S.A. (Yard No. 202) for the United States Maritime Commission, New York, U.S.A. (type T1-M-A1) and bareboat chartered by the War Shipping Administration, Washington, D.C., U.S.A. to the Ministry of War Transport, London (F.T. Everard & Sons Ltd., managers). *4.10.1944:* Mined and abandoned six miles off Port de Bouc. *2.1945:* Afterpart towed into Marseilles, temporary bow fitted and used as an oil hulk under French control. *2.1947:* Returned to United States Maritime Commission and sold to Carlo Cameli, Genoa, Italy and renamed PARAGGI. *1947:* Sold to Compagnia Maritima Corso, Rome, Italy. *1948:* Sold to Carlo Cameli, Genoa, Italy. *1964:* Sold to Petrolmar S.p.A. Trasporti Marittimi Costieri e Portuali di Prodotti Petroliferi, Genoa, Italy and renamed N.S. DI MONTALLEGRO. *1976:* Owners became Petrolmar S.p.A., Genoa, Italy. Still in service (1990).

SEVEN SISTERS *National Maritime Museum*

M15. SEVEN SISTERS (1943–1945) Tanker

O.N. 169725 1,185g 687n 1,600d 213.8 × 37.1 × 14.3 feet.
8-cyl. 4SA oil engine by Union Diesel Engine Co., Oakland, California, U.S.A.

9.1943: Completed by Grays Ironworks Inc., Galveston, Texas, U.S.A. (Yard No. 101) for the United States Maritime Commission, New York, U.S.A. (type T1-M-A1) and bareboat chartered by the War Shipping Administration, Washington, D.C., U.S.A. to the Ministry of War Transport, London (F.T. Everard & Sons Ltd., managers). *1945:* Managers became Anglo-Saxon Petroleum Co. (Eastern) Ltd., London. *4.1946:* Charterer became the Ministry of Transport, London. *10.1946:* Returned to United States Maritime Commission and sold to China Tanker Co. Ltd., Shanghai, China and renamed YUNG SUNG (Oil Number 114). *1952:* Managers became China Merchants Steam Navigation Co. Ltd., Kaohsiung, Taiwan. *1959:* Owners became China Merchants Steam Navigation Co. Ltd., Kaohsiung, Taiwan. *1959:* Broken up at Keelung, Taiwan.

LADY KATHLEEN

C. Reynolds

M16. LADY KATHLEEN (1943–1951) Ferro-concrete

O.N. 169566 1,832g 949n 266.3 × 41.9 × 20.3 feet.
8-cyl. 2SA 'O' type oil engine by the Newbury Diesel Co. Ltd., Newbury.

9.1943: Completed by W. & C. French Ltd., Newport, Monmouth for Concrete Maritime Ltd. (Wm. Cory & Son Ltd. and F.T. Everard & Sons Ltd., managers), London. *1948:* Sold to D/S A/S Phoenix, Bergen, Norway (Paal Wilson, Bergen & F.T. Everard & Sons Ltd., London, managers). *11.1951:* Drifted ashore in bad weather from an anchorage off Riga and wrecked in position 57.54N, 21.33E while on passage from Helsinki to Riga in ballast.

WALNUT BEND

National Maritime Museum

M17. WALNUT BEND (1943–1945) Tanker

O.N. 169751 1,124g 740n 1,600d 209.7 × 37.0 × 13.2 feet.
5-cyl. 2SA oil engine by Fairbanks Morse & Co., Beloit, Wisconsin, U.S.A.

10.1943: Completed by Barnes-Duluth Shipbuilding Co., Duluth, Minnesota, U.S.A. (Yard No. 11) for the United States Maritime Commission, New York, U.S.A. (type T1-M-A1) and bareboat chartered by the War Shipping Administration, Washington, D.C., U.S.A. to the Ministry of War Transport, London (F.T. Everard & Sons Ltd., managers). *1945:* Managers became Anglo-Saxon Petroleum Co. (Eastern) Ltd., London. *4.1946:* Charterer became the Ministry of Transport, London. *3.1947:* Returned to United States Maritime Commission and sold to China Tanker Co. Ltd., Shanghai, China and renamed YUNG WEI (Oil Number 129). *1952:* Owners became China Ocean Shipping Co., Peking, China. Still in service (1990).

M18. GOLDEN MEADOW (1943–1945) Tanker

O.N. 169792 1,184g 559n 1,528d 213.7 × 37.1 × 14.3 feet.
8-cyl. 4SA oil engine by Union Diesel Engine Co., Oakland, California, U.S.A.

12.1943: Completed by Lancaster Ironworks Inc., Perryville, Maryland, U.S.A. (Yard No. 204) for the United States Maritime Commission, New York, U.S.A. (type T1-M-A1) and bareboat chartered by the War Shipping Administration, Washington, D.C., U.S.A. to the Ministry of War Transport, London (F.T. Everard & Sons Ltd., managers). *1945:* Managers became Anglo-Saxon Petroleum Co. (Eastern) Ltd., London. *4.1946:* Charterer became the Ministry of Transport, London. *12.1946:* Returned to United States Maritime Commission and sold to China Tanker Co. Ltd., Shanghai, China and renamed YUNG TUNG (Oil Number 115). *1952:* Managers became China Merchants Steam Navigation Co. Ltd., Kaohsiung, Taiwan. *1959:* Owners became China Merchants Steam Navigation Co. Ltd., Kaohsiung, Taiwan. *3.1962:* Broken up at Keelung, Taiwan.

EMPIRE HARVEST as **SHELBRIT 5**. *J. Clarkson*

M19. EMPIRE HARVEST (1943–1946) Tanker

O.N. 169403 814g 332n 850d 193.0 × 30.7 × 13.8 feet.
T.3-cyl. steam engine by Aitchison, Blair Ltd., Clydebank.

12.1943: Completed by A. & J. Inglis Ltd., Glasgow (Yard No. 1225) for the Ministry of War Transport, London (F.T. Everard & Sons Ltd., managers). *4.1946:* Owners became the Ministry of Transport, London. *5.1946:* Sold to Shell-Mex & B.P. Ltd., London and renamed SHELBRIT 5. *1952:* Renamed B.P. ENGINEER. *5.1965:* Sold for breaking up to Scrappingco S.A., Brussels, Belgium. *31.5.1965:* Work commenced.

M20. CHANT 22 (1944–1946) Tanker

O.N. 180106 402g 215n 480d 142.2 × 27.0 × 8.5 feet.
4-cyl. 2SA oil engine by Crossley Brothers Ltd., Manchester.

1.1944: Completed by Goole Shipbuilding & Repairing Co. Ltd., Goole (Yard No. 410) for the Ministry of War Transport, London (F.T. Everard & Sons Ltd., managers). *4.1946:* Owners became the Ministry of Transport, London. *6.1946:* Sold to Skibs A/S Fratres (Jorgen Jahre, manager), Sandefjord, Norway and renamed TROND. *1946:* Sold to Bulls Tankrederi A/S, Sandefjord, Norway, same managers. *1948:* Sold to Skibs A/S Fratres (Bjorn Stenseth, manager), Sandefjord, Norway. *1949:* Sold to Polish Government and renamed WODNIK. *1961:* Deleted from Lloyds Register as no longer sea-going.

TRANSOIL *J. Wells*

M21. TRANSOIL (1944–1946) Twin screw tanker

O.N. 169935 1,719g 1,234n 2,550d 250.2 × 43.1 × 16.6 feet.
2 × 12-cyl. 4SA oil engines by National Superior Co., Springfield, Ohio, U.S.A.

1936: Completed by Ingalls Ironworks Co., Chickasaw, Alabama, U.S.A. (Yard No. 171) for American Tanker Corporation, Boston, Massachussets, U.S.A. *2.1944:* Bareboat chartered by War Shipping Administration, Washington, D.C., U.S.A. to the Ministry of War Transport, London (Anglo-Saxon Petroleum Co. Ltd., managers). *1944:* Managers became F.T. Everard & Sons Ltd. *4.1946:* Charterer became the Ministry of Transport, London. *8.1946:* Returned to U.S. ownership and sold to International Tankers S.A. (National Bulk Carriers Inc., managers), Montreal, Canada. *1948:* Sold to Associated Oil Transportation Co., New York, U.S.A. and renamed OIL TRANSPORTER. *1951:* Sold to Gayport Shipping Ltd., Toronto, Canada. *1951:* Re-engined with 2 × 12-cyl. 2SA oil engines made by General Motors Corp., La Grange, Illinois, U.S.A. *1959:* Sold to Hall Corporation of Canada, Montreal, Canada, and renamed OIL TRANSPORT. *1968:* Sold to Challenger Ltd., Hamilton, Bermuda and renamed WIT. *1968:* Sold to Wit Ltd. (West Indies Transport Co. Inc., managers), Hamilton, Bermuda. *1977:* Sold to Challenger Ltd., Hamilton, Bermuda. Still in service (1990).

TRANSOIL *J. Wells*

TRANSOIL *J. Wells*

EMPIRE PYM *J. Callis*

M22. EMPIRE PYM (1944–1946) Tanker

O.N. 169104 2,370g 1,281n 3,265d 291.0 × 44.0 × 19.1 feet.
T.3-cyl. steam engine by D. Rowan & Co. Ltd., Glasgow.

3.1944: Completed by the Grangemouth Dockyard Co. Ltd., Grangemouth (Yard No. 448) for the Ministry of War Transport, London (F.T. Everard & Sons Ltd., managers). *4.1946:* Owner became the Ministry of Transport, London. *7.1946:* Sold to Refast Steamship Co. Ltd. (Stevinson, Hardy & Co. Ltd., managers), London and renamed REFAST. *1953:* Sold to Nolido Compania de Navegacion S.A. (Marcou & Sons [Shipbrokers] Ltd., managers), Puerto Limon, Costa Rica and renamed CASSIAN. *1954:* Sold to Société Mazout Transport, Paris, France and renamed MOBILSUD. *1958:* Sold to Société Mobil Transports, Paris, France. *1964:* Sold to S.A. Monegasque d'Armement & de Navigation (Claude Audibert, manager), Monaco and renamed JANSON. *1966:* Sold to Sarda Bunker S.p.A., Naples, Italy and renamed CAPO MANNU. *1980:* Broken up in Italy.

M23. CHANT 24 (1944–1945) Tanker

O.N. 180109 402g 215n 480d 142.2 × 27.0 × 8.5 feet.
4-cyl. 2SA oil engine by Crossley Brothers Ltd., Manchester.

3.1944: Completed by Goole Shipbuilding & Repairing Co. Ltd., Goole (Yard No. 412) for the Ministry of War Transport, London (F.T. Everard & Sons Ltd., managers). *8.1945:* Transferred to Admiralty service. *1946:* Sold to A/S Troja Skipsrederi (Gunnar Jacobsen, manager), Oslo, Norway and renamed RINGA. *1950:* Sold to Ottario Novella S.p.A., Genoa, Italy. *1983:* Sold to Cantieri Navali del Golfo for breaking up at La Spezia, Italy where work commenced *4.7.1983*.

M24. CHANT 66 (1944–1945) Tanker

O.N. 180346 401g 210n 465d 141.7 × 27.1 × 8.5 feet.
5-cyl. 4SA oil engine by Ruston & Hornsby Ltd., Lincoln.

4.1944: Completed by Burntisland Shipbuilding Co. Ltd., Burntisland (Yard No. 291) for the Ministry of War Transport, London (F.T. Everard & Sons Ltd., managers). *5.1.1945:* Capsized while repairing at Grangemouth. *23.1.1945:* Refloated and sold to G. & W. Brunton for breaking up at Grangemouth where work was completed by *5.9.1945*.

M25. CHANT 67 (1944–1946) Tanker

O.N. 180347 401g 201n 465d 141.7 × 27.1 × 8.5 feet.
5-cyl. 4SA oil engine by Ruston & Hornsby Ltd., Lincoln.

4.1944: Completed by Burntisland Shipbuilding Co. Ltd., Burntisland (Yard No. 292) for the Ministry of Transport, London (F.T. Everard & Sons Ltd., managers). *4.1946:* Owner became the Ministry of Transport, London. *7.1946:* Sold to Sporveienes Bensindepot Nor A/S, Oslo, Norway and renamed NORBENSIN. *1952:* Sold to K.J. Rebensdorf & others, Gothenburg, Sweden and renamed REDO. *1956:* Sold to Knut Hermansson, Skarhamn, Sweden and renamed REDON. *1961:* Re-engined with a 6-cyl. 2SA oil engine made by Alpha Diesel A/S, Frederikshavn, Denmark. *1971:* Sold to Maritime Co. Ltd., Khorramshahr, Iran and renamed KAMBIZ. Still in service (1990).

M26. CHANT 68 (1944–1946) Tanker

O.N. 123110 401g 210n 465d 141.7 × 27.1 × 8.5 feet.
4-cyl. 2SA oil engine by Crossley Brothers Ltd., Manchester.

4.1944: Completed by Burntisland Shipbuilding Co. Ltd., Burntisland (Yard No. 293) for the Ministry of War Transport, London (F.T. Everard & Sons Ltd., managers). *4.1946:* Owner became the Ministry of War Transport, London. *5.1946:* Sold to Compania Maritima de Petrole S.A., Panama and renamed LEMAN. *1950:* Nicolas E. Vernicos Shipping S.A., Piraeus, Greece appointed managers. *1951:* Sold to K. Deliyiannos, Piraeus, Greece. *1961:* Sold to Nicolas E. Vernicos Shipping Co. Ltd., Piraeus, Greece and renamed MOTOL VI. *1969:* Sold to Cavership for breaking up at Piraeus, Greece where work commenced *28.11.1969*.

CHANT 60: a typical member of the class. *National Maritime Museum*

CHANT 69

National Maritime Museum

M27. CHANT 69 (1944) Tanker

O.N. 123109 401g 210n 465d 141.7 × 27.1 × 8.5 feet.
4-cyl. 2SA oil engine by Crossley Brothers Ltd., Manchester.

4.1944: Completed by Burntisland Shipbuilding Co. Ltd., Burntisland (Yard No. 294) for the Ministry of War Transport, London (F.T. Everard & Sons Ltd., managers). *16.6.1944:* Capsized off Normandy; wreck later sunk by gunfire.

Note: There is some evidence to suggest that CHANT 6 was managed at some time by F.T. Everard & Sons Ltd. However, this cannot be substantiated from official sources or from Lloyds Register and the ship has therefore not been included in this list.

M28. CHANT 26 (1944–1945) Tanker

O.N. 180111 402g 215n 480d 142.2 × 27.0 × 8.5 feet.
4.cyl. 2SA oil engine by Crossley Brothers Ltd., Manchester.

4.1944: Completed by Goole Shipbuilding & Repairing Co. Ltd., Goole (Yard No. 414) for the Ministry of War Transport, London (F.T. Everard & Sons Ltd., managers). *1945:* Managers became Coastal Tankers Ltd., London. *8.1945:* Transferred to Admiralty service. *6.1946:* Sold to La Sociedade de Navegacion Comagre S.A. (John Catapolis, manager), Panama. *6.1946:* Sold to Finska Angfartygs A/B, Helsingfors, Finland and renamed T.1. *1951:* Sold to Reuters Handels A/B (H.A. Reuter, manager), Kungsbacka, Sweden and renamed B.T. IX. *1958:* Re-engined with a 5-cyl. 2SA oil engine made by Nydqvist & Holm, Trollhattan, Sweden and renamed SVARTSKAR. *1959:* Sold to A/B Bensintransport (G. Reuter, manager), Stockholm, Sweden and renamed B.T. IX. *1963:* Sold to F. Visentini, Chioggia, Italy and renamed FOCA. *1967:* Sold to Daniele Corvetta & C., Ravenna, Italy. *1968:* Sold to Angelo Hopps, Trapani, Italy. *1969:* Sold to Foca-Miriam S.r.l., Trapani, Italy. *1974:* Broken up in Italy.

M29. EMPIRE TROTWOOD (1944–1946) Tanker

O.N. 180356 797g 380n 830d 193.0 × 30.7 × 14.1 feet.
T.3-cyl. steam engine by D. Rowan & Co. Ltd., Glasgow.

5.1944: Completed by the Grangemouth Dockyard Co. Ltd., Grangemouth (Yard No. 455) for the Ministry of War Transport, London (F.T. Everard & Sons Ltd., managers). *4.1946:* Owner became the Ministry of Transport, London. *1946:* Managers became Anglo-Saxon Petroleum Co. Ltd., London. *1947:* Sold to Kuwait Oil Co. Ltd., London and renamed AMIR. *1952:* Sold to Shell-Mex & B.P. Ltd., London and renamed B.P. DISTRIBUTOR. *5.1965:* Sold to Scrappingco S.A., Brussels for breaking up at Antwerp, Belgium where work commenced *31.5.1965*.

CHANT 28 after the war. *Port Autonome du Havre*

M30. CHANT 28 (1944–1945) Tanker

O.N. 180115 402g 215n 480d 142.2 × 27.0 × 8.5 feet.
7-cyl. 4SA oil engine by R.A. Lister (Marine Sales) Ltd., Dursley.

5.1944: Completed by Goole Shipbuilding & Repairing Co. Ltd., Goole (Yard No. 416) for the Ministry of War Transport, London (F.T. Everard & Sons Ltd., managers). *1945:* Managers became Coastal Tankers Ltd., London. *1946:* Sold to Port Autonome du Havre, Le Havre, France. *1986:* Sold to Fablon & Cie. for breaking up at Le Havre, France.

M31. CHANT 50 (1944–1945) Tanker

O.N. 180113 402g 215n 480d 142.2 × 27.0 × 8.5 feet.
4-cyl. 2SA oil engine by Crossley Brothers Ltd., Manchester.

5.1944: Completed by Goole Shipbuilding & Repairing Co. Ltd., Goole (Yard No. 435) for the Ministry of War Transport, London (F.T. Everard & Sons Ltd., managers). *8.1945:* Transferred to Admiralty service. *7.1946:* Sold to Lysaker Kemiske Fabrik A/S, Oslo, Norway and renamed TANK 1. *1956:* Sold to Rederi A/B Bjornsund (B.G. Gustafson, manager), Stockevik, Sweden and renamed TANKHOLM. *1961:* Re-engined with a 5-cyl. 4SA oil engine made by A/S Volund, Copenhagen, Denmark. *1965:* Sold to B.G. Gustafson Partrederi, Stockevik, Sweden. *1971:* Sold to R.A. Bjornsund, Molndal, Sweden and renamed VINGO. *1973:* Sold to R. Wallman, Molndal, Sweden. *1974:* Sold to K.H. Kindslatt, Molndal, Sweden. *1974:* Sold to Personner Attervinning A/B for breaking up at Ystad, Sweden.

EMPIRE DOMBEY as **ALLURITY (1)**.

T. Rayner

M32. EMPIRE DOMBEY (1944–1947) Tanker

For details see under ship No. 84 **ALLURITY (1)**.

M33. CHANT 51 (1944–1945) Tanker

O.N. 180116 402g 214n 480d 142.2 × 27.0 × 8.5 feet.
4-cyl. 2SA oil engine by Crossley Brothers Ltd., Manchester.

6.1944: Completed by Goole Shipbuilding & Repairing Co. Ltd., Goole (Yard No. 436) for the Ministry of War Transport, London (F.T. Everard & Sons Ltd., managers). *8.1945:* Transferred to Admiralty service. *6.1946:* Sold to Rederi A/B Diana (Tore Ulff, manager), Stockholm, Sweden and renamed DOLLIE. *1951:* Sold to N.V. Teerbedrijf, Uithoorn, Holland and renamed GEMMA. *28.12.1951:* Sank after developing engine trouble off Bilbao while on loaded passage from Bilbao to London.

M34. CHANT 56 (1944–1946) Tanker

O.N. 169131 401g 212n 450d 141.7 × 27.1 × 8.5 feet.
6-cyl. 2SA oil engine by British Auxiliaries Ltd., Glasgow.

3.1944: Completed by Furness Shipbuilding Co. Ltd., Haverton Hill-on-Tees (Yard No. 369) for the Ministry of War Transport, London (Coastal Tankers Ltd., appointed managers, but later transferred to F.T. Everard & Sons Ltd.). *4.1946:* Owner became the Ministry of Transport, London. *10.1946:* Sold to Anglo-Saxon Petroleum Co. Ltd., London. *2.1947:* Sold to N.V. Nederlandsch-Indische Tank-Stoomboot Maatschappij (Shell Tankers N.V., managers), The Hague, Holland and renamed MILO. *1955:* Owners became N.V. Petroleum Maatschappij 'La Corona' (Shell Tankers N.V., managers), The Hague, Holland. *7.1959:* Sold to the Indonesian Government for breaking up at Palembang, Sumatra.

M35. CHANT 57 (1944–1946) Tanker

O.N. 169133 401g 212n 450d 141.7 × 27.1 × 8.5 feet.
6-cyl. 2SA oil engine by British Auxiliaries Ltd., Glasgow.

3.1944: Completed by Furness Shipbuilding Co. Ltd., Haverton Hill-on-Tees (Yard No. 370) for the Ministry of War Transport, London (Coastal Tankers Ltd., appointed managers but later transferred to F.T. Everard & Sons Ltd.). *4.1946:* Owner became the Ministry of Transport, London. *5.1946:* Sold to Rethymnis & Kulukundis Ltd., London and renamed GRANDE. *1946:* Sold to Rederi A/B Staffen (J. Haag, manager), Gefle, Sweden and renamed GRAN. *1953:* Re-engined with a 5-cyl. 2SA oil engine made by Alpha Diesel A/S, Frederikshavn, Denmark. *1966:* Sold to Maritime Co. Ltd., Khorramshahr, Iran and renamed KAMRAN. *18.1.1989:* Foundered in heavy weather near Abu Musa in position 25.50N, 55.22E while on passage from Dubai to Iran.

EMPIRE FAIRHAVEN as FIXITY (1). *W.S.P.L.*

M36. EMPIRE FAIRHAVEN (1944–1946)

For details see under ship No. 70 **FIXITY (1)**.

M37. EMPIRE MULL (1944–1945) Tanker

O.N. 180358 797g 380n 850d 193.0 × 30.7 × 14.1 feet.
T.3-cyl. steam engine by Aitchison, Blair Ltd., Clydebank.

8.1944: Completed by the Grangemouth Dockyard Co. Ltd., Grangemouth (Yard No. 456) for the Ministry of War Transport, London (F.T. Everard & Sons Ltd., managers). *1945:* Managers became Anglo-Saxon Petroleum Co. Ltd., London. *3.1946:* Transferred to the French Government (Ministère de la Marine Marchande), Marseilles, France. *1946:* Renamed MEDEA (Compagnie des Bateaux à Vapeur du Nord, managers). *1948:* Managers became S.A. de Gerance & d'Armement, Paris, France. *1951:* Sold to Gebruder Loffler, Hamburg, West Germany and renamed CHRISTINE. *1952:* Lengthened to 221.0 feet, tonnages became 903g, 428n and 1,050d. *1956:* Sold to Bulk Oil Steamship Co. Ltd., London and renamed PASS OF KINTAIL. *1963:* Sold to Navalpetroli Societa di Navigazione A.R.L., Genoa, Italy and renamed PASSAMARE. *1965:* Sold to Seka S.A., Piraeus, Greece and renamed KALI LIMENES. *1986:* Deleted from Lloyds Register due to lack of information.

M38. NORTH STAR (1944–1947) Twin screw tanker

O.N. 180561 1,429g 697n 242.5 × 36.9 × 19.7 feet.
Steam turbine driving two electric motors by Ridgeway Dynamo & Engine Co., Ridgeway, Pennsylvania, U.S.A.

12.1918: Completed by Alabama-New Orleans Transportation Co., Violet, Louisiana, U.S.A. (Yard No. 24) for the Mexican Petroleum Co., New York, U.S.A. as PANOIL *1920:* Sold to the Pan-American Petroleum & Transport Co., Los Angeles, California, U.S.A. *1921:* Fitted with new boiler and two C.2-cyl. steam engines made by Staten Island Shipbuilding Co., New York, U.S.A. *1923:* Sold to the Mexican Petroleum Corp. Inc., New York, U.S.A. *1924:* Renamed CRUDOIL. *1926:* Sold to Huasteca Petroleum Co. Inc., New York, U.S.A. *1930:* Sold to Allied Oil Transport Co. Inc., Cleveland, Ohio, U.S.A. *1937:* Managers became Cleveland Tankers Inc. *1942:* Sold to Cleveland Tankers Inc., Cleveland, Ohio, U.S.A. and renamed NORTH STAR. *12.1944:* Bareboat chartered by War Shipping Administration, Washington, D.C., U.S.A. to Ministry of War Transport, London (F.T. Everard & Sons Ltd., managers). *4.1946:* Charterer became the Ministry of Transport, London. *1947:* Returned to United States Maritime Commission and sold to Carlo Cameli, Genoa, Italy and renamed CERVARA. *1954:* Broken up in Italy.

M39. EMPIRE DRURY (1944–1945) Tanker

O.N. 180360 797g 380n 835d 193.0 × 30.7 × 14.1 feet.
T.3-cyl. steam engine by D. Rowan & Co. Ltd., Glasgow.

12.1944: Completed by the Grangemouth Dockyard Co. Ltd., Grangemouth (Yard No. 460) for the Ministry of War Transport, London (F.T. Everard & Sons Ltd., managers). *1945:* Managers became Anglo-Saxon Petroleum Co. Ltd., London. *4.1946:* Owner became the Ministry of Transport, London. *1947:* Sold to Shell-Mex & B.P. Ltd., London and renamed SHELBRIT 6. *1952:* Renamed B.P. REFINER. *1964:* Sold to Compagnia Siciliana Navigazione Cisterna S.p.A., Palermo, Sicily, Italy and renamed COSINA. *6.1973:* Sold to V. Ferrara & C. for breaking up at Palermo, Sicily where work commenced *25.6.1973.*

EMPIRE GANGES as **ASTRALITY (2)**. *A. Duncan*

M40. EMPIRE GANGES (1945–1946) Tanker

For details see under ship No. 131 **ASTRALITY (2)**.

M41. EMPIRE TAVISTOCK (1945) Tanker

For details see under ship No. 105 **ALLEGRITY**.

M42. EMPIRE NEWT (1945–1947) Tanker

O.N. 145446 1,548g 1,033n 241.0 × 41.0 × 15.6 feet.
T.3-cyl. steam engine by the shipbuilder.

1903: Built by Chicago Shipbuilding Co., Chicago, Illinois, U.S.A. (Yard No. 61) for the Great Lakes & St. Lawrence Transport Co., Chicago, Illinois, U.S.A. as the dry cargo vessel JOHN CRERER. *1917:* Sold to Chemins de Fer de l'Etat Francais (Société Maritime National, managers), Le Havre, France and renamed FOURAS. *1921:* Sold to Glen Steamships Ltd. (J. Playfair, manager), Midland, Ontario, Canada and renamed GLENGARNOCK. *1927:* Sold to Canada Steamship Lines Ltd., Montreal, Canada and renamed COURTRIGHT. *1937:* Sold to be broken up but only laid up. *1940:* Converted to a tanker by Marine Industries Ltd., Sorel, P.Q., Canada. *1940:* Sold to Branch Lines Ltd., Montreal, Canada and renamed CEDARBRANCH. *1945:* Sold to the Ministry of War Transport, London (F.T. Everard & Sons Ltd., managers) and renamed EMPIRE NEWT. *4.1946:* Owner became the Ministry of Transport, London. *3.1947:* Sold to BISCO and allocated to T.W. Ward Ltd. for breaking up at Inverkeithing.

M43. EMPIRE SEACOAST (1946)

O.N. 180455 522g 308n 400d 142.6 × 27.1 × 16.0 feet.
4-cyl. 2SA oil engine by British Polar Engines Ltd., Glasgow.

10.1945: Completed by H. Scarr Ltd., Hessle (Yard No. S470) for the Ministry of War Transport, London (Singapore Straits Steam Shipping Co. Ltd., London, managers). *1946:* Managers became F.T. Everard & Sons Ltd. *4.1946:* Owner became the Ministry of Transport, London. *7.1946:* Sold to Middle East Coastal Services Ltd., Famagusta, Cyprus (J. Fisher & Sons Ltd., Barrow-in-Furness, managers) and renamed BIRHAKIM. *1949:* Sold to British India Steam Navigation Co. Ltd., London. *1949:* Sold to the Indian General Navigation & Railway Co. Ltd., Calcutta, India and renamed TANDA. *1963:* Sold to Pakistan River Steamers Ltd., Chittagong, East Pakistan. *1972:* Owners became Bangladesh River Steamers Ltd., Chittagong, Bangladesh. *1975:* Owners became Bangladesh Inland Water Transport Corp., Chittagong, Bangladesh and renamed C5-212. Still in service (1990).

EMPIRE SEAFRONT: a typical member of the class. *R. Dunston Ltd.*

M44. EMPIRE SEAPORT (1946)

O.N. 180457 522g 308n 400d 142.6 × 27.1 × 16.0 feet.
4-cyl. 2SA oil engine by British Polar Engines Ltd., Glasgow.

11.1945: Completed by H. Scarr Ltd., Hessle (Yard No. S475) for the Ministry of War Transport, London (Singapore Straits Steam Shipping Co. Ltd., London, managers). *1946:* Managers became F.T. Everard & Sons Ltd. *4.1946:* Owner became the Ministry of Transport, London. *7.1946:* Sold to Middle East Coastal Services Ltd., Famagusta, Cyprus (J. Fisher & Sons Ltd., Barrow-in-Furness, managers) and renamed ELADEM. *1949:* Sold to British India Steam Navigation Co. Ltd., London. *1949:* Sold to Rivers Steam Navigation Co. Ltd. (Macneill, Barry & Co., managers), Calcutta, India and renamed TORILLA. *1963:* Sold to Pakistan River Steamers Ltd., Chittagong, East Pakistan. *1972:* Owners became Bangladesh River Steamers Ltd., Chittagong, Bangladesh. *1975:* Owners became Bangladesh Inland Water Transport Corp., Chittagong, Bangladesh and renamed C5-216. Still in service (1990).

FORMER GERMAN VESSELS

M45. EMPIRE TIGOMBO (1945–1946) Twin screw tanker

O.N. 180759 604g 249n 800d 179.5 × 29.6 × 13.0 feet.
2 × 7-cyl. 2SA oil engines by Halburg Maschinenbau & Geisseri A.G., Ludwigshafen, Germany.

1944: Completed by Greifenwerft G.m.b.H., Stettin, Germany (Yard No. 142) for the Deutsche Kriegsmarine as HOWACHT. *5.1945:* Taken as prize by Allied forces. *9.1945:* Taken over by the Ministry of War Transport, London (F.T. Everard & Sons Ltd., managers) and renamed EMPIRE TIGOMBO. *4.1946:* Handed over to U.S.S.R. and renamed UTRISH. *1965:* Used as a target and destroyed by the Russian Navy in the Black Sea.

M46. EMPIRE TIGACHI (1945–1946) Tanker

O.N. 180783 685g 254n 185.7 × 29.6 × 13.0 feet.
14-cyl. 2SA oil engine by Halburg Maschinenbau & Geisseri A.G., Ludwigshafen, Germany.

1942: Completed by Elsflether Werft A.G., Elsfleth, Germany (Yard No. 235) for the Deutsche Kriegsmarine as FLEMHUDE. *5.1945:* Taken as a prize in damaged condition by Allied forces. *7.1945:* Taken over by the Ministry of War Transport, London (Anglo-Saxon Petroleum Co. Ltd., London, managers) and renamed EMPIRE TIGACHI. *1945:* Management transferred to F.T. Everard & Sons Ltd. *3.1.1946:* Ran onto a submerged wreck off Nidingen while on passage from Helsingborg to London with a cargo of tar and became a total loss.

M47. EMPIRE TEGADOS (1945–1946) Tanker

692g 452n 820d 186.1 × 28.2 × 13.3 feet.
8-cyl. 4SA oil engine by Deutsche Werke A.G., Kiel, Germany.

1938: Completed by F. Schichau, Konigsberg, Germany (Yard No. 1384) for the Deutsche Kriegsmarine as GABELSFLACH. *16.9.1944:* Damaged by fire in an air-raid on Kiel. *5.1945:* Taken as a prize by Allied forces at Kiel. *9.5.1945:* Wreck sank in tow west of Fehmarn Island, later salved and repaired under British supervision. *8.1945:* Taken over by the Ministry of War Transport, London (Anglo-Saxon Petroleum Co. Ltd., London, managers) and renamed EMPIRE TEGADOS. *1945:* Managers became F.T. Everard & Sons Ltd. *3.1946:* Handed over to U.S.S.R. and renamed ALEXI TOLSTOI. *1964:* Broken up at Baku, Azerbaijan.

M48. EMPIRE TEGIDAD (1945–1946) Tanker

O.N. 180733 642g 434n 1,046d 176.4 × 28.3 × 13.3 feet.
8-cyl. 4SA oil engine by the shipbuilder.

1934: Completed by Deutsche Werke A.G., Kiel, Germany (Yard No. 230) for the Deutsche Reichsmarine as SYLT. *1935:* Transferred to the Deutsche Kriegsmarine. *5.1945:* Taken as a prize by Allied forces at Trondheim, Norway. *10.1945:* Taken over by the Ministry of Transport, London (F.T. Everard & Sons Ltd., managers) and renamed EMPIRE TEGIDAD. *4.1946:* Owner became the Ministry of Transport, London. *8.1946:* Transferred to the Allied Control Commission and sold to Carl W. Hansen Tankschiffahrt, Hamburg, West Germany and renamed SYLT. *1969:* Sold to Compania de Navegacion Lomamer S.A., Panama and renamed ROVENSCA. *1982:* Sold to Sidemar S.p.A. for breaking up at Trieste, Italy.

EMPIRE TEGIDAD as **SYLT**.

T. Rayner

EMPIRE TIGITY as ANTHONY M.

T. Rayner

M49. EMPIRE TIGITY (1945–1946) Tanker

O.N. 180755 465g 216n 545d 143.9 × 25.6 × 11.9 feet.
6-cyl. 4SA oil engine by Motorenwerke Mannheim A.G., Mannheim, Germany.

1944: Completed by H. Peters, Wewelsfleth, Germany (Yard No. 449) for the Deutsche Kriegsmarine as GOHREN. *5.1945:* Taken as a prize by Allied forces. *10.1945:* Taken over by the Ministry of War Transport, London (F.T. Everard & Sons Ltd., managers) and renamed EMPIRE TIGITY. *1946:* Management transferred to Metcalf Motor Coasters Ltd., London. *4.1946:* Owner became the Ministry of Transport, London. *4.1947:* Sold to Metcalf Motor Coasters Ltd., London and renamed ANTHONY M. *1953:* Re-engined with a 8-cyl. 4SA oil engine made by Blackstone & Co. Ltd., Stamford. *1971:* Sold to Effluents Services Ltd., Stockport and renamed KINDER. *4.1983:* Sold to Pemberton & Carlyon for breaking up at Garston.

M50. EMPIRE TEGAMAS (1945–1946) Tanker

O.N. 180722 708g 452n 1,000d 176.1 × 28.3 × 14.8 feet.
8-cyl. 2SA oil engine by Deutsche Werke A.G., Kiel, Germany.

1939: Completed by F. Schichau G.m.b.H., Konigsberg, Germany (Yard No. 1440) for the Deutsche Kriegsmarine as ODERBANK. *5.1945:* Taken as a prize by Allied forces at Trondheim, Norway. *10.1945:* Taken over by the Ministry of War Transport, London (F.T. Everard & Sons Ltd., managers) and renamed EMPIRE TEGAMAS. *2.1946:* Handed over to U.S.S.R. and renamed KHERSONES. *1965:* Used as a target and destroyed by the Russian Navy in the Black Sea.

M51. EMPIRE TEGUDA (1945–1946) Tanker

O.N. 180729 670g 404n 1,000d 177.1 × 28.3 × 13.2 feet.
8-cyl. 4SA oil engine by Deutsche Werke A.G., Kiel, Germany.

1938: Completed by Danziger Werke A.G., Danzig (Yard No. 84) for the Deutsche Kriegsmarine as AMRUM. *5.1945:* Taken as a prize by Allied forces at Kiel. *10.1945:* Taken over by the Ministry of War Transport, London (F.T. Everard & Sons Ltd., managers) and renamed EMPIRE TEGUDA. *2.1946:* Handed over to U.S.S.R. and renamed NARGEN. Still in service as a supply vessel at Baku, Azerbaijan (1990).

M52. EMPIRE TIGOON (1945–1946) Tanker

O.N. 180760 674g 252n 186.2 × 29.6 × 13.0 feet.
14-cyl. 2SA oil engine by Gebruder Sulzer A.G., Ludwigshafen, Germany.

8.1942: Completed by Dok & Werf Maatschappij Wilton-Fijenoord N.V., Rotterdam, Holland (Yard No. 686) for the Deutsche Kriegsmarine as STEINGRUND. *5.1945:* Taken as a prize by Allied forces. *1945:* Taken over by the Ministry of War Transport, London (Anglo-Saxon Petroleum Co. Ltd., London, managers) and renamed EMPIRE TIGOON. Later managers became F.T. Everard & Sons Ltd. followed by Anglo-Saxon Petroleum Co. (Eastern) Ltd., London. *6.1946:* Managers became M.T.R., Singapore. *1.1947:* Ship chartered to Oci Koh Trading Co., Singapore. *7.1947:* Sold to the Greek Government, Athens and renamed XANTHI. *1956:* Transferred to Royal Hellenic Navy and renamed VIVIIS (A471). Still in service as a water tanker (1990).

POST WAR MANAGED VESSELS

DAVID DORMAN

J.K. Byass

M53. DAVID DORMAN (1978–1984)

O.N. 366438 664g 394n 943d 57.51 × 10.09 × 3.37 metres.
6-cyl. 4SA oil engine by Mirrlees Blackstone Ltd., Stamford.

6.1978: Completed by Jadewerft (Wilhelmshaven) G.m.b.H., Wilhelmshaven, West Germany (Yard No. 143) for Shamrock Shipping Co. Ltd., Larne (F.T. Everard & Sons Management Ltd., managers). *10.1981:* Company and ship sold to J. Fisher & Sons p.l.c., Barrow-in-Furness, same managers. *8.1984:* Managers became J. & A. Gardner & Co. (Management) Ltd., Glasgow. *11.1988:* Managers became Dennison Shipping Ltd., Kirkwall. *5.1989:* Renamed DEER SOUND. Still in service (1990).

EDGAR DORMAN

J.K. Byass

M54. EDGAR DORMAN (1978–1984)

O.N. 366445 664g 393n 953d 57.51 × 10.09 × 3.37 metres.
6-cyl. 4SA oil engine by Mirrlees Blackstone Ltd., Stamford.

10.1978: Completed by Jadewerft (Wilhelmshaven) G.m.b.H., Wilhelmshaven, West Germany (Yard No. 144) for Shamrock Shipping Co. Ltd., Larne (F.T. Everard & Sons Management Ltd., managers). *10.1981:* Company and ship sold to J. Fisher & Sons p.l.c., Barrow-in-Furness (same managers). *3.1984:* Managers became J. & A. Gardner & Co. (Management) Ltd., Glasgow. *9.1988:* Managers became Dennison Shipping Ltd., Kirkwall. *2.1989:* Renamed BRESSAY SOUND. Still in service (1990).

LIGAR BAY *V. Young*

M55. LIGAR BAY (1979–1985) Twin screw

O.N. 316442 1,297g 400n 1,449d 69.07 × 1.92 × 4.28 metres.
2 × 8-cyl. 4SA oil engines driving electric motors by English Electric Co. Ltd., Newton-le-Willows.

10.1964: Completed by Henry Robb Ltd., Leith (Yard No. 488) as a self discharging bulk cement carrier for Tarakohe Shipping Co. Ltd. (D.O. Whyte, manager), Wellington, New Zealand. *12.1979:* Sold to Blue Circle Industries Ltd., London (F.T. Everard & Sons Management Ltd., managers). *3.1985:* Sold to West Indies Cement Carriers Ltd., Cayman Islands. *1988:* Sold to Seaward Shipping & Dredging Ltd., Cayman Islands (H. & A. Trading Co. Inc., Puerto Rico, managers). Still in service (1990).

NORTHRIDGE *C. Hill*

M56. NORTHRIDGE (1980–1986)

O.N. 357517 1,598g 892n 3,440d 96.45 × 14.13 × 5.19 metres.
8-cyl. 4SA oil engine by Klockner-Humboldt-Deutz A.G., Koln, West Germany.

5.1973: Completed by Martin Jansen Schiffswerft & Maschinenfabrik, Leer, West Germany (Yard No. 101) for William Robertson Shipowners Ltd., Glasgow as CAIRNGORM. *6.1977:* Sold to North Africa Line Ltd. (Comben Longstaff & Co. Ltd., managers), London and renamed NORTHRIDGE. *2.1980:* Managers became F.T. Everard & Sons Management Ltd. *10.1986:* Sold to Fastnet Shipping Co., Limassol, Cyprus (Sea River Line N.V., Essen, Belgium, managers) and renamed FASTNET. *1988:* Sold to Global Marine Lines Inc., Panama and renamed GENESIS I. Still in service (1990).

DURHAMBROOK *J.K. Byass*

M57. DURHAMBROOK (1980)

O.N. 379689 18,042g 11,504n 31,200d 188.75 × 23.14 × 10.6 metres.
4-cyl. 2SA oil engine by Doxford Engines Ltd., Sunderland.

10.1978: Completed by Sunderland Shipbuilders Ltd., North Sands, Sunderland (Yard No. 739) for Gold Fields Mining and Industrial Ltd. (Comben Longstaff & Co. Ltd., managers), London. *11.1979:* Transferred to County Ships Ltd., Hove (same managers). *4.1980:* Transferred to Gold Fields Mining and Industrial Ltd., London (same managers). *4.1980:* Managers became F.T. Everard & Sons Management Ltd. *8.1980:* Sold to Hemisphere Shipping Co. Ltd. (Ocean Tramping Co. Ltd., managers), Hong Kong and renamed HANDYMARINER. *1988:* Sold to Habilma Shipping Corp., Liberia (same managers). Still in service (1990).

DEVONBROOK *Comben Longstaff & Co. Ltd.*

M58. DEVONBROOK (1980–1981)

O.N. 379849 18,042g 11,504n 31,200d 188.75 × 23.14 × 10.6 metres.
4-cyl. 2SA oil engine by Doxford Engines Ltd., Sunderland.

4.1979: Completed by Sunderland Shipbuilders Ltd., North Sands, Sunderland (Yard No. 740) for Consolidated Gold Fields Ltd. (Comben Longstaff & Co. Ltd., managers), London. *4.1980:* Managers became F.T. Everard & Sons Management Ltd. *4.1981:* Sold to Hemisphere Shipping Co. Ltd. (Ocean Tramping Co. Ltd., managers), Hong Kong and renamed APTMARINER. *1984:* Sold to Aptoma Shipping Corp., Liberia (same managers). Still in service (1990).

M59. MERCURIUS/BC MERCURIUS (1980–1988)

O.N. 713059 499g 332n 861d 55.61 × 9.10 × 3.55 metres.
8-cyl. 4SA oil engine by Klockner-Humboldt-Deutz A.G., Koln, West Germany.

1959: Completed by Scheepswerf C. Meyntjens & Zoon, Antwerp, Belgium (Yard No. 333) for Rederij m.s. "Ank T" (Scheepvaart Kantoor J. Tavenier, managers), Zaandam, Holland as ANK T. *1969:* Sold to H. Buitenkamp (N.V. Wijne & Barends, managers), Groningen, Holland and renamed MARITTA JOHANNA. *1972:* Sold to N.V. Johanna Transport & Trading Co., Groningen, Holland (same managers). *1974:* Sold to J.P. de Vries (Wijne & Barends B.V., managers), Zuidlaren, Holland and renamed RIET. *1974:* Sold to B.V. Zand en Grind Exploitatie Maatschappij Holland, Heemstede, Holland, renamed MERCURIUS and converted into a self-discharging bulk cement carrier. *1977:* Owners became Cebo Marine B.V., Heemstede, Holland. *1980:* Sold to Glen Scheepvaart Maatschappij N.V. (N.V. Trias & F.T. Everard & Sons Management Ltd., managers), Rotterdam. *1984:* Re-engined with a 12-cyl. 4SA oil engine made by the Caterpillar Tractor Co., Peoria, Illinois, U.S.A. *1.1988:* Sold to Blue Circle Industries p.l.c., Aldermaston (F.T. Everard & Sons Management Ltd., managers), transferred to British flag and renamed BC MERCURIUS. *22.10.1988:* Vessel arrived in tow of local motor fishing vessel A MHAICHDEAN HEARACH at Uig, Skye after being abandoned by her crew the previous day when a fire broke out in the engine room off Harris while on a ballast passage from Stornoway to Larne. The vessel was considered beyond economical repair and left Uig on *22.11.1988* under tow of the motor tug AFON GOCH 232/67 arriving at Garston *24.11.1988* for breaking up by S. Evans & Sons Ltd., Widnes who commenced work on *5.12.1988*.

BC MERCURIUS *Author's collection*

RIVER DART *C. Hill*

M60. RIVER DART (1981–1985)

O.N. 391006 499g 348n 825d 50.02 × 9.28 × 3.36 metres.
5-cyl. 4SA oil engine by Aabenraa Motorfabrik, H. Callesen A/S, Aabenraa, Denmark.

6.1981: Completed by A/S Nordsovaerftet, Ringkobing, Denmark (Yard No. 148) for General Freight Co. Ltd., London (F.T. Everard & Sons Management Ltd., managers). *7.1985:* Sold to Ensign Express Shipping Ltd., London. Still in service (1990).

RIVER TAMAR C. Hill

M61. RIVER TAMAR (1981–1985)

O.N. 398843 498g 345n 824d 49.97 × 9.28 × 3.36 metres.
5-cyl. 4SA oil engine by Aabenraa Motorfabrik, H. Callesen A/S, Aabenraa, Denmark.

8.1981: Completed by J.W. Cook & Co. (Wivenhoe) Ltd., Wivenhoe (Yard No. 1465) for General Freight Co. Ltd., London (F.T. Everard & Sons Management Ltd., managers). *3.1985:* Sold to Custodian Leasing Ltd., London (Whitbury Shipping Co. Ltd., Rochester, managers). *1986:* Owners became Clientcare Ltd., London (same managers). *11.1990:* Sold to Ramsey Steamship Co. Ltd., Douglas, Isle of Man and renamed BEN ELLAN. Still in service (1990).

SHAMROCK ENTERPRISE C. Hill

M62. SHAMROCK ENTERPRISE (1982–1986)

O.N. 387685 995g 652n 1,694d 69.30 × 11.10 × 4.29 metres.
8-cyl. 4SA 'V' oil engine by B. & W. Alpha Diesel A/S, Frederikshavn, Denmark.

4.1982: Completed by Scheepswerf Bodewes Gruno B.V., Foxhol, Holland (Yard No. 252) for Lazard Leasing Services Ltd., London and leased to Shamrock Shipping Co. Ltd., Larne (a subsidiary company of J. Fisher & Sons p.l.c., Barrow-in-Furness) (F.T. Everard & Sons Management Ltd., managers). *6.1986:* Managers became Coe Metcalf Shipping Ltd., Liverpool. *6.1990:* Renamed SILVERTHORN. Still in service (1990).

SHAMROCK ENDEAVOUR *C. Hill*

M63. SHAMROCK ENDEAVOUR (1982–1986)

O.N. 387866 995g 652n 1,694d 69.30 × 11.10 × 4.30 metres.
8-cyl. 4SA 'V' oil engine by B. & W. Alpha Diesel A/S, Frederikshavn, Denmark.

5.1982: Completed by Scheepswerf Gebroeder Coops B.V., Hoogezand, Holland (Yard No. 283) for Lloyds Industrial Leasing Ltd., London and leased to Shamrock Shipping Co. Ltd., Larne (a subsidiary company of J. Fisher & Sons p.l.c., Barrow-in-Furness) (F.T. Everard & Sons Management Ltd., managers). *3.1986:* Managers became Coe Metcalf Shipping Ltd., Liverpool. *7.1990:* Renamed ROSETHORN. Still in service (1990).

DORIS I *Author's collection*

M64. DORIS I (1982–1990) Tanker

668g 303n 877d 64.78 × 9.91 × 3.45 metres.
6-cyl. 4SA oil engine by Maschinenbau Kiel G.m.b.H., Kiel, West Germany.

4.1964: Completed by Norderwerft Koser & Meyer, Hamburg, West Germany (Yard No. 854) for Schiffahrts & Speditionskontor 'Elbe' G.m.b.H., Hamburg, West Germany as DORIS. *1981:* Sold to Salvatore Compania Naviera S.A., Panama (Seaspan Manning & Technical Services Ltd., Longfield, managers) and renamed DORIS 1. *3.1982:* Managers became Glen Salvesen Ltd., Greenhithe. *10.1990:* Managers became Haggerstone Marine Ltd., Romford. Still in service (1990).

FARNESE — *Author's collection*

M65. FARNESE (1983–)

O.N. 700677 992g 616n 1,470d 80.02 × 9.02 × 3.20 metres.
8-cyl. 4SA oil engine by V.E.B. Schwermaschinenbau Karl Liebknecht, Magdeburg, East Germany.

12.1975: Completed by Schiffswerft Gebruder Schloemer, Oldersum, West Germany (Yard No. 231) for Bereederungsgesellschaft m.b.H., m.s. "Cargoliner III" K.G. (G. Wessels, manager), Berlin, West Germany as CARGOLINER III. *1981:* Sold to DAL Drittvertrieb-Vermietungs G.m.b.H., Mainz, West Germany (same manager) and renamed AMY. *1982:* Sold to Bulk Freighters Ltd., Jersey and converted to a self discharging bulk cement carrier. *1983:* Renamed FARNESE. *1983:* Company and ship acquired by Blue Circle Industries p.l.c., London (F.T. Everard & Sons Management Ltd., managers). *1988:* Re-registered in London. Still in service (1990).

ROCQUAINE — *C. Hill*

M66. ROCQUAINE (1983–1986)

O.N. 377823 985g 641n 1,559d 66.91 × 10.77 × 4.12 metres.
8-cyl. 4SA oil engine by Mirrlees Blackstone Ltd., Stamford.

12.1977: Completed by J.W. Cook & Co. (Wivenhoe) Ltd., Wivenhoe (Yard No. 1455) for Rocquaine Shipping Co. Ltd. (Onesimus Dorey [Shipowners] Ltd., managers), Guernsey. *4.1983:* Company and ship acquired by J. Fisher & Sons p.l.c., Barrow-in-Furness. *4.1983:* Managers became F.T. Everard & Sons Management Ltd. *1984:* Owner became J. Fisher & Sons p.l.c., Barrow-in-Furness. *5.1986:* Managers became S.R.B. International, Belfast. *7.1986:* Re-registered in Nassau, Bahamas. *1988:* Owner became Rocquaine Shipping Co. Ltd. Still in service (1990).

BELGRAVE *C. Hill*

M67. BELGRAVE (1983–1986)

O.N. 379000 985g 641n 1,559d 66.91 × 10.77 × 4.12 metres.
8-cyl. 4SA oil engine by Mirrlees Blackstone Ltd., Stamford.

4.1978: Completed by J.W. Cook & Co. (Wivenhoe) Ltd., Wivenhoe (Yard No. 1456) for Onesimus Dorey (Shipowners) Ltd., Guernsey. *4.1983:* Company and ship acquired by J. Fisher & Sons p.l.c., Barrow-in-Furness. *4.1983:* Managers became F.T. Everard & Sons Management Ltd. *1985:* Owner became J. Fisher & Sons p.l.c., Barrow-in-Furness (same managers). *1.1986:* Chartered to Spray Shipping Corp., Panama (Alexanders Partners [Shipbroking] Ltd., London, managers). *6.1986:* Re-registered in Nassau, Bahamas. Still in service (1990).

PERELLE *C. Hill*

M68. PERELLE (1983–1986)

O.N. 386923 985g 641n 1,559d 66.91 × 10.77 × 4.12 metres.
8-cyl. 4SA oil engine by Mirrlees Blackstone Ltd., Stamford.

1.1979: Completed by J.W. Cook & Co. (Wivenhoe) Ltd., Wivenhoe (Yard No. 1458) for Onesimus Dorey (1972) Ltd., Guernsey. *4.1983:* Company and ship sold to by J. Fisher & Sons p.l.c., Barrow-in-Furness. *4.1983:* Managers became F.T. Everard & Sons Management Ltd. *1985:* Owner became J. Fisher & Sons p.l.c., Barrow-in-Furness (same managers). *1.1986:* Chartered to Sun Shipping Corp., Panama (Alexanders Partners [Shipbroking] Ltd., London, managers). *7.1986:* Re-registered in Nassau, Bahamas. Still in service (1990).

WILLONIA

C. Hill

M69. WILLONIA (1984–1986)

For details see under ship No. 233 **WILLONIA/SANGUITY (2)**.

GWYN

Company archives

M70. GWYN (1985) Twin screw

O.N. 390492 794g 552n 1,397d 58.27 × 9.40 × 3.89 metres.
2 × 6-cyl. 4SA oil engines by Cummins Engine Co. Inc., Columbus, Indiana, U.S.A.

7.1985: Completed by Yorkshire Dry Dock Co. Ltd., Hull (Yard No. 290) for Graig Shipping Co. Ltd., Cardiff (F.T. Everard & Sons Management Ltd., managers). *3.11.1985:* Sank two miles north east of Borkum Riff Light Vessel in position 53.45N, 06.08E while on passage from Hamburg to Seaham with a cargo of steel. All crew rescued by the motor vessel HOOP 460/57. *23.9.1986:* Raised, subsequently declared a constructive total loss and sold to Heuvelman & Jansen Beheer B.V., Krimpen aan-den-Ijssel, Holland. *4.1988:* Sold to D.W. den Herder Scheepvaartbedrijf, Yerseke, Holland. Rebuilt as a trailing suction dredger and re-engined with two 6-cyl. 4SA oil engines made by A/B Volvo Penta, Gothenburg, Sweden and renamed HENDRIKA. Still in service (1990).

WILKS

C. Hill

M71. WILKS (1985–1986) Twin screw

O.N. 366101 495g 310n 1,002d 44.10 × 9.96 × 3.90 metres.
2 × 6-cyl. 4SA oil engines by Caterpillar Tractor Co., Peoria, Illinois, U.S.A.

4.1976: Completed by Yorkshire Dry Dock Co. Ltd., Hull (Yard No. 238) for Eggar Forrester (Holdings) Ltd., London (R. Lapthorn & Co. Ltd., Rochester, managers). *2.1985:* Managers became Wilks Shipping Co. Ltd., London. *10.1985:* Managers became F.T. Everard & Sons Management Ltd. *6.1986:* Sold to J. Harker Ltd., Hull, renamed TEESDALE H. and converted into a tanker. Still in service (1990).

WIS

C. Hill

M72. WIS (1985–1986) Twin screw

O.N. 377191 491g 408n 1,036d 45.93 × 9.96 × 3.88 metres.
2 × 6-cyl. 4SA oil engines by Caterpillar Tractor Co., Peoria, Illinois, U.S.A.

1.1977: Completed by Yorkshire Dry Dock Co. Ltd., Hull (Yard No. 241) for Eggar Forrester (Holdings) Ltd., London (R. Lapthorn & Co. Ltd., Rochester, managers). *2.1985:* Managers became Wilks Shipping Co. Ltd., London. *10.1985:* Managers became F.T. Everard & Sons Management Ltd. *6.1986:* Sold to Breydon Marine Ltd., Great Yarmouth and renamed BREYDON VENTURE. *4.1989:* Re-engined with two 6-cyl. 4SA oil engines made by A/B Volvo Penta, Gothenburg, Sweden. Still in service (1990).

WIB

C. Hill

M73. WIB (1985–1986) Twin screw

O.N. 379856 498g 320n 1,046d 45.73 × 9.50 × 3.88 metres.
2 × 8-cyl. 4SA oil engines by Caterpillar Tractor Co., Peoria, Illinois, U.S.A.

2.1979: Completed by Yorkshire Dry Dock Co. Ltd., Hull (Yard No. 257) for Eggar Forrester (Holdings) Ltd., London (R. Lapthorn & Co. Ltd., Rochester, managers). *2.1985:* Managers became Wilks Shipping Co. Ltd., London. *10.1985:* Managers became F.T. Everard & Sons Management Ltd. *6.1986:* Sold to Breydon Marine Ltd., Great Yarmouth. *3.1987:* Renamed BREYDON ENTERPRISE. Still in service (1990).

LU

C. Hill

M74. LU (1985–1988) Twin screw

O.N. 390744 497g 384n 1,140d 45.55 × 9.50 × 4.03 metres.
2 × 8-cyl. 4SA oil engines by Caterpillar Tractor Co., Peoria, Illinois, U.S.A.

12.1980: Completed by A/S Nordsovaerftet, Ringkobing, Denmark (Yard No. 144) for Eggar Forrester (Holdings) Ltd., London (R. Lapthorn & Co. Ltd., Rochester, managers). *2.1985:* Managers became Wilks Shipping Co. Ltd., London. *10.1085:* Managers became F.T. Everard & Sons Management Ltd. *6.1988:* Sold to Atlantic Conbulk Maritime Corp., Monrovia, Liberia, bareboat chartered to Atlantska Plovidba, Dubrovnik, Jugoslavia and renamed BOBARA. Still in service (1990).

WIGGS *C. Hill*

M75. WIGGS (1985–1988) Twin Screw

O.N. 390745 497g 384n 1,140d 45.55 × 9.50 × 4.03 metres.
2 × 8-cyl. 4SA oil engines by Caterpillar Tractor Co., Peoria, Illinois, U.S.A.

1.1981: Completed by A/S Nordsovaerftet, Ringkobing, Denmark (Yard No. 145) for Eggar Forrester (Holdings) Ltd., London (R. Lapthorn & Co. Ltd., Rochester, managers). *2.1985:* Managers became Wilks Shipping Co. Ltd., London. *10.1985:* Managers became F.T. Everard & Sons Management Ltd. *6.1988:* Sold to Atlantic Conbulk Maritime Corp., Monrovia, Liberia, bareboat chartered to Atlantska Plovidba, Dubrovnik, Jugoslavia and renamed DOLI. Still in service (1990).

WIRIS *C. Hill*

M76. WIRIS (1985–1988) Twin screw

O.N. 398974 496g 384n 1,140d 45.55 × 9.50 × 4.05 metres.
2 × 8-cyl. 4SA oil engines by Caterpillar Tractor Co., Peoria, Illinois, U.S.A.

3.1982: Completed by A/S Nordsovaerftet, Ringkobing, Denmark (Yard No. 153) for Eggar Forrester (Holdings) Ltd., London (R. Lapthorn & Co. Ltd., Rochester, managers). *2.1985:* Managers became Wilks Shipping Co. Ltd., London. *10.1985:* Managers became F.T. Everard & Sons Management Ltd. *6.1988:* Sold to Atlantic Conbulk Maritime Corp., Monrovia, Liberia, bareboat chartered to Atlantska Plovidba, Dubrovnik, Jugoslavia and renamed ORASAC. Still in service (1990).

STEVONIA *C. Hill*

M77. STEVONIA (1986)

For details see under ship No. 234
STEVONIA/SOCIALITY (2).

LIZZONIA with original pale blue hull. *C. Hill*

M78. LIZZONIA (1986)

For details see under ship No. 231
LIZZONIA/CAPACITY (3).

ANGELONIA with later black hull. *C. Hill*

M79. ANGELONIA (1986)

For details see under ship No. 232
ANGELONIA/COMITY (2).

COTINGA *C. Hill*

M80. COTINGA (1986–)

O.N. 366301 1,599g 1,187n 3,089d 83.52 × 14.13 × 5.19 metres.
8-cyl. 4SA oil engine by MaK. Maschinenbau G.m.b.H., Kiel, West Germany.

11.1976: Completed by Scheepswerven Bodewes B.V., Martenshoek, Holland (Yard No. 528) for Hadley Shipping Co. Ltd. (Warwick & Esplen Ltd., managers), London. *4.1986:* Managers became F.T. Everard & Sons Management Ltd. Still in service (1990).

CHARLES CRUZ

Company archives

M81. CHARLES CRUZ (1986–1989)

O.N. 364682 499g 333n 1,397d 75.70 × 11.00 × 3.58 metres.
8-cyl. 4SA oil engine by Motorenwerke Mannheim A.G., Mannheim, West Germany.

1969: Completed by Scheepswerf 'Hoogezand' J. Bodewes, Bergum, Holland (Yard No. 154) for Johannes Bos, Hamburg, West Germany as BELL VISION. *1971:* Sold to Partenreederei m.s. 'Christina Bos' (Johannes Bos, manager), Hamburg, West Germany and renamed CHRISTINA BOS. *1972:* Sold to Peter Dohle Schiffahrts K.G., Hamburg, West Germany and renamed CHRISTINA I. *1974:* Sold to Dr. Ing. T. Hinckeldey, Hamburg, West Germany and renamed SUFFOLK. *1976:* Sold to Windle Shipping Co. Ltd. (Uiterwyk Corp., managers), Liverpool and renamed WINDLE STAR. *1980:* Sold to Brora Shipping Co. Ltd. (The Hybury Co. Ltd., managers), London and renamed BRORA. *1982:* Owners became the Hybury Co. Ltd., London. *8.1982:* Sold to P.L. Harding & A.R. Reid (The Hybury Co. Ltd., managers), London and renamed CHARLES CRUZ. *11.1985:* Owner became J.E. Hyde Shipowners Ltd., London (same managers). *4.1986:* Managers became F.T. Everard & Sons Management Ltd. *4.1989:* Sold to Pegasus Air & Sea Services Ltd., Gibraltar (same managers). *8.1989:* Sold to Shipping Anglo Marocaine (SHIAMA), Casablanca, Morocco and renamed TARIK. Still in service (1990).

RIVER TRADER

Company archives

M82. RIVER TRADER (1989–)

O.N. 717276 1,223g 874n 2,607d 88.47 × 12.20 × 4.05 metres.
6-cyl. 4SA oil engine by Anglo-Belgian Corp. N.V., Ghent, Belgium.

5.1982: Completed by N.V. Scheepswerf van Rupelmonde, Rupelmonde, Belgium (Yard No. 446) for Sea River Line N.V., Essen, Belgium as RIVER TRADER. *6.1989:* Sold to Upstream Navigation Co. Ltd. (Marlow Navigation Co. Ltd., managers), Limassol, Cyprus. *7.1989:* Acquired by Short Sea Europe p.l.c., London (F.T. Everard & Sons Management Ltd., managers). *5.1990:* Tonnages became 1,220g, 787n and 2,607d. Still in service (1990).

LADY PATRICIA C. Hill

M83. LADY PATRICIA (1990–)

O.N. 708388 1,547g 791n 2,538d 80.75 × 11.33 × 5.31M
6-cyl. 4SA oil engine by Motorenwerke Mannheim A.G., Mannheim, West Germany.

12.1970: Completed by Angyalfold Shipyard, Hungarian Ship and Crane Works, Budapest, Hungary (Yard No. 2222) for K.G. Lubischer Seetransport G.m.b.H. & Co. (Otto A. Muller, manager), Lubeck, West Germany as DIABAS (original tonnages 1,399g, 675n, 2,306d and length 74.83m). *1972:* Transferred to Singapore flag. *1974:* Sold to Dolomit Hamburger Seereederei G.m.b.H., Singapore (same manager). *11.1975:* Lengthened at Bremerhaven, tonnages and dimensions becoming those shown in line 1. *1977:* Sold to Diabas K.G. Lubische Seetransport G.m.b.H. & Co., Singapore (same manager). *1978:* Sold to m.s. Diabas Dolomit Hamburger Seereederei G.m.b.H., Singapore (same manager). *1983:* Sold to Sailfast Shipping (Pte.) Ltd., Singapore and renamed ORCHID WAVE. *4.1985:* Sold to Thomas Watson (Shipping) Ltd., Rochester, registered in Gibraltar and renamed LADY PATRICIA. *4.1987:* Sold to Lakehead Shipping Ltd., Gibraltar (Thomas Watson (Shipping) Ltd., Rochester, managers) and registered in the Bahamas. *7.1990:* Chartering managers became F.T. Everard & Sons Management Ltd. Still in service (1990).

M84. SHORT SEA TRADER

3,100d 99.9 × 12.60 × 4.20m
8-cyl. 4SA oil engine by Alpha Diesel A/S, Frederikshavn, Denmark.

1.1990: Ordered from Cochrane Shipbuilders Ltd., Selby (Yard No. 168) by Short Sea Europe p.l.c., London (F.T. Everard & Sons Ltd., managers) for delivery in *7.1991.*

M85. NORTH SEA TRADER

3,100d 99.99 × 12.60 × 4.20m
8-cyl. 4SA oil engine by Alpha Diesel A/S, Frederikshavn, Denmark.

5.1990: Ordered from Cochrane Shipbuilders Ltd., Selby (Yard No. 170) by Short Sea Europe p.l.c., London (F.T. Everard & Sons Ltd., managers) for delivery in *9.1991.*

TUGS AND SERVICE CRAFT

CO-OPERATOR

T. McLaren

T1. CO-OPERATOR (1919–1940) Tug/tender

O.N. 133430 60g 41n 74.2 × 15.0 × 6.2 feet.
4-cyl. 4SA petrol/paraffin motor by J.I. Thornycroft & Co. Ltd., Southampton.

1913: Completed by W.H. Warren, New Holland (Yard No. 109) for the Lincoln Equitable Co-operative Industrial Society Ltd., Lincoln. *1915:* Sold to Vickers Ltd.(T.K. North, manager), London. *1919:* Acquired by F.T. Everard. *1940:* Sold to Arthur Rutland, Gravesend. *1985:* Sold for use as a houseboat.

STONEBOW

V. Allen

T2. STONEBOW (1919–1953) Tug/tender

O.N. 136716 57g 39n 72.0 × 14.9 × 6.6 feet.
2-cyl. 2SA oil engine by Robey & Co. Ltd., Lincoln.

1913: Completed by J.S. Watson Ltd., Beckingham Yard, Gainsborough for the East Anglian Navigation Co. Ltd. (T. Johnson, manager), Sleaford. *10.1915:* Sold to Vickers Ltd. (T.K. North, manager), London. *5.1919:* Acquired by F.T. Everard. *1924:* Re-engined with a 2-cyl. 2SA oil engine made by Plenty & Son Ltd., Newbury. *12.1953:* Vessel broken up at Greenhithe by the owner.

T3. FAVEROLLE (1921–1938) Tug

O.N. 144564 67g 10n 75.0 × 15.1 × 7.4 feet.
C.2-cyl. steam engine by T. & J. Hosking Ltd., Bermondsey.

1919: Completed by Henry Scarr Ltd., Hessle for the Admiralty, London as BANTAM. Later renamed FAVEROLLE. *21.2.1921:* Acquired by F.T. Everard. *1.1938:* Vessel broken up at Greenhithe by the owner.

Steam tugs bunkering at Greenhithe.

Company archives

T4. FRED EVERARD (1)/F.T. EVERARD (1) (1921–1928) Tug

O.N. 145218 56g 13n 63.1 × 16.2 × 7.3 feet.
T.3-cyl. steam engine by Bolnes B.V., Krimpen aan-de-Lek, Holland.

1916: Completed by H. Paans, Roodvaart, Holland for The Shipping Controller, London. *5.1921:* Acquired by F.T. Everard and renamed FRED EVERARD. *9.1926:* Renamed F.T. EVERARD. *8.1928:* Vessel broken up at Greenhithe by the owner.

F.T. EVERARD (2)

P. Thomas

T5. F.T. EVERARD (2) (1928–1951) Tug

O.N. 160596 124g 83.0 × 21.6 × 11.0 feet.
T.3-cyl. steam engine by Plenty & Son Ltd., Newbury.

1928: Completed by Fellows & Co. Ltd., Great Yarmouth (Yard No. 321) for the company. *1951:* Sold to Fowey Tug Co. Ltd., Fowey and renamed TOLBENNY. *1965:* Sold to W.J. Reynolds Ltd., Plymouth and renamed TACTFUL. *1980:* Sold to Davis & Camm Ltd. for breaking up at Plymouth.

T6. FRANK PINK (1930–1948) Coaling barge

O.N. 147995 139g 95n 106.6 × 21.0 × 7.3 feet.
2-cyl. 2SA oil engine by J.V. Svenson, Augustendal, Sweden.

1915: Completed by Short Bros. Ltd., Sunderland for the Admiralty, London as dry cargo lighter X71. *9.1922:* Sold to Thomas Ensor & Son. *11.1924:* Sold to Pirbright Co. Ltd., London and renamed FRANK PINK. *1.1930:* Acquired by the company. *1948:* Sold to T.W. Ward Ltd. for breaking up at Grays.

S.A. EVERARD *T. Rayner*

T7. S.A. EVERARD (1939–1990) Tug

O.N. 167348 124g 84.0 × 21.6 × 10.0 feet.
8-cyl. 2SA 'L' type oil engine by the Newbury Diesel Co. Ltd., Newbury.

11.1939: Completed by Fellows & Co. Ltd., Great Yarmouth (Yard No. 342) for the company. *1976:* Re-engined with a 8-cyl. 4SA oil engine made by Lister Blackstone Ltd., Stamford. *3.1990:* Sold to H.C.H. Services Ltd., Greenhithe and renamed HAZEL E. Still in service (1990).

T8. JOKER (1) (1939–1942) Launch/tug

Unregistered 45.0 × 10.5 × 3.7 feet.
4-cyl. 4SA petrol/paraffin 'Kelvin' engine by Bergius Co. Ltd., Glasgow.

1932: Completed by T. van Duivendijk's Scheepswerf N.V., Lekkerkerk, Holland for Greenhithe Lighterage Co. Ltd., Greenhithe as TATTOO. *1935:* Re-engined with a 4-cyl. 2SA oil engine made by the Atlantic Engine Co. (1920) Ltd., Wishaw. *1939:* Acquired by the company and renamed JOKER. *5.1942:* Requisitioned by the Admiralty. *16.7.1942:* Lost in heavy weather south of Bolt Head while in tow of the salvage tug CAROLINE MOLLER 444/19.

T9. JOKER (2)/JESTER (2) (1944–1963) Launch/tug

Un-registered 12g 40.8 × 10.9 × 3.3 feet.
4-cyl. 4SA 'C' type oil engine by the Newbury Diesel Co. Ltd., Newbury.

1944: Completed by Fellows & Co. Ltd., Great Yarmouth (Yard No. No. 346) for the company as JOKER. *1949:* Renamed JESTER. *1963:* Engine removed and hull broken up at Greenhithe by the owner.

JOKER (3)

Author

T10. JESTER (1)/JOKER (3) (1947–1990) Launch/tug

Un-registered 12g 40.8 × 11.0 × 3.6 feet.
4-cyl. 4SA 'C' type oil engine by the Newbury Diesel Co. Ltd., Newbury.

1947: Completed by Fellows & Co. Ltd., Great Yarmouth (Yard No. 358) for the company as JESTER. *1949:* Renamed JOKER. *1977:* Re-engined with a 6-cyl. 4SA oil engine made by Dorman Diesels Ltd., Stafford. *1983:* Leased to South Thames Shiprepairers Ltd., Greenhithe. *1985:* Reverted to F.T. Everard & Sons Ltd. *3.1990:* Sold to H.C.H. Services Ltd., Greenhithe. Still in service (1990).

E.A. EVERARD

Company archives

T11. E.A. EVERARD (1948–1965) Tug

O.N. 169275 54g 65.0 × 17.0 × 7.4 feet.
C.2-cyl. steam engine by J. Dickinson & Son Ltd., Sunderland.

5.1943: Completed by R. Dunston (Thorne) Ltd., Thorne (Yard No. T403) for the Ministry of War Transport, London as TID 5. *4.1946:* Owner became the Ministry of Transport, London. *9.1948:* Acquired by the company and renamed E.A. EVERARD. *1950:* Re-engined with a 6-cyl. 2SA 'G' type oil engine made by the Newbury Diesel Co. Ltd., Newbury. *1952:* Re-engined with a 4-cyl. 2SA 'G' type oil engine made by the Newbury Diesel Co. Ltd., Newbury. *1965:* Taken out of service and engine removed. *6.1971:* Hull sold to L. Todd for breaking up at Greenhithe.

P.B. EVERARD (1) *W.S.P.L.*

T12. P.B. EVERARD (1) (1955–1969) Tug

O.N. 169364 54g 65.0 × 17.0 × 7.4 feet.
C.2-cyl steam engine by North Eastern Marine Engineering Co. (1938) Ltd., Sunderland.

2.1944: Completed by R. Dunston (Thorne) Ltd., Thorne (Yard No. T473) for the Ministry of War Transport, London as TID 64. *4.1946:* Owner became the Ministry of Transport, London. *5.1946:* Sold to French owners and renamed CLAUDE. *8.1955:* Acquired by the company and renamed P.B. EVERARD. *1969:* Sold to Stour Salvage Ltd. for breaking up at Harwich.

STRIKER *J. Hines*

T13. STRIKER (1956–1964) Twin screw tender

Un-registered 112.0 × 25.0 × 6.7 feet.
2 × T.3-cyl. steam engines by the shipbuilder.

10.1933: Completed by J. Samuel White & Co. Ltd., Cowes for the Admiralty, London as the R.N. Torpedo School tender REDWING. *11.1956:* Acquired by the company and renamed STRIKER. *12.1964:* Sold to A.E. Peirce for breaking up at Canvey Island. Resold to Brugse Scheepsloperij for breaking up at Bruges, Belgium where she arrived during *1.1965.*

T14. SPINNAKER (1957–1985) Launch/tug

O.N. 187542 37g 58.5 × 14.3 × 6.3 feet.
6-cyl. 4SA oil engine by Crossley Brothers Ltd., Manchester.

1949: Completed by Clelands (Successors) Ltd., Wallsend (Yard No. 140) for the Burmah Oil Co. (Burmah Trading) Ltd., London as B.O.C. 39. *1.1957:* Acquired by the company and renamed SPINNAKER. *1959:* Re-engined with a 6-cyl. 4SA 'C' type oil engine made by the Newbury Diesel Co. Ltd., Newbury. *1983:* Leased to South Thames Ship Repairers Ltd., Greenhithe. *1985:* Sold to J. Marsh & Sons Ltd., Greenhithe. Still in service (1990).

SPINNAKER

Author

T15. SPANKER (1957–1985) Launch/tug

O.N. 187543 37g 58.5 × 14.3 × 6.3 feet.
6-cyl. 4SA oil engine by Crossley Brothers Ltd., Manchester.

1949: Completed by Clelands (Successors) Ltd., Wallsend (Yard No. 141) for the Burmah Oil Co. (Burmah Trading) Ltd., London as B.O.C. 40. *1.1957:* Acquired by the company and renamed SPANKER. *1960:* Re-engined with a 6-cyl. 4SA 'C' type oil engine made by the Newbury Diesel Co. Ltd., Newbury. *1973:* Re-engined with a 6-cyl. 4SA oil engine made by Dorman Diesels Ltd., Stafford. *1983:* Leased to South Thames Ship Repairers Ltd., Greenhithe. *1985:* Sold to J. Marsh & Sons Ltd., Greenhithe. Still in service (1990).

STALKER

W.S.P.L.

T16. STALKER (1957–1970) Launch/tug

O.N. 301234 37g 58.5 × 14.3 × 6.3 feet.
6-cyl. 4SA oil engine by Crossley Brothers Ltd., Manchester.

1949: Completed by Clelands (Successors) Ltd., Wallsend (Yard No. 142) for the Burmah Oil Co. (Burmah Trading) Ltd., London as B.O.C. 41. *1.1957:* Acquired by Fellows & Co. Ltd., Great Yarmouth and renamed STALKER. *1970:* Sold to J.T. Palmer & Sons, Gravesend. *1972:* Sold to A.M. & R.C. Dinwoodie, Granton. *1984:* Sold to R. Lyons, Glasgow. *1985:* Sold to McConnell Salmon Ltd., Clydebank. Still in service (1990).

R.A. EVERARD *Company archives*

T17. R.A. EVERARD (1961–1990) Tug

O.N. 168410 88g 71.2 × 20.5 × 10.6 feet.
T.3-cyl. steam engine by Plenty & Co. Ltd., Newbury.

3.1943: Completed by R. Dunston (Thorne) Ltd., Thorne (Yard No. T377) for the River Lighterage Co. Ltd., London as PINKLAKE. *1960:* Sold to W.E. White & Sons (Towage) Ltd., London. *1961:* Acquired by the company and renamed R.A. EVERARD. *1962:* Re-engined with a 7-cyl. 2SA 'L' type oil engine made by the Newbury Diesel Co. Ltd., Newbury. *1975:* Re-engined with an 8-cyl. 4SA oil engine made by Lister Blackstone Ltd., Stafford. *3.1990:* Sold to H.C.H. Services Ltd., Greenhithe and renamed CAROLE H. Still in service (1990).

JESTER (3) and JOKER (3) *Author*

T18. JESTER (3) (1963–1985) Launch/tug

Un-registered 12g 40.7 × 11.0 × 3.6 feet.
4-cyl. 4SA 'C' type oil engine by the Newbury Diesel Co. Ltd., Newbury.

1963: Completed by F.T. Everard & Sons Ltd., Greenhithe for their own account. *1974:* Re-engined with a 6-cyl. 4SA oil engine made by Dorman Diesels Ltd., Stafford. *1985:* Sold to M. Imms for breaking up at Shepperton.

P.B. EVERARD (2) *M. Gaston*

T19. P.B. EVERARD (2) (1970–1981) Tug

O.N. 184562 74g 70.7 × 18.1 × 7.3 feet.
6-cyl. 2SA oil engine by British Polar Engines Ltd., Glasgow.

1952: Completed by Cochrane & Sons Ltd., Selby (Yard No. 1374) for Charrington, Gardner & Locket (London) Ltd., London as MARGARET LOCKET. She had been launched as MARGARET. *1970:* Acquired by the company and renamed P.B. EVERARD. *1981:* Sold to W.G.S. Crouch & Sons Ltd., Greenhithe and renamed JAYNE SPEARING. *1984:* Sold to Riverway Development Co. Ltd., London. *1988:* Sold to J.G. Jakubait & Sons, London. Still in existence (1990).

CAPABLE (2) *Author*

T20. CAPABLE (2) (1973–1985) Tug

O.N. 337014 52.8 × 15.0 × 8.1 feet.
8-cyl. 4SA 'V' oil engine by Rolls Royce Motors Ltd., Shrewsbury.

3.1968: Completed by J.W. Cook (Wivenhoe) Ltd., Wivenhoe (Yard No. 1359) for the Port of London Authority, London as PLATONIC. *1973:* Acquired by the company and renamed CAPABLE. Re-engine and conversion work commenced but not completed. *1985:* Sold to L. Tester, Faversham. *1987:* Sold to M. Street, Gravesend. Still in existence (1990).

FUNNEL MARKS AND HOUSEFLAGS

No documentary evidence appears to have survived concerning the adoption of the red and white funnel mark and houseflag. Its inspiration appears to have been the painted shutters to be seen on houses in Holland and one of its virtues is that it is reversible and thus the same viewed from either side.

Photographic evidence suggests that it was in use shortly after the First World War, certainly by the time the limited company was formed in 1922; indeed, it might have been the formation of the company that prompted the adoption of the houseflag. The 1906 photograph of the launch of the sailing barge CAMBRIA shows no such design amongst the decoration on her bowboards, nor does her sister HIBERNIA in an early photograph. Such photographs as exist of the early steamers purchased during the First World War show them in what was probably the livery of their previous owners.

However, both funnel mark and houseflag are well in evidence in the launch and trials photographs of the second GRIT in 1923. Other small motor vessels – PAMELA HOPE and CAPABLE – also carried the funnel mark in the early twenties.

Over the years the proportions of the houseflag seem to have remained fairly constant at 2 to 1. The funnel mark, however, has varied considerably; in some cases to fit particular funnels. In the early days it appears as an uninterrupted band of red and white diagonal quarterings but by the mid-thirties new ships had a smaller and separate mark on each side of the funnel.

A comprehensive description of the vagaries of each ship's colour schemes would fill a book in itself and these notes should only be taken as a general guide. Any intending modelmaker is advised to obtain good photographs of the ship taken during the chosen period to get the scheme right.

Before the Second World War the ships had black hulls with brown or buff superstructures. After the wartime grey the ships returned to their black hulls with red boot topping and white superstructures. From about 1950 the new dry cargo ships of the larger type were painted yellow with green boot topping but this reverted to red after only a few years. Originally the yellow was quite bright but has been toned down and is now officially described as cream. At about the same time the tankers adopted a grey hull colour although some of the old ships either did not change or else soon reverted to black.

In general, yellow and grey ships have yellow funnels and black ships have black funnels. There have been exceptions of course and while at least one black tanker had a yellow funnel, some grey tankers had black funnels. The blue hulls of the newer Comben Longstaff vessels were retained and the mark on their black funnels was changed about a year after the purchase. The former Wharton ships retained their black hulls but they too had their funnel marks changed.

One noteworthy variation from the normal colour schemes was that of the ships attending the 1935, 1937 and 1953 Spithead Reviews, ANGULARITY, SUAVITY and SINGULARITY, which were all painted white for the occasion. The FRED EVERARD, attending the 1977 Review, retained the contemporary company colour scheme.

After the page of representative Everard funnels comes a page of the funnels and houseflags of companies purchased by Everards or jointly owned as in the case of the West River Shipping Co. Ltd. Here the normal Everard mark had a green letter 'T' superimposed to represent the Tunnel Portland Cement Co. Ltd., the other partner in the company. This funnel mark and flag was only carried by the vessels GUARDIAN CARRIER and WESTPORT. The funnel marks of Martin's Coastal Steamships Ltd., Thun Tankers Ltd. and Comben Longstaff & Co. Ltd. were changed soon after those companies were purchased but, whereas the names of the ships belonging to the first two were changed to Everard names, the former Longstaff ships retained their 'brook' names. The tall steamship funnels of the ships purchased with J. Hay & Sons Ltd. retained their distinctive colours until sold. The ALFRED EVERARD came into service with the pink and black funnel but this was soon changed and other ships coming into the titular ownership of J. Hay & Sons Ltd. also had Everard funnels. Similarly the former Glen ships retained their striking red and black funnels but curiously they had a small Everard flag painted at the bottom of the black band. The Glen funnel colours have not been used since the sale of the original ships.

Finally there is a page of the funnel marks of the various companies for whom Everards have managed ships. The plain grey funnel of the wartime Empire ships has been omitted. Short Sea Europe plc is also not represented because the company has not adopted a funnel mark. The funnel of the company's first ship, RIVER TRADER, is an insignificant structure not suitable for any identifying embellishment. Neither will the newbuildings from Selby have funnel marks but in their case the company name will be displayed on the poop bulwarks.

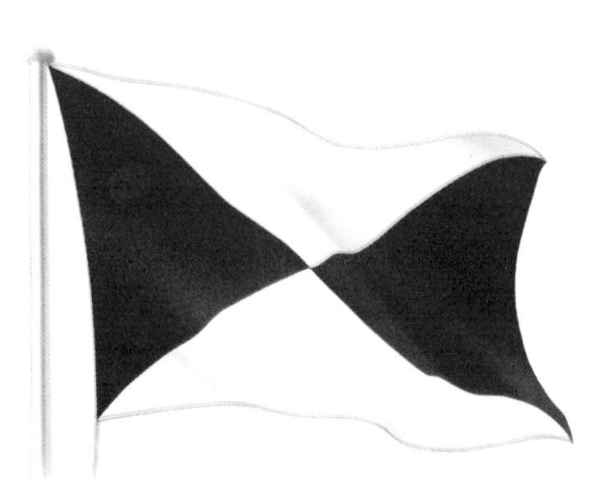

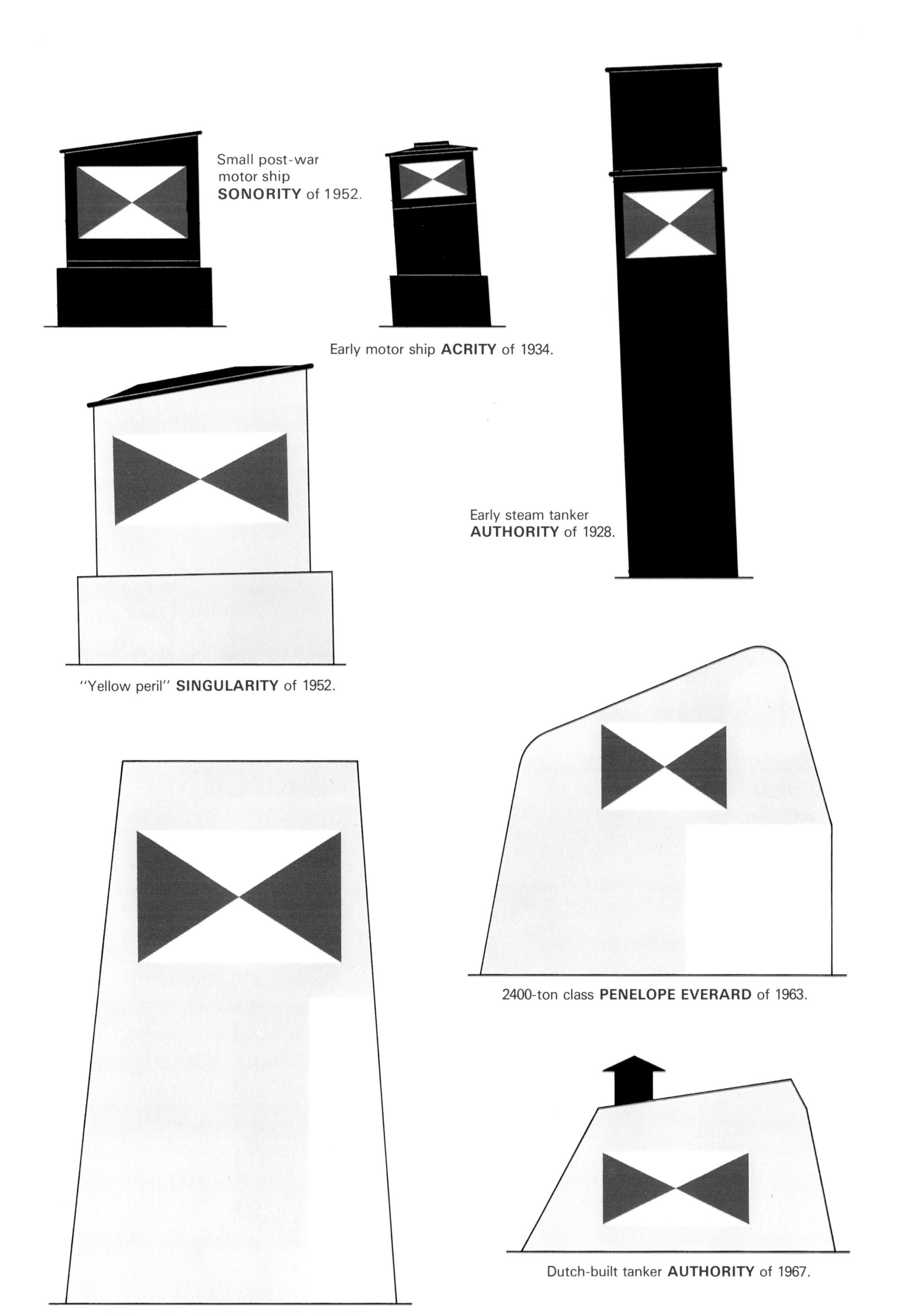

Small post-war motor ship **SONORITY** of 1952.

Early motor ship **ACRITY** of 1934.

Early steam tanker **AUTHORITY** of 1928.

"Yellow peril" **SINGULARITY** of 1952.

2400-ton class **PENELOPE EVERARD** of 1963.

Dutch-built tanker **AUTHORITY** of 1967.

4000-ton class **SINGULARITY** of 1977.

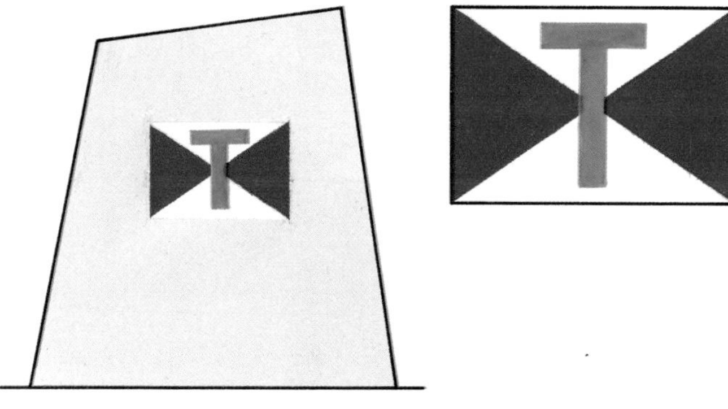

West River Shipping Co. Ltd.

Thun Tankers Ltd.

Martin's Coastal Steamships Ltd.

Comben Longstaff & Co. Ltd.

J. Hay & Sons Ltd.

Glen & Co. Ltd.

Shamrock Shipping Co. Ltd.

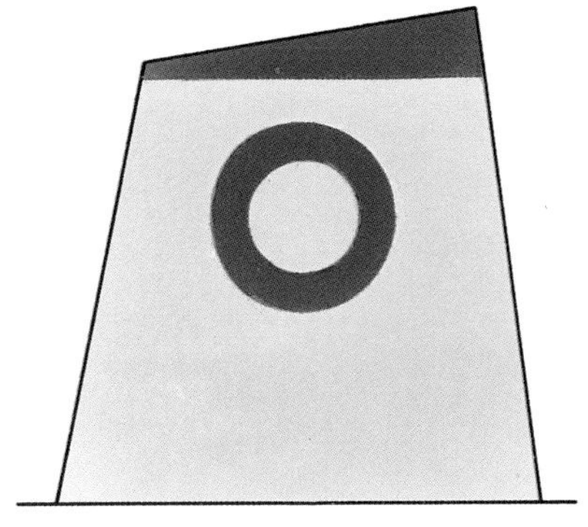

Blue Circle Industries Ltd.

North Africa Line Ltd.

General Freight Co. Ltd.

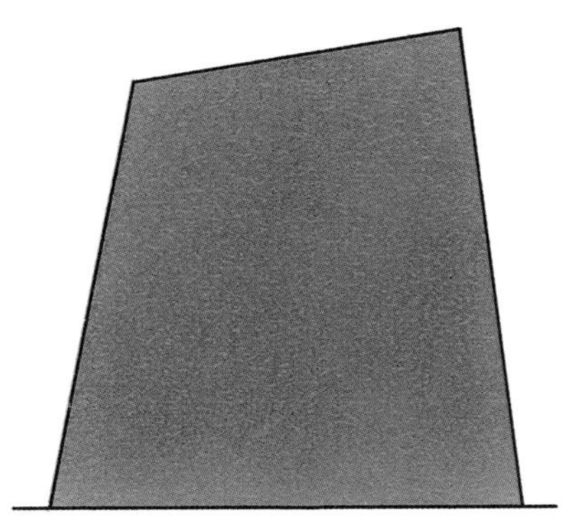

Salvatore Cia. Nav. S.A.

Onesimus Dorey (Shipowners) Ltd.

J. Wharton (Shipping) Ltd.

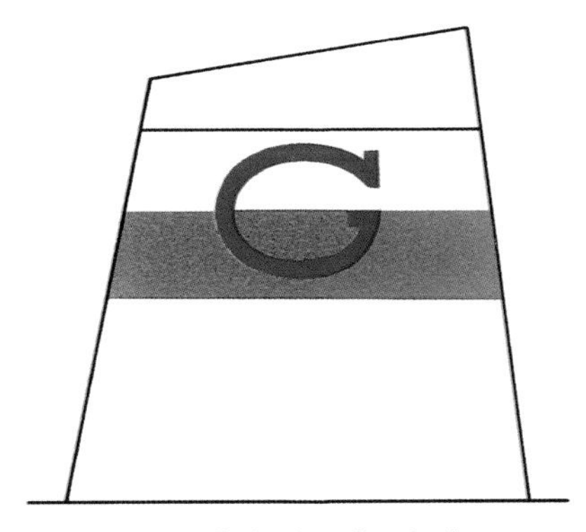

Graig Shipping Co. Ltd.

Eggar Forrester (Holdings) Ltd.

Hadley Shipping Co. Ltd.

J.E. Hyde Shipowners Ltd.
(Pegasus Line charter)

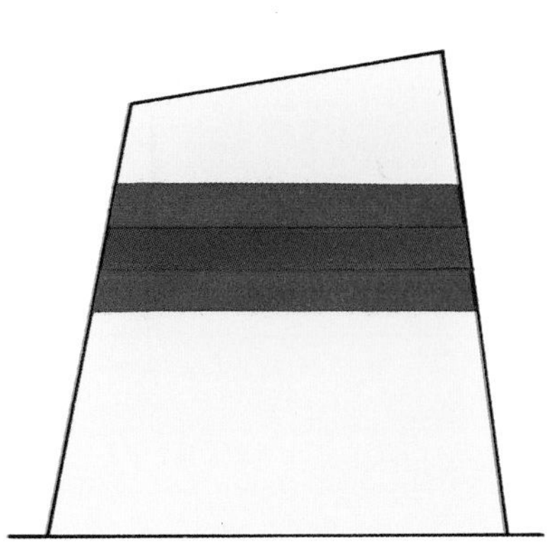

Thomas Watson (Shipping) Ltd.

INDEX OF SHIPS

Index to ships owned or managed by F.T. Everard & Sons Limited and Group companies showing the fleet number and pages where there is a reference to or a picture of the ship. The names in capitals are those carried whilst in Everard ownership or management. The notation 1, 2, etc. in brackets after the name in the fleet list indicates that the ship is the first, second etc. of that name in the fleet. The prefix 'S' indicates a sailing vessel, the prefix 'M' indicates a ship managed for another owner including the British Government and the prefix 'T' indicates a tug or other auxiliary craft.

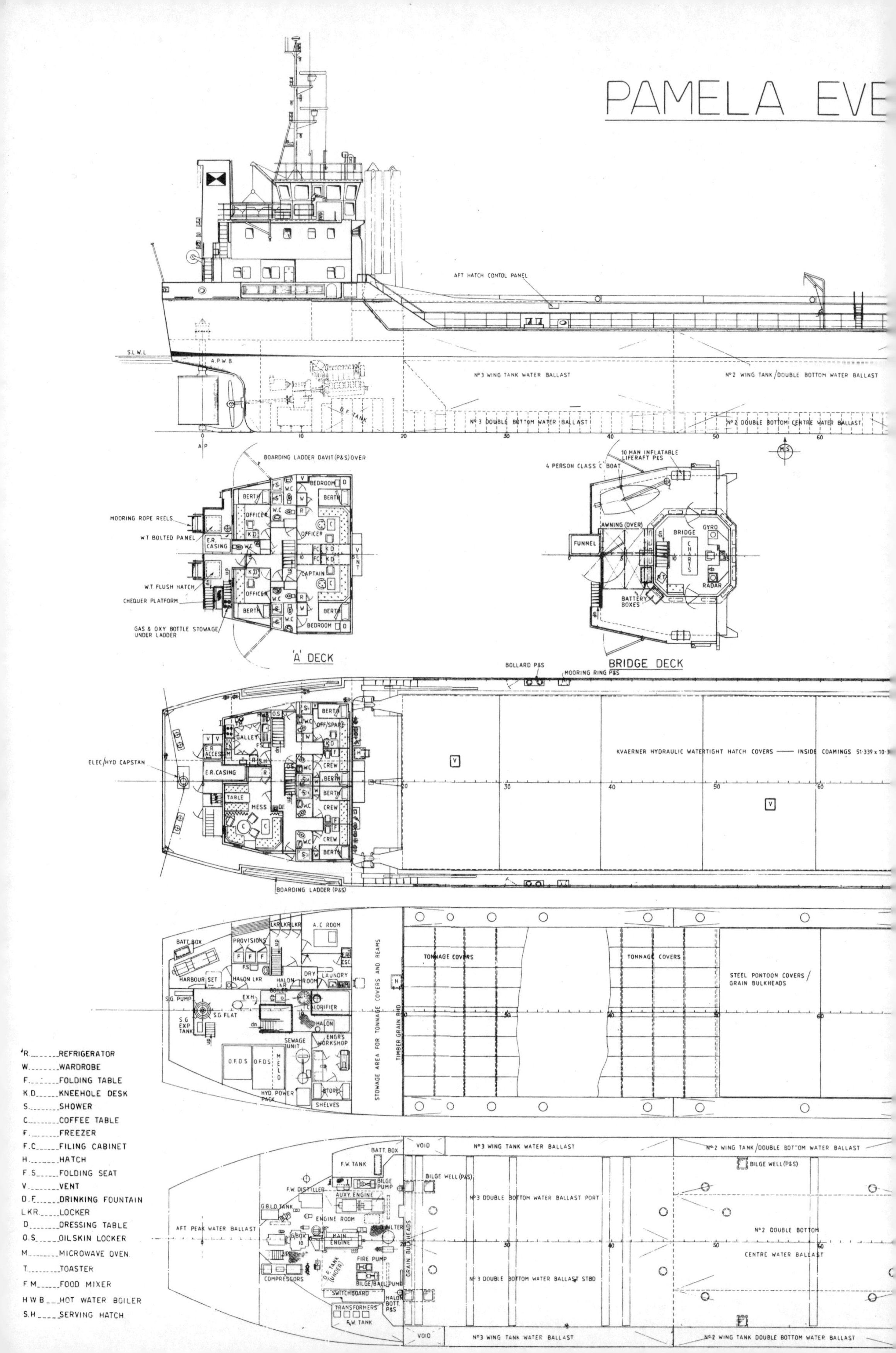

PAMELA EVE
AFT HATCH CONTOL PANEL
S.L.W.L
A.P.W.B.
Nº3 WING TANK WATER BALLAST
Nº2 WING TANK/DOUBLE BOTTOM WATER BALLAST
Nº3 DOUBLE BOTTOM WATER BALLAST
Nº2 DOUBLE BOTTOM CENTRE WATER BALLAST
D.F. TANK
A.P
BOARDING LADDER DAVIT (P&S) OVER
MOORING ROPE REELS
W.T. BOLTED PANEL
W.T. FLUSH HATCH
CHEQUER PLATFORM
GAS & OXY. BOTTLE STOWAGE UNDER LADDER
E.R. CASING
BERTH
OFFICER
CAPTAIN
BEDROOM
W.C
VENT
'A' DECK
10 MAN INFLATABLE LIFERAFT P&S
4 PERSON CLASS 'C' BOAT
AWNING (OVER)
FUNNEL
BRIDGE
CHARTS
GYRO
RADAR
BATTERY BOXES
BRIDGE DECK
BOLLARD P&S
MOORING RING P&S
ELEC/HYD CAPSTAN
E.R. ACCESS
GALLEY
MESS
TABLE
OFF/SPARE
CREW
KVAERNER HYDRAULIC WATERTIGHT HATCH COVERS — INSIDE COAMINGS 51·339 x 10·3
BOARDING LADDER (P&S)
BATT BOX
PROVISIONS
A.C ROOM
HARBOUR SET
HALON LKR
DRY ROOM
LAUNDRY
S.G. PUMP
S.G FLAT
S.G EXP TANK
BOILER
CALORIFIER
HALON
SEWAGE UNIT
ENGR'S WORKSHOP
O.F.D.S
HYD. POWER PACK
STORE
SHELVES
STOWAGE AREA FOR TONNAGE COVERS AND BEAMS
TIMBER GRAIN BHD
TONNAGE COVERS
STEEL PONTOON COVERS / GRAIN BULKHEADS
R. REFRIGERATOR
W. WARDROBE
F. FOLDING TABLE
K.D. KNEEHOLE DESK
S. SHOWER
C. COFFEE TABLE
F. FREEZER
F.C. FILING CABINET
H. HATCH
F.S. FOLDING SEAT
V. VENT
D.F. DRINKING FOUNTAIN
LKR. LOCKER
D. DRESSING TABLE
O.S. OILSKIN LOCKER
M. MICROWAVE OVEN
T. TOASTER
F.M. FOOD MIXER
H.W.B. HOT WATER BOILER
S.H. SERVING HATCH
VOID
BATT. BOX
F.W. TANK
F.W. DISTILLER
BILGE PUMP
AUXY ENGINE
BILGE WELL (P&S)
G.B.L.O TANK
ENGINE ROOM
AFT PEAK WATER BALLAST
MAIN ENGINE
D.F. TANK (UNDER)
FIRE PUMP
BILGE/BALL PUMP
COMPRESSORS
SWITCHBOARD
TRANSFORMERS
HALON BOTT. P&S
GRAIN BULKHEADS
Nº3 DOUBLE BOTTOM WATER BALLAST PORT
Nº3 DOUBLE BOTTOM WATER BALLAST STBD
Nº2 DOUBLE BOTTOM CENTRE WATER BALLAST
Nº2 WING TANK DOUBLE BOTTOM WATER BALLAST

Forgotten Fleets

F T EVERARD & Sons
Part One
by
Mark Rowbotham

When writing about shipping companies, it is always gratifying to know that there is a significant wealth of resources available to use, including contact with those who were actively involved in the operation and management of such companies. The case of F T Everard Ltd is no exception, and indeed highlights the illustrious nature of a well-known and highly-respected British shipping company. The name Everard exemplifies everything good and respectful about a typical British shipping company, and its significant impact on the UK shipping scene over many decades. Despite the company's takeover by James Fisher of Barrow in recent times, Everard vessels are still very much a part of maritime activities around the UK coasts, and account for a significant portion in revenue gained in the marine transportation of various kinds of bulk cargoes.

At the end of 2006, the British shipping line James Fisher acquired the long-established British shipping company F T Everard Ltd. Both companies had long been involved in the short sea shipping sector, and were both engaged in the predominantly coastal shipping trade, although in general, the ships of F T Everard were somewhat smaller than those of James Fisher. Nevertheless, F T Everard, from its base on the River Thames in Greenhithe, near Dartford, Kent, had carved out a niche market for itself in the maritime carriage of mainly oil products over many years, and was long regarded as a major player in the British shipping scene, even when changes in cargo trends had long since decimated most of the major British shipping lines. Such was the importance of Everards as a shipping company, that James Fisher agreed to incorporate the Everard name in the new, expanded company, and admit two of the Everard Directors to the James Fisher board. The new company of James Fisher Everard now controls the British short sea bulk shipping sector, and appears to be holding its own in the face of one of the worst recessions the UK has ever experienced.

The shipping company F T Everard and Sons Limited was established by Frederick T Everard at Greenhithe, near to Dartford, Kent, in 1922. However, Frederick had originally worked at Keep's barge yard at Greenhithe as foreman shipwright, and by 1880 he had become the yard's manager. It was in 1880 that Frederick Everard acquired the yard for himself and continued to build and repair the traditional spritsail Thames Barges. The company both built and repaired these vessels for some time, and eventually had the opportunity to own a vessel, a barge called Industry, in 1892. Another barge, the Elizabeth, was purchased in 1895, following her salvage from the riverbed where she had lain as a result of being sunk following a collision. The first barge built by the company for its own use was the Lord Kitchener of 1889, and she was duly followed by several other large barges for several owners, and some of these vessels were later acquired by Everards. Two other barges were built by William and Frederick, the sons of Frederick T Everard, and they were named Cambria and Hibernia respectively in 1906. The same year, three sailing barges which had been built at Berqvara, Sweden, were purchased by the company from the Berqvara Syndicate Ltd, and were renamed Lina, Marguerite and Spencer on their arrival in England in 1901. They all enjoyed long careers with the company, and the last was only retired in 1950.

The early years of the 20th century saw radical changes in marine propulsion, and the company duly built its first motor vessel at Greenhithe, which entered service in 1913. She was named Grit, and was powered by a 45 hp diesel engine. She was informally known as a "boomy barge", although in more formal terms she was described as an auxiliary ketch with leeboards. Her name has been ascribed to several theories, but a popular theory is that her name portrayed the enduring human quality needed to build, operate and sail the vessel. Another theory suggested that she was intended to be one of a pair of identical vessels, the other to be called Determination. In the event, the Grit was lost before the completion of the second vessel of the pair, and the latter of the two repeated the earlier name. A further theory, it is said, refers to the length of time taken to build the vessel, and that the name

The 522 grt tanker Agility was built in 1924 by George Brown at Greenock. She was the first ship of fleet to be named with the 'ity' suffix. She is seen here at Poole in May 1939. In 1956 she was broken up by T W Ward at Grays.

the difference. Five canal locks have a height difference of 10 metres, located in Genk, Diepenbeek, Hasselt, Kwaadmechelen and Olen, and the sixth, the canal lock of Wijnegem, has a difference of 5.45 metres. In the 1930s, it took about 7 days to travel from Antwerp to Liège over water, compared with the same distance presently covered in 18 hours. Since the completion of the Rhine-Main-Danube Canal in 1992, a barge can now travel from Antwerp all the way across Europe to the Black Sea.

All terminals in the port are connected with the European railway network. With a total of 1000 km railways and free capacity this modus will be the most important growth sectors for the future of rail transport, with heavy investments being made in equipment, rail infrastructure and terminals. Antwerp is one of the leading European rail ports, with more than 23 million tonnes of freight being carried annually by rail. On an average working day some 250 goods trains are loaded and unloaded in Antwerp, representing more than 40% of all rail freight in Belgium. The port itself has a network of nearly 1,000 km of rail lines serving practically every terminal, warehouse and company in the port. The fully automatic Antwerp North marshalling yard covers an area of 500 hectares. Anyone wishing to send goods by rail can choose between three types of rail service. The most frequent of these is the block train, i.e. a complete train reserved for a single customer, usually for carrying one type of goods from one point to another. There are also trains with wagons for several customers, with many travelling going to different destinations. Finally, there is multimodal or combined transport, with regular services connecting Antwerp quickly and reliably with the main industrial centres in Europe. Germany, France, Italy, the Netherlands, Austria, Spain and Switzerland are served on a daily basis, while other European countries are served several times per week.

Antwerp has four rail container terminals, namely the main hub and the Zomerweg, Schijnpoort and Circeldyck terminals. In addition all the large shipping container terminals in the port have their own rail terminal offering direct connections to the main economic centres of Europe. Antwerp Intermodal Solutions (AIS), a joint project by Antwerp Port Authority and the freight handling companies PSA HNN and P&O Ports, with support from the rail infrastructure operator Infrabel, has succeeded in attracting more rail container traffic to the port. This has led to six new rail connections being set up, and four existing services being expanded. These are rail shuttles linking Antwerp between two and five times per week with destinations in North Rhine Westphalia, central Germany, North-East France and Austria. In most cases they are "open trains", on which any company can reserve container space.

The port of Antwerp is putting a significant amount of effort into raising the proportion of freight carried by rail. Two important elements in this strategy are reactivating the "Iron Rhine" and construction of the Liefkenshoek rail tunnel. The Iron Rhine is the most efficient rail route between the port of Antwerp and the Ruhr regions, the industrial heart of Germany. This line is some 50 km shorter than the present route between Montzen and Aachen, and has lower gradients. The International Arbitration Tribunal in the Hague confirmed in 2005 that Belgium is entitled to use the Iron Rhine, but that the Netherlands may impose a number of conditions for the protection of the environment. According to the agreed schedule, the definitive route will begin full operation before 2015. In the meantime, Belgium has insisted upon the Netherlands complying with earlier agreements for limited, temporary use to be made of the historic route. At the request of the Belgian rail company Dillen & Lejeune Cargo, the Dutch government has already opened part of the Iron Rhine for limited use between Weert and Budel, close to the Belgian-Dutch border. The planning process for the Liefenshoek rail tunnel, the proposed second rail link between the left and right banks of the Schelde, has entered its final phase. In December 2006, the Flemish government took a definitive decision on the route, having already given its approval for a system of pre-financing, in order to enable work on the tunnel to start earlier than originally planned. The intention is that according to the existing schedule, work on the tunnel's construction will start in late 2008/early 2009, in order to allow the tunnel to enter service at the end of 2012.

Another form of transport, although less evident, is the port's pipeline network. The port has more than 300 km of pipeline, making it the most important central hub within the European pipeline network.

Concerning short-sea and feeder connections, Antwerp aims to be a full-service partner with most main shipping lines, and the port is constantly expanding its network of connections. Short-sea shipping involves the carriage of cargo or passengers by sea, but without any long ocean crossings, and to this extent, it is continental, not intercontinental, in its concept and structure. In European terms, it covers the Baltic States, Scandinavia and Iceland, the UK and Ireland, the mainland of Western Europe, the Iberian Peninsula, the Mediterranean countries (including North Africa) and the Black Sea area. Short-sea shipping accounts for 45% of the cargo volume in Antwerp, while short-sea container carrying makes up 40% of all the port's container trade. This success is due to the widespread network of short-sea and feeder services, with the port of Antwerp offering 280 short-sea departures per month to more than 150 destinations. Liquid bulk accounts for 33% of the short-sea freight, containers 46% and dry bulk 12%. Conventional/break-bulk traffic accounts for slightly more than 5%, and ro-ro traffic accounts for 3%.

Owing to the feeder services which connect directly with deepsea liner services, the port of Antwerp is continually reinforcing its position as a hub for European transhipment trade. Indeed, the feeder traffic guarantees on-time, cost-effective handling. With the recent opening of two new container terminals in the Deurganck dock, Antwerp is attracting even more deepsea and feeder services. This capacity expansion ensures plenty of room for growth, with close integration of deepsea and feeder services. As a port, Antwerp is well aware that short-sea shipping is an important part of the range of options that it aims to offer. For longer distances, for instance from Scandinavia to the Iberian Peninsula, short-sea shipping provides an excellent alternative to the often congested European road network, and the use of these services based on the port of Antwerp can yield cost savings of up to 60% compared with traditional road haulage. To promote the use of short-sea services, the Port Authority has amended the structure of port dues so that they no longer form a significant part of the total transport cost, with discounts for regular short-sea services. This promotion policy will be continued in the future, thanks among other things to the EU subsidies for encouraging "motorways of the sea."

In parallel with this, the port of Antwerp will put additional efforts into further simplifying the customs and administration procedures, especially given EU initiatives to streamline and simplify the existing pan-EU Customs systems. There will also be additional exemptions from the pilotage obligation for coastal shipping, in that ships with an LOA (Length Overall) of less than 80 metres will automatically be exempt from the obligation to take on a pilot, while ships with an LOA of 80 to 95 metres can obtain exemption if the ship's crew is able to meet various criteria concerning their knowledge of the port's harbours and channels leading from the Schelde estuary.

The editor would like to thank the Port of Antwerp for providing the photographs that accompany this article.

The 229 grt Fred Everard leaving Poole on 18th April 1939. She was built in 1926 by Fellows & Co of Great Yarmouth as a sailing barge, being converted to a motor coaster in 1938. She sank after a collision off Margate on 9th May 1956.

was derived from the phrase "Got Ready In Time", but this theory appears to have been invented by an employee of the shipyard to suit the second vessel. The first Grit was sunk in the Channel in 1916 by the German U-Boat UB-29, while carrying military stores across to France. It transpired that it took several rounds of gunfire by the U-Boat to sink the vessel, and when the submarine's commander asked the sunken vessel's crew what materials had been used in her construction, he was told that she was built with English oak. The second vessel to be named Grit entered service in 1923. Unlike her predecessor, she was a proper motor coaster, designed as such and not as a sailing vessel with an auxiliary engine. However, even as a motor vessel, she was still equipped with sails to take advantage of a favourable wind. However, her career was to prove short-lived, as she was run down and sunk in thick fog off Hythe in February 1934 by the Latvian steamship Gaisma. However, it was maintained by some of her survivors that the guilty vessel was in fact the German Nord-Deutscher Lloyd liner Europa inbound to Bremen from New York following a stop in Southampton. Following an examination of issues of the marine journal Lloyd's List from the time, the Europa could well have passed through the area at the time of the collision. Several other vessels to be named Grit followed, the last being built in 1976 and the seventh vessel to bear the name. However, it would appear that the name was not associated with good fortune, as four out of the seven vessels to bear the name were lost either as a result of collisions or as a result of enemy action during hostilities. Indeed, the seventh and final vessel to bear the name Grit was lost following a collision in 1988.

During World War I, three small steam-powered vessels were purchased. These were the dry cargo vessels Norseman, Tosca and Bellavale, and they survived the war. By 1920, the Norseman and Bellavale had been sold by 1920 to enable the company to concentrate on the development of the coastal motorship, but the Tosca remained in the Everard fleet until 1926. She was immediately replaced by the slightly larger vessel Tirydail, which was joined in 1929 by the vessel Glen Mary. Both of these vessels were steamships and were purchased second-hand, and it is interesting to note that although the company operated steamships throughout much of its existence, it never built any vessels using such propulsion. Around this time, the tanker business was developing, and the company purchased the steam-powered tanker Alchymist in 1919. She had originally been built to carry wood tar for a company of timber merchants, and she was duly modified for the bulk carriage of edible oils, without the need to carry the cargo in barrels which were prone to leakage as well as incurring substantial handling costs, such was the technology which had been used to construct her holds. She proved very successful in service, and over the next few years, four new tankers were ordered with a design based on the experience gained from the Alchymist. The first to emerge from the shipyard was the vessel Agility, built by George Brown & Co of Greenock at a cost of £15,350. Everards had formed a link with George Brown during World War I, when William J Everard served in the Royal Navy at Glasgow, and he apparently stated his intention to have built at least 12 vessels at the Garvel Shipyard belonging to George Brown. In the end, this estimate proved wildly conservative, and in reality no less than 28 vessels were built for Everards at Greenock, the last Everard vessel to emerge from the yard being the tanker Atonality in 1949. Following the end of hostilities in 1945, the company purchased three "Empire" tankers which had also been built by George Brown.

The company had continued its association with barges, and several more were purchased during and after World War I, to the point that in 1919 a total of 36 barges were owned by the company. The larger barges operated on coastal voyages chiefly around the south and east coasts of the UK, while the smaller barges were employed on river traffic, in particular cement from the works to the larger ocean-going vessels berthed in the docks. Other sailing barges, usually those coming to the end of their operational life, were engaged in the carriage of mud or clay to the cement works, especially the

The 350 grt Assiduity was built in 1930 by George Brown at Greenock. She was broken up by T W Ward at Grays where she arrived on 20th June 1961. She is seen here leaving Poole on 29th June 1939.

The 359 grt Actuosity was built in 1933 by George Brown at Greenock. She is seen here at Poole in May 1939. On 3rd October 1940 she sank off Cromer.

plant at West Thurrock on the lower Thames. However, this traffic ended abruptly when the cement works obtained alternative sources of supply, and in any case the barges operating this traffic had come to the end of their working life. Shortly after the end of World War I, two ex-Government steam tugs were purchased by the company, along with a number of dry cargo and tank lighters for the river work to supplement the barges. Some of the lighters had been built in the Netherlands, while others were built for the company at Faversham, in Kent, and Great Yarmouth, in Norfolk. A few were designed to operate in the creeks and canals leading off the Thames, particularly in the river's upper reaches. Although it had been forecast for some time that the lighterage work would eventually cease, such activities have continued for many years, albeit at significantly lower levels of activity compared with past trading.

In the mid-1920s, Frederick T Everard ordered four large sailing barges from Fellows & Co of Great Yarmouth, the largest sailing barges ever to be built. They were enlargements of the "Greenhithe" design, a barge originally laid down in Ipswich in 1923 but completed for Everards and rigged at Greenhithe. The quartet were named Will, Fred, Alf and Ethel Everard, and were known affectionately as the "iron pots" because of their steel hulls. Between them they amassed a number of record passages and also performed very well in the Thames and Medway barge races. The Ethel was abandoned at Dunkirk during the evacuation of the beaches in 1940, while the Fred and the Alf were cut down and converted into motor coasters. The Fred Everard was chartered by the Admiralty as a stores vessel during World War II and was stationed at Scapa Flow in the Orkney islands, where she supplied stores and ammunition to the Royal navy battlecruiser HMS Hood before the latter's fateful last patrol in the North Atlantic in mid-1941. Only the Will Everard survived as a sailing barge, and she had a small auxiliary diesel engine fitted in 1950. She was eventually sold in 1966, and then became actively engaged in charter work with her name shortened to Will.

The annual barge matches on the rivers Thames and Medway had always been major events, and Frederick T Everard was keen to ensure that his barges could effectively compete in these races, this tradition being passed down to his sons. In 1929, Frederick senior dies and the five barges were withdrawn from that year's races as a mark of respect. He was succeeded by his eldest son, Frederick W Everard, who remained chairman of the company until his death in 1964. Throughout this time, the Everard barges brought several trophies to the company's shelves as a result of their victories. Up until the centenary matches of 1963, after which the Everard barges no longer competed, they had won 22 Thames races and 23 on the river Medway in addition to many second and third places and other awards. The traditional Thames Barge race had been re-established to celebrate the Coronation of Queen Elizabeth II in 1953, and although there was a decline in the number of commercial barges, entries remained high due to the number of barges sold out of their original trade and used as yachts. The rivalry of two companies in particular, namely F T Everard & Sons and the London & Rochester Trading Company, led to the development of the rig and leeboards beyond their daily working performance into full racing vessels, the results of which are still copied today. In 1963, the Centenary of the first match, the Committee of the day decided to end the race as a formal event, but Thames Barge racing is still popular, and sailing barges still maintain a regular presence in the Thames estuary.

In the early 1920s, a number of other smaller motor vessels were purchased by the company. Among these were four ex-government vessels known as "X-Lighters" or "Beetles". Over 200 of these vessels had been built in 1915 by shipyards all around the UK, many being used in the

The 434 grt tanker Aptity was built in 1939 by George Brown at Greenock, leaving Poole in May 1939. In 1969 she was converted into a barge and was eventually broken up by R G Fry at Greenhithe in February 1987.

The 554 grt Spirality in Poole in November 1967. She was built in 1939 by the Goole Shipbuilding and Repair Co. In 1968 she was broken up by J Boel at Antwerp where she arrived on 18th November.

Dardanelles campaign in Turkey of the same year. They were the forerunners of the World War II landing craft, and were designed around the dimensions of the army Howitzer gun carriage. Following completion, some of these vessels were converted into tankers and those purchased by Everards were named Lobster, Oyster, Mussel and Shrimp. However, they were re-named with curiously pedestrian names and duly became the Roam, Wander, Ramble and Saunter. The first two foundered in bad weather, possibly as a result of water accumulating on deck and held there by the flush decks and bowboards. The other two vessels, however, had half-height fo'c'sle heads built on to improve their seakeeping qualities.

By 1939, the sailing barges, which had enjoyed their heyday in the early 1920s, were declining in numbers, despite the fact that they were still carrying a significant amount of cargo right up to the outbreak of war that year. The steamships and motor vessels were making an increasing contribution to the company's trading activities, and were replacing the barges which had so well served the fleet for so long. Because they did not need to rely on the wind, they could travel faster and could function more predictably, and could also negotiate the narrow rivers unaided where a traditional sailing barge would probably require the assistance of a tug. Everards had operated sail-powered vessels through the turn of the century, and only turned to motorised barges in the 1920s, but their designs were still basic, and navigational aids comprised the ship's wheel and a compass. Even communication was rudimentary, with the first Everard vessel only apparently being equipped with a radio in 1939. Even on more recent post-war vessels of the 1950s, Decca Navigator equipment was fitted but the vessels did not apparently have a proper radar system on board, with only one vessel at the time, the Astrality, apparently being fitted with radar. However, the company was already showing its capabilities in the 1930s which would later make it a UK leader in coastal bulk transportation, as some of the 1930s-built vessels were built as tankers which were designed to carry edible oils. However, Everards still maintained a link with sail-powered vessels, as the last Thames barge to trade entirely under sail was the Everard-built Cambria in 1970, owned by Captain A W Roberts. Captain Roberts had sailed the Cambria for more than twenty years, and gained a reputation for his handling of other Everard barges.

Trades came and went, especially in the dry cargo market, but a particular market which blossomed for the company was that of the carriage of oils. The company's tanker fleet was particularly occupied with the carriage of not only edible oils for Unilever but also with petroleum products for the major oil companies, and the fleet often traded away from UK shores to areas such as the Baltic Sea and beyond. A further tanker innovation was the vessel Acclivity of 1931. Her profile was kept very low to enable her to negotiate the bridges on the river Seine during her voyages with edible oil from Zwijndrecht in the Netherlands to Paris. She was equipped with double-bottom ballast tanks, a feature which was unusual in small ships of the time and particularly rare in small tankers. However, they were needed to overcome the problem of the low bridges on the Seine, as well as to ease the problem of cleaning the cargo tanks, and in reality anticipated the overall use of ballast tanks in coastal tankers by fifty years. Another feature was the very large daily service fuel oil tank which enabled the ship to make the return passage from Le Havre, at the mouth of the Seine, to Paris without needing to draw fuel from the main bunker tanks and thereby incurring fuel duties.

The expansion of the fleet was steady rather than sudden, and was always based on sound finances, in that the company never needed to borrow money to finance the construction or purchase of its vessels. The vessels

Above: The 2,535 grt Georgina V Everard was built in 1955 by the Goole Shipbuilding and Repairing Co. In 1978 she was sold to Mohamed Ali Mohamed Dib Sawalhi of Lebanon and renamed Myassa, the following year being renamed Myassar. Later that year she was sold to Al Saad Shipping of Libya before being broken up in 1985.

Below: The 1,577 grt Sanguity was built in 1956 by the Grangemouth Dockyard. In 1978 she was sold to Lisca Shipping and renamed Ramona. In 1986 she was sold to Lotus shipping of St Vincent without changing her name. She was broken up in Bruges where she arrived on 24th December 1994. She is seen here passing Gravesend in May 1977.

The 1,543 grt Alfred Everard was built in 1957 by the Grangemouth Dockyard Company. In 1978 she was sold to Rapid Transit Shipping of the Cayman Islands and renamed Marys Ketch. In 1982 she was sold to Linea Caribe Pacifico of Honduras and renamed Aldebaran. She was deleted from Lloyds Register in 1992.

of the period were all purchased with cash with the company holding the 64 shares, unlike the previous situation before the formation of the limited company in 1923, when individual family members held the shares of some of the ships. Following the company's establishment as a limited venture, sufficient money was accumulated for the specification of the vessel to be decided upon and the order placed for a new ship. Costings for new ships were also very tight, and in 1933 a ship from the George Brown yard was cancelled because the Chancellor of the Exchequer of the time had increased the duty on fuel oil in his budget. However, all the ships were financed form the company's own resources and it was not until the building of the vessel Security at Hessle in 1970 that external sources of finance were used.

Starting with the tanker Agility, the family company's vessels were either named after family members or given the suffix "ity" e.g. Amity and Annuity, and Frederick Everard and Gillian Everard. These names were originally selected by Annie E Everard from the book "Nuttalls Standard Pronouncing Dictionary", which had originally been published by Frederick Warne & Co in about 1872. This particular volume had originally belonged to her mother, and apparently still exists. Since the series was started, over 100 names ending in "...ity" have been used, many of them more than once, the majority beginning with the letters A or S, but others also with the letters C, F or T. Some names were invented, but all have been quite appropriate to the vessels on which they were bestowed, and they have created a distinct identity and individual style of the years of the company's existence, even lasting into the period following the merger of Everards with James Fisher. One vessel, the Antiquity, apparently gained her name as a result of the length of time it took to build her. Her new owner, William Everard, is reputed to have declared that she would be an antique before she even entered service, and on his return to the yard some time later he found the name "Antiquity" painted on her stern. Other vessels, such as the Scarcity and Austerity, reflected the difficult period when the vessels were built immediately following the end of hostilities in 1945. The vessel Tankity reflected a humorous touch, as the name, however much it had been invented, referred to her description, a tanker. The vessel Centurity, built in 1956, reflected the fact that she was the hundredth vessel to enter the fleet. As time progressed, the initial letters of the vessels' names came to signify the type of vessel which they belonged to. The "S...ity" names were used for the larger dry cargo ships, the "C...ity" names for smaller dry cargo ships and the "A...ity" names for the tankers. However, family names continued to be used in the dry cargo fleet and also until more recently for tugs.

By the outbreak of hostilities in 1939, the fleet had expanded to 36 motor vessels, 7 steamships, three tugs, 24 sailing barges and a large number of lighters and service craft. During the war, fifty ships were managed at some stage for the Government. There was little respite from wartime service activity, and the ships were involved in the Norwegian campaign, the evacuation from Dunkirk, many Channel and North Sea convoys, the D-day Normandy landings and the liberation of Europe. A total of 22 ships were lost during the war and two of the managed ships were also lost. The vessel Serenity was lost to enemy action off Whitby in 1939, and the vessel Summity was hit by a German bomber, but she was later repaired. The tanker Acclivity had an incredible escape while she was discharging whale oil in spring 1940 at Zwijndrecht in the Netherlands, a port which she often visited. The guns of the rapidly-advancing German forces could be heard and it was decided not to finish the discharge, but to cut and run. The ship was fired upon as she passed through Rotterdam and out past the Hook of Holland where it is thought that she sailed straight through a minefield. The ship arrived in the Thames the following day largely unscathed and survived the war, although she was often in the midst of heavy activity. The vessel Antiquity was

The 1,589 grt William J Everard was built in 1963 by the Goole Shipbuilding and Repair Co. In 1982 she was sold to Wimpey Marine and converted into the drillship Wimpey Geocore. In 1988 she was sold to Olympia Shipping of Gibraltar who rebuilt her as a freighter and renamed her Seaburn Girl. A further sale in 1990 to Leighton Shipping saw her renamed Husum. Two further sales in 1992 saw her sail initially as Epson and then Ecowas Trader I for the Nigerian Company East West Coast Marine. She disappered from Lloyds Register in 2002.

fitted out as a rescue ship early in the war, and was given extra food stores and water tanks, and her cargo hold was made more suitable for accommodating people. She was involved in the evacuation of 475 people from the island of Jersey in June 1940, and later took part in several convoys, including CW8 which was badly bombed in the Strait of Dover in July 1940. In that same convoy was the Everard vessel Summity mentioned earlier. She was bombed and severely damaged, and was beached at Shakespeare Cliff by her master, before being towed to Dover and later repaired. The vessel Acrity was used to transport ammunition to Norway early in the war, despite the fact that none of her crew had the necessary certification for such transportation. She successfully completed the trip, and returned to the UK without incident. The Aridity was mined in the Thames estuary in October 1940 while inbound with a cargo of wheat, but all the crew managed to escape safely. The ship did not sink but drifted ashore, and the sedulity was sent downriver to stand by the stricken vessel until the Acrity could be towed back to Greenhithe, where she was duly repaired. The Acrity was later involved in the Normandy landings, despite having been officially declared a war loss. The Sedulity herself was attacked off Cromer in February 1942, but was safely towed to Great Yarmouth. The Supremity, which had entered service in November 1939, was only in wartime service for 13 months. In December 1940, while part of convoy FS53, she hit a mine in the Thames estuary and settled to the riverbed. Her crew escaped, except for the chief engineer who fell overboard and disappeared.

During the war, the company managed some 50 vessels for the Ministry of War Transport, many of them "Empire" vessels and several of which were built at the George Brown yard at Greenock. The dry cargo vessels Empire Cliff and Empire Foreland were based on the earlier Everard vessel Sequacity, and were forerunners of the later Everard vessels Ability and Amenity, but eventually they were transferred along with other dry cargo vessels to the management of other owners, leaving Everards to concentrate on the tanker sector. The vessel Empire boy was the first of a number of steam-powered tankers to be managed by Everards, and she was followed by several vessels from the "Empire Cadet" class, built at either the Grangemouth Dockyard Company or A & J Inglis of Glasgow. Another group of vessels managed by Everards were six American T1-M-A1 tankers, which were given the names of US oilfields such as Walnut Bend and Rio Bravo. The largest group of vessels in terms of the number of identical vessels which was managed by Everards was a group of tankers with the name "Chant" followed by a number, excluding the number 13, which was considered unlucky. The name "Chant" was supposed to be derived from "Channel Tanker", and all the vessels were of pre-fabricated construction. They were intended for use in supporting the Allied invasion of Europe, and the intention was to build 68 of them. At an early stage in the construction programme, it was decided to complete 25 of the vessels as dry cargo ships, and instead of "Chant" names they were given "Fabric" numbers, but these too were changed in favour of "Empire F..." names before the vessels were completed. Everards succeeded in purchasing two of these vessels from foreign owners in later years, and they were renamed Auspicity and Averity (401 gt). They operated for 18 years in Everard colours before being withdrawn and sold. Many of the company's vessels took part in the Allied invasion of

Europe in 1944, and in one convoy alone, namely ETC8 which sailed from Southend on 13 June 1944 bound for the Sword and Juno beaches, there were three Everard vessels, namely the Ability, Signality and Sedulity, the latter having been attacked off Cromer on the Norfolk coast in 1942.

In total, the company lost 22 employees during the conflict, a small number compared with the losses suffered by other, larger, British shipping companies, but sufficient to take its toll on the company considering its more limited scope of activities. A memorial was erected as a tribute to the employees killed during the war in the parish church at Greenhithe. Also during the war, the company's London office was moved from Great Tower Street to Fenchurch Buildings following an air raid in 1941, and the company's Chartering department remained there until 1984, when more suitable accommodation was found in the Baltic Exchange Chambers in St Mary Axe. However, this move was relatively short-lived, and in 1989 the London office again moved, this time to outside the City and from the prestigious district of EC3 in the square mile to the more down-market Elder Street in E1. However, the Greenhithe office and the adjacent shipyard remained on the same site throughout the war, and there was a total commitment to repairing war-damaged ships and to maintain the efficient operation of the company's fleet of vessels. The shipyard also built two Mk 3 tank landing craft for the Government, number 334 being launched in early 1942 and number 364 launched a year later. At about the same time, the Fellows' drawing office undertook design work for the construction of three dry cargo coastal vessels, and they were allocated yard numbers 101, 192 and 193, suggesting that they were to be constructed at two different yards, neither of which was Fellows' yard. Their design was very similar to the George Brown-built vessels Summity and Supremity, both of which had entered service in 1939, however none of them were ever built, at least not to their design specification. Shortly after the end of hostilities, a similar vessel to the design of yard number 101 was laid down at Greenhithe using steel prepared at Great Yarmouth. Work proceeded very slowly, but was eventually abandoned with little more than the keel, some floors and frames in position.

After the cessation of hostilities, the company carried various cargoes including coal, grain, cement and china clay plus outsized machinery and timber, and was engaged in regular trade with Scandinavia. However, the company's recovery from the war was tinged with sadness, owing to the death of Alfred Everard, the youngest son of the company's founder, in 1945. the post-war construction of vessels commenced with the construction of vessels at Goole and Grangemouth, whilst a number of "Empire" vessels were purchased from the Government, some of which had been managed by Everards for the Ministry of War Transport. By far the largest group of former Government vessels which were purchased by Everards were the nine dry cargo vessels belonging to the "Fabric" or "Empire F" class. These vessels were all given names beginning with the letter "F". They were very successful vessels and carried a wide variety of cargoes on coastal voyages until 1961 when they were sold for scrap.

In 1948, the company acquired a controlling interest in Fellows & Co Ltd and Crabtree (1931) Ltd, both of Great Yarmouth, and ships were built and repaired at Great Yarmouth until the shipyard and works were sold in 1970. Fellows also built a number of tank and dry cargo lighters for the Thames lighterage business, and on completion, these vessels were towed along the coast to London by Everard ships. During the catastrophic East Coast floods of 1953, the Everard vessels Sedulity and Flexity were berthed alongside together at Great Yarmouth. The river was so high that baulks of timber pulled from the water had to be jammed between the ships and the quay so as to stop them from mounting

Don Smith/Pictureships

The 1,599 grt Rosemary Everard was built in 1964 by Clelands at Wallsend. In 1984 she was sold to Sikeon Shipping of Malta and renamed Theodoros G. In 1988 she was sold to Galatia Shipping of Honduras without a name change. Further sales in 1993 and 1997 saw her sail as Berlice and Rosemary Eve before she sank between San Carlos and Zapara Island on 22nd April 2001. She is photographed here by Don Smith passing Gravesend in October 1978.

the dockside itself.

Apart from the two larger vessels Supremity and Superiority which had been built at Goole, most of the post-war vessels were relatively small and resembled their pre-war sisters. However, in 1949 the construction programme took a major leap forward with the construction at Goole of the vessel Stability, characterised by a forward wheelhouse. She and her sister Security had originally been painted with black hulls, they were repainted with yellow hulls, and along with the other 10 similar vessels of the class, they were collectively known as the "Yellow Perils". At approximately 1800 dwt and 1600 gross tons they were diminutive versions of the two earlier vessels built at Goole, but they were considered to be good-looking vessels. In early 1953, the vessel Singularity was moved to Greenhithe and prepared for the Coronation Review at Spithead. She was fully cleaned out and temporary accommodation was added to house all the company's guests. The same class, along with the vessels Georgina V Everard and Frederick T Everard, as well as the former "Empire" ships, expanded the company's trading activities northwards to the Baltic Sea with coal outwards and timber and wood pulp inwards. The vessels also ventured south to North Africa, returning home with cargoes of phosphate from Casablanca. The vessel Similarity was involved in the coal trade for many years, carrying coal from Goole to Kingsbridge, in Devon. Grain was also a frequent cargo, and later on so was the carriage of soya beans to the Erith Oil Works on the Thames.

The post-war expansion of the company's dry cargo fleet was greatly exceeded by that of the tankers, although the growth in the tanker fleet was mainly achieved by the purchase of the former "Empire" and other ex-Government vessels, with relatively few newbuildings. In total, 36 tankers were purchased by the company between 1945 and 1957, and the sizes of the vessels ranged from the 180 dwt tons former military oil barge Attunity to the 5,127 dwt tons Astrality (ex Empire Ganges), the second vessel to bear this name. The work carried out by these vessels depended not only upon demand but also upon their suitability for the work involved, which varied considerably. Some of the vessels carried edible oils, molasses and lubricating oils, while others carried motor spirit and other clean petroleum products. Other vessels carried more "dirty" cargoes, such as fuel oil for power stations and bunkering for larger vessels. The vessels Conformity and Candourity carried fuel oil from Coryton up the river Thames to Hammersmith, but were also engaged on bunkering operations on the rivers Thames and Medway and the Bristol Channel. Further small-scale bunkering work was undertaken by four former military oil barges, of which two, namely the Apexity and Attunity, were purchased in 1952 and the other two, the Tankity and the Totality, were purchased in 1956. the larger vessels Argosity and Arduity were lengthened and were then used for the carriage of vegetable oils, lubricating oils and clean petroleum products, the Arduity also making trips to Iceland to load quantities of fish oil for the Mersey. Her unlengthened sister vessel Amity successfully carried loads of lard from Brussels to Liverpool, setting a trend which would not only expand the trade into the regular carriage of lard but would also include the carriage of tallow. By 1956, F T Everard had 100 ships including several coastal tankers whose size increased gradually with successive builds of new vessels. Until the late 1960s, most of the newbuild vessels were chartered out on a time-charter basis to the major oil companies for the carriage of clean petroleum products and fuel oil. However, by this time, the oil companies were also operating more of their own vessels, and this, together with the increasing age of the Everard ships meant that the number of Everard vessels declined rapidly. Most of the older tankers were sold for scrapping by 1970, leaving a smaller but more modern fleet of versatile tankers to maintain the company's business. F T Everard had both dry bulk and tanker types of vessels in its fleet, and in keeping with the company's policy they were all named with an "...ity". The tankers had grey hulls and the dry bulk vessels had black hulls. The names of the tankers commenced with "A", as in Alacrity, and the dry bulk ships were all "F", as in Frivolity and Fortuneity. The first letters were later to change, as other vessels were built with names such as Supremity and Superiority.

There were further casualties in the early 1960s, when the vessel Security (1,490 grt, built 1950) was struck by the German vessel Carpathia in the River Elbe in thick fog on 2 February 1964. She subsequently sank, but was raised a month later and broken up in Hamburg. She was later succeeded by another vessel to bear the same name, built in 1971. The vessel Frederick T Everard (2,535 grt) ran aground at Robin Hood's Bay on the North Yorkshire coast in 1965 during a storm, apparently with a cargo of paper pulp from Norway, and was declared a total loss. All the crew were rescued by RNLI lifeboat.

Also, at this time, the company diversified into other activities, including the purchase of other wharves. The company became more involved in the carriage of hydrocarbon mineral oils, and purchased and developed Cattedown Wharves in Plymouth in 1957, which became the main oil terminal for Plymouth. Cattedown Wharves became a marine service company owned by Everard but operating as a separate entity within the overall business which handled cargo shipped through Plymouth. Although it also dealt in animal feed, fertilisers, fish meal and clay, much of Cattedown's business involved petroleum products for the major oil companies. Meanwhile, the shipyard at Greenhithe continued as a service to the fleet and carried out both major and minor repairs on the company's vessels, although many of the vessels were too large for the slipways and had to be dry-docked elsewhere. The management of the shipyard was split from the fleet activities in 1968, and in 1973, ships belonging to other owners came to the yard for repair for the first time. However, economic adversities forced the yard to close in December 1982, and shortly afterwards the ship repair facilities were leased to South Thames Shiprepairers Ltd, who continued to operate the yard with a much-reduced labour force before they too were forced to close the yard in July 1985.

Everards also purchased a number of shipping companies over many years. The first of these was Martins Coastal Steamships Ltd of Plymouth in 1950, and their two vessels, the Dalesmeet and the Watersmeet, duly became the Capacity and Celebrity in the Everard fleet. The next acquisition took place in 1956 of the shipping company J Hay & Sons Ltd of Glasgow. Seven elderly steam-powered coasters were integrated into the Everard fleet, but all of these vessels had been sold or scrapped by 1963. However, the name of J Hay & Sons was maintained for some time following the demise of their original ships.

Towards the end of 1961, the company Glen & Co, also of Glasgow, was acquired. This company was more involved in vessel management, particularly concerning vessels belonging to shipping companies engaged in transatlantic and Scandinavian trading. At the time of purchase, only two of these companies, Clydesdale Shipowners Ltd and Scottish Navigation Co Ltd, were still active, and between them owned six vessels, all of which were sold by 1967, although by the 1970s Everards had itself moved increasingly into ship management. With the purchase of Glen & Co, Everards also acquired J T Salvesen & Co Ltd and David Traill & Sons Ltd of Grangemouth, along with Urban Korner A/B of Gothenburg, thus establishing Everards in the liner trades between Scandinavia, the UK and Ireland. Following an offer by the Forth Ports Authority, the stevedoring company of David Traill & Sons Ltd was sold in

The 1,599 grt Ethel Everard was built by Clelands at Wallsend in 1966. In 1984 she was sold to Mortek Shipping of Piraeus and renamed Angie. On 15th August 1985 she ran aground off Crete when en route from Bar to Triploi and sank on 2nd September.

1977. The company J T Salvesen remained under Everard control for a while as forwarding and general ships' agents, but this company was also sold in 1985. An interesting note about J T Salvesen is that Johan Theodor Salvesen's can claim some degree to fame in that he installed his youngest brother Christian as manager of his Scottish office at Leith in 1851. The rest, as it is said, is history. William J Everard died in 1958, leaving his brother Frederick W Everard, the last surviving son of the founder, to continue running the business, until he too died in 1964. He was succeeded by his nephew Frederick A Everard as chairman, and Ethel Everard became the Managing Director. The new chairman's eldest daughter became a Director of the company in 1969, followed by his two sons A M (Michael) Everard and William D Everard in 1972.

The company has for many years operated coastal dry cargo vessels, tankers and tugs from its base near Dartford on the River Thames and, until its takeover by James Fisher, operated a modern fleet of product tankers trading throughout the United Kingdom and the near continent. The sister vessels Actuality and Apricity were ordered in 1966 especially for the timber trade from Scandinavia, and were equipped with steel hatches, hydraulic winches for the derricks and steel stanchions for the deck cargoes of timber. To maximise their deadweight capacity, their construction was kept as light as possible, and, at the time of their delivery, they were considered to be the largest ships which could safely navigate the lower part of the river Trent, making them ideal vessels for the wharf at Gunness with their deadweight of 1,160 tons. However, they were soon eclipsed and more recently vessels with a deadweight of over 3,000 tons are regular visitors to the wharf. Altogether, during the 1960s a total of 22 vessels were built, and another 12 were purchased from elsewhere, including two tugs and those vessels acquired through the purchase of Glen & Co. The dry cargo vessels varied from the 2,500 deadweight ships built by Clelands and at Goole, all with family names, two low air draft vessels Capacity and The Duchess, built by J Pollock Sons & Co Ltd at Faversham for service up the river Seine to Paris, to 5 small vessels built by Clelands and Fellows. Four tankers came from Goole and four other Dutch-built tankers from Groningen, namely the Authority (sold in 1985 to Greek interests) and Asperity, both of which were delivered in 1967, and the Activity and Allurity, which followed in 1969. The vessel Capacity was also involved in trade from Felixstowe to Zeebrugge, Silloth to Drogheda, Preston to the Isle of Man, and in between these runs, carrying East Anglian malted barley to the whisky distillery at Port Ellen on the Scottish island of Islay. This latter trade was later continued by the larger vessel Clarity and later still by the vessel Commodity. The smaller 'F'-type vessels, at 199 gross tons, fell just short of the international marine conventions. The first two of the series of five vessels, Frivolity and Festivity, were both built at Great Yarmouth in 1963, and they were followed by the improved Fixity in 1966. The vessels Futurity and Formality were built to an improved XL400 design, which was also used for the construction of vessels for other owners at Wallsend-on-Tyne and Malta. The vessel Festivity was abandoned during a gale in the North Sea in November 1971, and this incident made her the subject of a formal marine inquiry, which led to conclusions which were to influence the operation of small coastal vessels in general. These five small ships lasted for several years, the last being sold in 1987. The vessels Activity and Allurity were employed on charter as standby anti-pollution vessels for offshore drilling rigs between 1984 and 1986, before being taken out of service to complete their special surveys. They were then laid up at Greenhithe before being sold. The Audacity was built at Goole as a UK version of the Dutch tankers, and proved to have a better deadweight capacity than her Dutch-built counterparts, relieving the Assiduity on the Mobil Oil Co Ltd, charter from Coryton to Ipswich and King's Lynn. A smaller vessel, the Acclivity, was built in 1968 and operated with the fleet until her sale to Moroccan interests based in Casablanca in 1981.

Continued next month

Editor's Mailbox

From: **Roger Wormsley, Ko Sichang, Thailand**

I would like to add to the artcles re Ben Line and Banana Boats in the April and May issues of S.T.& Y.

Until the Bangkok Bar was dredged in the late 1950's Ben Line's main line service ships could not reach that port and cargo for that destination was discharged in Singapore and taken there by a feeder ship the 'BENVEG'. This vessel was one of a number of MOT designed ships built especially for the Far East theartre of war being a 'B type coaster' of 1,200 tons deadweight. The 'BENVEG' was built at Blyth Dry Dock & Engineering Co., Ltd. as the "EMPIRE PARK" in 1946 and aquired by Ben Line in 1952. The vessel was sold to Ta Hing of Hong Kong in 1962 and traded for some years afterwards in Indonesia as the "GRANDHING".

The "BENDORAN" was sunk on D.Day the 6th June 1944 as one of ten block ships forming the 'Gooseberry 4' barrier off 'Juno Beach' near Coursauelles several miles to the east of Arromanches. It was demolished in-situ after the end of WW-2.

A charming and distinctive thing about the Ben Line livery was that the external bulkheads of the bridge block were painted to emulate grained wooden panelling. This can be seen, but not identified, on the illustration of the "BENREOCH".

With regard to Elders & Fyffes, I travelled out the West Indies in their "GOLFITO" to work in the West Indies in1954 and at that time she was in service from Southampton to Barbados, Trinidad, Kingston Jamaica and back to the UK. Other Banana Boats than those mentioned in the article were also still in service, namely the "JAMAICA PRODUCER" managed by Kaye & Sons Ltd., running from Jamaica to London and a couple of Scandinavian ships that served Dominica, St.Lucia, St.Vincent and Grenada delivering their banana cargoes to Fleetwood in the U.K

For those readers who do not have a marine bakground although Banana Boats are technically speaking Reefer Ships, the carriage of bananas needs continuous care and attention as the temperature of the cargo chambers must be continually monitored. When the bananas are loaded they are green but by adjusting the temperatures of the banana chambers during transit they are discharged in such a condition that they are not quite ripe, the finall few days of ripening taking place naturally after discharge so that they reach the market in prime condition.

From: **Markus Berger, www.swiss-ships.ch**

I read with interest the article of Mr. Norman L. Middlemiss, but found out that some parts of that article, are not correct. For example the charters of all the Rethymnis & Kulukundis ships had started already in 1939, so for example the ATLANTICOS sailed from Newcastle on 11/10/1939 for Santos. The last one was the MOUNT LYCABETTUS which departed for her first voyage in charter for the Swiss Government on 23/12/1939.

The CARITAS I, CARITAS II and the HENRY DUNANT, were owned during the war by the Swiss Comité international de la Croix-Rouge, according to the so-called réméré agreement (sale under the condition that the seller may buy the ship back within a certain period of time). The management of those ships were allocated to Schweizerische Reederei A.G. (Swiss Shipping Co. Ltd.), Basel.

Schweizerische Reederei does not exist anymore under this name and they own only two River Rhine containerships the ALPINA and the self-propelled barge VELA which is connected to the ALPINA. The company is named Rhenus Alpina, Basel now and is owned by the German Rhenus Group. The former manager of the ocean going ship department has set up the Alpina Reederei AG, Chur in 2001 with a German shipowner.

The KELLER (KELLER LINE & Swiss Mediterranean Shipping Co.) family took over the bankrupt NAUTILUS Line 1954 and their liner service from the Mediterranean ports to West Africa, named NAUTILUS LINE.

The ANZÈRE was ordered and built 1978 for Compagnie de Navigation Transocéanique Suisse S.A., Genève and was not built 1970 as stated in the article.

The Suisse-Outremer S.A. de Gérance et d'Affretement Maritimes, Genève has nothing to do with the so called Zurich banking gnomes. Suisse-Outremer S.A. de Gérance et d'Affretement Maritimes, Genève was set up by the private banking houses Pictet & Co. & Ferrier Lullin & Co. of Geneva and it has nothing to do with the CMB of Belgium or a so called Outremer Bank. After the private bankers lost their interests in the shipping business in 1963, they sold the ANUNCIADA, ALLOBROGIA, and the ARIANA to Suisse-Atlantique Société d'Armement Maritime S.A. of Lausanne.

The office of Suisse-Outremer S.A. de Gérance et d'Affretement Maritimes, Genève was purchased 15/11/1963 by Hans Heinrich von Thyssen-Bornemisza and moved to Zürich. About the mentioned "C" class ships: the CALANCA and are small reefers built by Werf "Gusto", the CASTAGNOLA a general cargo ship, with near sisters built for the Halcyon Line, was built in Flensburg, and the CARIBIA and CASSARATE in Warnemünde. Unfortunately the childeren of H.H. Thyssen having lost interest in the shipping business and Swiss Overseas Ship Management Ltd. was sold on 07/05/2002 to a captain-owner and this company owned and managed several smaller ships until 07/04/2005 when the company was liquidated.

A company named Suisse-Outremer AG was newly founded at Amriswil on 23/12/2004.

Swissmarine is not, a so called ship manager, Swissmarine is a cargo broker/operator and chartering company.

MACS (Maritime Carrier AG) is no longer situated in Altendorf. They moved to Zürich on 07/02/2005, but all the operating and ship management action is done in Hamburg.

ABC Maritime is not located as mentioned in Basel. This shipowning and management company is situated at Nyon, Canton Vaud in the French part of Switzerland.

Vinalmar was founded on 26/09/1946, and does no longer exist since 11/12/2007 and is no longer in the ocean going wine transportation business.

The mentioned ships VINDEMIA and VINIA were never owned or managed by Vinalmar SA or Ermefer SA.

The mentioned MSC NAPOLI was not owned by MSC, Geneva. She was instead owned by Zodiac Maritime Agencies, London and only chartered out to MSC, Geneva.

I thought this additional information would be informative to the author and the readers of Shipping Today & Yesterday.

From: **Richard Hagon, Flat 9, The Beeches, 15 Heald Road, Bowdon, Altrincham WA14 2HZ**

Reading about various cargo ships in the magazine reminded me of a ship my class adopted when I was at Bradbury Secondary School in Hale near Altrincham. It was about 1968 and the name of the cargo ship was 'Antilochus'. At the time it was under the command of a Captain Hill and was based at Birkenhead.

Our Teacher arranged a day trip to see the ship. After being shown around the various areas we were given tea and cakes in the mess. A great adventure!

I wondered what had happened to the vessel since, so I researched it on the internet and came up with the following information:

This was the second ship of this name. It was built by Harland & Wolff, Belfast in 1947 for A Holt & Co, Liverpool (Better known as the Blue Funnel Line). There was also mention of the Ocean Steam Ship Co but I am not sure how that fits in. In 1975 ownership transferred to Elder Dempster Lines and in 1977 it was sold to Gulf (Shipowners) Ltd London and renamed 'Gulf Orient'. It was broken up in Gadani Pakistan in 1978.

Readers Corner
This month's unknown ship

This photograph was taken at Southampton in the mid 1960s. Can any reader identify the coaster?

December's unknown ship brought many replies most of whom identified her as the Onitsha. I believe that the Federal/NZ ship is the Piako.

Please reply to :-
The Editor, Shipping Today and Yesterday, PO Box 55, Alderney, Channel Islands GY9 3BL
or by e-mail: editor@shippingtandy.com

Chris Barton writes: I am not able to offer any suggestion for the main freighter, but after studying the NZS/Federal ship in dry dock and with use of a magnifying glass I would offer either Piako or Somerset. They were 10k grt ships built in 1962 and broken up in 1984 having been sold out of the P&O fleet to Greek owners towards the end of their service. I am basing this identification on the fact that mystery ship has a main mast, only two hatches aft, and does not appear to have any substantial heavy lift derrick on the fore mast.

Alan Dean writes: This ship is easily identifiable as Elder Dempster's 150 ton heavy lift ship Onitsha of 1952.

Mike West wries: The ship is the 1955 built vessel Owerri of the 'O' class of Elder Dempster ships. The Federal/NZ ship is more than likely one of the 1952 built ships of the Surrey, Cornwall class.

John Powell writes: The unknown Elder Dempster ship in the August issue is clearly identified by the jumbo derrick at No.2 hatch as the Onitsha built by Harland and Wolff in 1952. Sold in 1972 to Cisne Cia.Nav.S.A. of Piraeus and renamed Amvourgon. On 8th January 1975 an engine room fire caused the crew to abandon ship and she was later broken up at Santander in June 1975.

A D Frost writes: August's Unknown Ships are Elder Dempster's Onitsha (distinguished by the 150t. Jumbo),sisters Obuasi & Owerri. Built 1952 by H&W, Belfast, sold 1972 r/n Amvourgon, b/u Santander 1975.The ship in dry-dock is Federal's Essex built 1954 by J. Brown, sold 1975 r/n Golden Gulf, b/u Gadani Beach 1977.

Robert Blackwell writes: I believe the Unknown Ship for August to be Elder Dempster's Onitsha, 1952, 5,802gt. Clearly recognisable by the heavy 'jumbo' derrick at no.2 hatch for the purpose of loading locomotives. She is alongside T shed, Royal Edward Dock discharging West African logs into barges. In drydock is N.Z's Piako, 1962, 9,986gt undergoing repairs by Jefferies Ltd of Avonmouth. She is in 'Federal' livery as were all N.Z ships early in 1966. But from 1967 all were registered under Federal ownership. A frequent caller at the 'mouth' she was always a joy to behold and with her sister, Somerset, the pair were probably the last 'classical' ships built for the company. The tugs are C.J King's Sea Alert on the left and the veteran steamer Sea Alarm alongside the caisson. I would reckon the year the photo was taken was 1969-70.

Graham Carter writes: The unknown ship on the right of the photograph I think you will find is the Elder Dempster Lines cargo liner Onitsha built in 1952 of 5,802gt. She was in a class of three, the other two being the Owerri and Obuassi. She was however the only one of the three that was fitted with a 10 ton derrick which can be clearly seen in the photograh. Sold in 1972 she was condemned in 1975 after being abandoned following an engine room fire.

R J Whittaker writes: The Elder Dempster ship is the Onitsha, built 1952. Together with the rest of the 'O' class, she was sold for further trading out of the Ocean Group in about 1972. Note that, although good looking, she appears top heavy. That type of superstructure was identical to that used on the larger Eboe/Ebani class of 1952. Also, note the tall mast just ahead of the funnel which dates the photo to the late 1960s, when those masts were added to Elder Dempster ships. The tall funnelled tug is the Sea Alert or Sea Alarm. I think the Federal ship is the Essex.

Gregor Morcom writes: The ship is Elder Dempster Lines "O" class and appears to be Onitsha, on which class I never sailed, (but recall party times at the "Turtle Club",on sister ship Oti, whilst in Lagos in the '60s). My last trip with ED was as 3rd Eng on Pegu and left at Avonmouth in September 1970.

Eric McIntyre writes: The freighter on the right of the photo looks like the Onitsha of Elder Dempster Lines, showing her heavy lift derrick capable of lifting locomotives. She was built in 1952 at Harland & Wolff, Belfast. She was 5,082 gross tons, 5cyl B&W oil engine, 13knots and had accommodation for 12 passengers. She was sold on 26.5.1972 to Cisne Cia Nav sa, Piraeus and renamed Amvourgon. On 8.1.1975 she had a fire in the engine room and was abandoned by the crew 7 miles off Fox River near Cape Gaspe. She was taken in tow to Halifax arriving 11.1.1975. She left halifax on 7th May and arrived at Santander on 9.6.1975 for demolition. Her sister ships were Obuasi and Owerri. To the left in dry dock the ship looks like Federal Line's Essex built by John Brown & Co., Clydebank in 1954. She was 10,936gt, very similar to her sister ship Otaki, 10,934gt also built by J.Brown in 1953. Essex was sold in December 1975 and became the Golden Gulf of Guan Guan shipping of Singapore. She lasted until 1977 when she was broken up at Gadani Beach.

Laurence Ward writes: The freighter on the right in the picture is the Onitsha (Elder Dempster Lines Limited). The ship was the lead ship of a class of three i.e. 'Onitsha' class, and was designed for the carriage of heavy locomotives. The other two ships in the class being the Obuasi completed 1952 (Cadet Ship for number of years) and the Owerri completed in 1955. All three ships were built by Harland & Wolff Ltd., Belfast. All three had a similar superstructure, but, there were differences in overall ships dimensions. The main things that visually points to the ship being the Onitsha is the fact that the mainmast masthouse is small (large in the other two ships) and the derricks for No. 2A hold (I think it was) were stowed in cradles (these can be seen in the photo) just ahead of the superstructure. The Onitsha had eight derricks (excluding the heavy lift derrick) for the foredeck holds, whilst the other two only had six (plus the heavy lift derrick), the derricks for No 2 also covered No 2A.
All three were designed to carry 12 passengers. The Federal/NZSC ship is either the Somerset (Federal Steam Nav. Co - built by John Brown & Co [Clydebank] Ltd., Glasgow - delivered 17.11.1962) or the Piako (NZSC - built by A. Stephen & Sons Ltd., Glasgow - delivered 11.01.1962). The photo shows a ship with a bulky funnel, a foremast that appears not to have a heavy lift derrick and crow's nest and, both masts without mast tables. This fits the profiles of both of these ships.

Forgotten Fleets

F T EVERARD & Sons

Part Two

by

Mark Rowbotham

The vessel Agility was the first of a more modern type of tanker to enter service. Initially she carried motor spirit and gas oil from Coryton to Gunness for Mobil Oil Co Ltd, but this work ceased when the Associated Petroleum Terminal came into operation at Immingham. Later, she was engaged in time charters to ICI and carried their motor spirit from the tees to the Tyne for several years before being replaced by a larger vessel in 1976. The next tanker from Goole, the Annuity, was almost twice the size of the Agility and she was mainly engaged in the carriage of lubricating oils from Rotterdam to Barton on the Manchester Ship Canal, and later from Rotterdam to Silvertown on the river Thames for Gulf Oil (Great Britain) Ltd. Other vessels built included the Assiduity, which was never seen as being totally satisfactory, and the Audacity, which was more successful. The Alacrity was converted into a chemical tanker soon after entering service, and was eventually sold in 1986 to Liberian interests. Two much larger vessels joined the fleet in 1971 when Everards purchased Thun Tankers Ltd, the British subsidiary of a Swedish company, and changed the subsidiary's name to Thames Tankers Ltd. The two tankers which were absorbed into the Everard fleet became the Amity and Anteriority, and the deadweight tonnage of each vessel was slightly lower than that of the Astrality of 1955. The Anteriority was engaged in coastal activities, including trips to the Mediterranean and the Black Sea, as well as voyages to the Middle East at the time when the Suez Canal was temporarily closed to traffic, carrying lubricating oils to Jeddah, in Saudi Arabia. The Amity was engaged on time charter activities to Sweden, carrying fuel oils from Gothenburg to various Baltic sea ports. When this time charter ended, she was placed on bareboat charter to a French company. However, the French did not keep up payments on the charter, and the vessel was eventually arrested. Following more than a year of legal proceedings, the ship was recovered in 1977 and was duly sold.

The 1,596 grt Security was built in 1971 by R Dunston at Hessle. She is seen her at Leith in 1974. In 1986 she was sold to Carisbrooke Shipping and renamed Mark which was later changed to Mark C. She then served as Elizabeth C (1995), Eliza (1999), Elizabeth (2000), Phoenix (2000), Agemar (2002), before being sold to Vibrani Shipping of Monrovia in 2005 and renamed Sea Lion I. She is still in service for them today.

The 499 grt Candourity was built in 1975 by Scheepswerf Bijlholt B. V. at Foxhol in the Netherlands. In 1992 she was sold to D J Goubert Shipping without changing her name. In 2003 she was sold to Queen Makoua Charlotte of Cameroon and renamed Makou Express the following year. A further sale in 2007 saw her renamed Alexandra Express. She is still in service.

In the 1970s, a large building programme took place, mostly of dry cargo vessels but ending with the first two vessels of a group of three tankers. The first of the dry cargo vessels came from the Groningen yard and was named Supremity, and she was designed primarily for the liner trade between Scandinavia and Ireland. She was followed by eight gearless dry cargo vessels of 1,599 gross tons, two of which were built by Richard Dunston of Hessle, closely followed by two more from Goole. These four were immediately followed by a further four vessels of the Fred Everard class which had the same gross tonnage but could achieve an extra 400 tons deadweight by the extension of various loopholes in several paragraphs of international tonnage regulations. They were initially involved in coastal trade, but soon their activities extended to Mediterranean work carrying steel and china clay, and returning with phosphates or other bulk minerals. These were followed by trips to northern Russia to load timber, as well as trips to Sweden to load timber, general cargo and containers. Eventually, the Mediterranean work declined, and they returned to coastal work around UK and North-West European waters. The mid-1980s proved a difficult period, and following a short period of lay-up, they were all sold by 1987 with the exception of the Sagacity, which lasted in the fleet a little longer. Another bulk vessel, the Mairi Everard, was built in 1974 with a similar size to the other vessels, except that she had a box hold, where all the internal frames are constructed within the wing ballast tanks, thus facilitating flush sides to the hold. Although particularly suitable for the carriage of grain, the ship started on the Swedish timber trade, and later went on to carrying steel pipes from Glasgow for the North Sea oil operations and eventually reverted back to timber-carrying operations interspersed with the occasional bulk cargoes.

In 1975 and 1976, the company took delivery of six smaller dry cargo vessels, two from Wivenhoe and the other four from Groningen. The Dutch-built vessels were slightly smaller than their British-built counterparts, and with the same operating costs carried some 70 tons less cargo. However, they had a better hull form and were therefore more economical on fuel, and being better sea boats, could often make passages in heavy seas where the other two could not. Two of the Dutch-built vessels, Conformity and Candourity, were able to pass beneath the toll bridge at Selby on the river Ouse, but after this, a limit was placed on the beam of vessels permitted to pass through the bridge. This limit thus precluded the Everard vessels from continuing to visit the port. Although this was seen as a serious matter at the time, the Olympia Oil & Cake Mills Ltd. at Selby changed from crushing imported soya beans to concentrate on locally-produced rape seed. It was not considered worthwhile in pursuing any protest against this decision, and the toll bridge enjoyed the protection originally given it by Act of Parliament in 1791. The vessel Commodity spent several years carrying malted barley to the whisky distillery at Port Ellen on Islay. Eventually, production declined, and supplies of barley to the distilleries were maintained by trucks using the regular MacBrayne ferry from the Scottish mainland. The Commodity then joined the Celebrity on the same general coastwise trading as their Dutch-built sisters.

Following the completion of these six vessels, orders were placed for a further four, much larger, vessels. They had the same hull form as the previous six, two were gearless and the other two geared ("geared" being the reference to the fact that such vessels have their own derricks for loading and unloading of cargo), and although they were below 1,600 gross tons, their deadweight exceeded 4,000 tons. This was achieved by each vessel containing a non-load bearing 'tween deck, which increased the permitted deadweight tonnage in terms of international tonnage regulations. These four Everard ships had probably the highest deadweight for any 1,599 gross ton ships anywhere in the world. The construction contract for three of these vessels was given to Swan Hunter

The 461 grt Capacity was built by J Pollock & Sons of Faversham. In January 1981 she was sold to R W Fielding of Liverpool and, in May of that year, she was sold to Shipbreaking (Queenborough) Ltd, for breaking up.

Shipbuilders Ltd. The first vessel to be delivered, the Singularity, was built at the company's Readhead yard at South Shields, and the two gearless ships, the Stability and the Speciality, were built at Goole. The fourth vessel, the Jack Wharton, was built for J Wharton (Shipping) Ltd. by Richards (Shipbuilders) Ltd. at Lowestoft. Everards supervised the construction of this vessel, and on her completion, bareboat chartered the vessel which appeared in the Everard livery until sold in 1987. The Singularity, however, was the last vessel to be built at the Readhead yard, and it closed soon afterwards. Towards her completion, the yard was plagued by industrial action and a "work to rule", which made sea trials and her handover date uncertain. The ship had been nominated to represent the company at the Queen's 1977 Jubilee Review at Spithead, but as the date approached, there were still doubts about her completion, and as a result, the vessel Fred Everard, then undertaking special survey at the neighbouring Tyne Dock Engineering Co Ltd. yard, was prepared and made into a worthy substitute. The two new geared vessels were soon engaged on voyages to the Mediterranean and West Africa, as well as to the Russian port of Archangel in the summer months. However, even these voyages were soon eclipsed by longer-distance ventures across the Atlantic to Canada, the USA, the West Indies, Guyana and the Azores. The Singularity undertook two voyages to Brazil and even ventured up the Amazon to the port of Manaus. Later, in 1981, she passed through the Panama Canal en route to Buenaventura on the Colombian Pacific Coast. Meanwhile, the Speciality started her career on the run between Ireland and Sweden, and was also placed on time charter work with the Central Electricity Generating Board (CEGB) in 1985 carrying coal to power stations. The Stability was even more restricted in her activities, and started out in the soya bean carrying trade from Rotterdam to Erith, later going to the Swedish service and also on to a CEGB time charter. Both ships later reverted to general coastwise trade, which included trips to Sweden and Archangel.

In 1982, Everard vessels traded to the Falkland Islands in the period following the end of the Falklands campaign and the surrender of the Argentine forces, using the company's geared ships, and, for that matter, the only British-flagged ships which could load and discharge containers at the small port of Port Stanley, which was not equipped to handle the larger cargo vessels. Various cargoes were carried on a regular basis by the Everard vessels Singularity and Jack Wharton, together with the Comben Longstaff vessels Lincolnbrook and Leicesterbrook, to Port Stanley and Ascension Island, and these comprised both military supplies, in particular helicopters and spare parts and explosives, and other more general stores, as well as buildings and other vehicles. Indeed, anything which was required to support and maintain the British forces in the Falklands was carried by these vessels. They were not as such designed for this kind of role, but with a certain degree of improvisation and modification, they made a useful contribution to the campaign. Following the cessation of the 1982 hostilities, the Falklands work declined and the geared vessels were both sold.

Once these four cargo ships were in operation, the company initiated design studies for several new tankers, which would be more sophisticated than the earlier tankers and which would be equipped with deep-well pumps for each pair of cargo tanks. Three ships of some 2,400 tons deadweight were ordered and built in Goole, the lead vessels being the Ability, which entered service in March 1979, and which was the first Everard vessel to sport two funnels, each located on either side of the vessel behind the accommodation quarters. Although they were designed to carry a variety of petroleum cargoes, they were limited to the carriage of clean petroleum products and lubricating oils to ports in the Northern European area.

Between the construction of the second and third vessels of the tanker construction programme, a significant event occurred in the company's history in April 1980 when Everards purchased Comben Longstaff & Co Ltd., along with its subsidiaries County Ships Ltd., Williamstown Shipping Ltd.

and Gowan Shipping Ltd. The Comben Longstaff fleet comprised 'S...brook' vessels, including the Solentbrook, four more modern 'L...brook' vessels, including the Lincolnbrook and Leicesterbrook, and the two much larger 'D...brook' vessels. The last two vessels were not originally part of the transaction, but Everards managed them for a short period of time while they were being sold by Longstaff's former parent company Consolidated Gold Fields Ltd. Comben Longstaff & Co.Ltd. was one of the most prominent shipowners in the UK and European trades, owning a wide variety of coasters and larger ships mostly with names ending in ...brook. The company was notable for building some of the last steamships for the coal trade, and followed these with an attractive series of motor ships.

The Comben Longstaff ships were soon integrated into the Everard fleet and gradually their funnel markings were changed to the Everard motif, although they retained their names and overall colour schemes. Longstaff had been serious competitors to Everards on the coastal trade for many years, but at the time of the purchase all their vessels were trading further afield. The 'S...brook' vessels were conventional, geared, two-hold cargo vessels and continued to operate on the Mediterranean, Baltic and Russian trades for some time, but all these vessels were sold by mid-1983, owing to operational unreliability caused mainly by the difficulty encountered in maintaining their DC electrical installations. The 'L...brook' vessels had, however, been constructed to a more modern design, and were in reality the main attraction for Everards. They all had single holds with single hatches which made them good ships for the carriage of grain, although portable bulkheads had to be fitted for safety and stability reasons when handling heavier cargoes. The gearless vessels Lancasterbrook and Londonbrook, with their grain bulkheads in place were soon engaged in the regular trade from Rotterdam to Erith with cargoes of soya beans. However, this trade ended when the Erith mill stopped crushing soya beans, and the vessels were transferred to general trading activities, the regular Swedish trade and they also spent periods on time charters to the CEGB, as had some of the other Everard vessels. The geared pair of Longstaff vessels, the Lincolnbrook and Leicesterbrook, were engaged on general trading work, with summer voyages to Archangel and the regular Swedish runs. Their cranes became particularly useful when they were engaged in the Falklands campaign, and enabled them to successfully carry the large RAF Chinook helicopters. The vessels took them both to and from the Falkland Islands, because overhauls could only be undertaken in the UK. Shortly after the Falklands work ended, one of each pair of vessels was sold, leaving the Lancasterbrook and Leicesterbrook to continue in the Everard fleet for a little longer.

Everards has also managed ships for other owners, including bulk cement carriers and tankers, as well as conventional dry cargo ships. As far back as 1978, management work had been undertaken by Everards, starting with the vessels David Dorman and Edgar Dorman of Shamrock Shipping Ltd. Both ships and the owning company were later acquired by James Fisher & Sons plc of Barrow-in-Furness, and Everards retained the management of these vessels for a while until the ships were placed on bareboat charter to J & A Gardner & Co Ltd. of Glasgow in 1984. Everards supervised the building of two further Shamrock ships, the Shamrock Endeavour and Shamrock Enterprise, which were also taken by J Fisher with Everards continuing with the management until this was transferred to Coe Metcalfe Shipping Ltd., a subsidiary of James Fisher, in 1986. Everards became more involved with further Fisher acquisitions when the Barrow company purchased the fleet of Onesimus Dorey (Shipowners) Ltd. of Guernsey in 1983. The three Dorey

The 499 grt Grit was the seventh company vessel to bear the unusual name which was most likely derived from the concept of "True Grit". She was built in 1976 by N.V. Scheepswerf Ferus Smit at Westerbroek. On 25th January 1988 she sank in Hull Roads after a collision with the dredger Bowprince and was subsequently broken up by D Cook Ltd. of New Holland.

The 1,926 grt Activity was built in 1982 by Clelands at Wallsend as the Shell Technician. In 1993 Shell reanmed her Arianta before she was transferred to Everards in 1999. In 2007 she was sold to Flagship SPB of St Petersburg and renamed Flagship 3.

vessels Belgrave, Perelle and Rocquaine, were managed by Everards until they were handed over to demise (bareboat) charterers in 1986. Management of other vessels followed, a variety of dry cargo carriers, including the Ligar Bay, a self-discharging cement carrier, the Dutch-registered Mercurius, and the Jersey-registered vessel Farnese. The Mercurius and the Farnese were transferred to UK registry in 1988, but the Mercurius, now renamed BC Mercurius, did not last long and was sold for scrap before the end of 1988 following an engine room fire. In 1982, the Panamanian-registered vessel Doris I became the first tanker to be managed by Everards since the 'Empire' tankers of World War II. The ship had been built in 1964, and was specially equipped to carry edible oils.

After the delivery of the vessel Amenity in 1980, there was a gap of nearly four-years before the company took delivery of another new vessel. This ship, named Selectivity, was the first of a class of four vessels of 799 gross tons. Their keels were laid before the imposition of the new London Tonnage Rules in 1982. If the vessels had been measured according to the new rules, their gross tonnage would have been much greater. Tonnage measurements are now governed by an IMO Convention (International Convention on Tonnage Measurement of Ships, 1969 -London Rules), which applies to all ships built after July 1982. In accordance with the Convention, the correct term to use now is GT, which is a function of the moulded volume of all enclosed spaces of the ship. The tonnage of ships above 24 metres in length which are engaged on international voyages is determined according to the International Convention on Tonnage Measurement of Ships, 1969 (London-Rules). Under the Convention system, the volume of all ship's enclosed spaces, i.e. from keel to funnel, is measured to the inside of the hull framing, whereas special open spaces are excluded, so they are not considered in the total volume. The gross tonnage indicates a vessel's total volume, not her weight or deadweight, which is a common misconception.

Two vessels of the class, namely the Selectivity and the Pamela Everard, were built to the account of the company Investors in Industry plc and were leased to Everards, while the other pair, Willonia and Stevonia, were built for J Wharton (Shipping) Ltd. of Gunness, on the river Trent, although Everards superintended the construction of both vessels and managed the Willonia from when she was completed. The original plan was that Everards should manage the vessel for two years and then, once the Stevonia was delivered, both ships would revert to their owners. However, in 1986 a complex deal was arranged, where Everards relinquished their share of the Gunness operation in exchange for the five vessels of the Wharton fleet, namely the Angelonia, Lizzonia, Willonia, Stevonia and the Jack Wharton. In order to achieve this transaction, F T Everard Shipping Ltd. was formed to take over the vessels.

The company took over the management of the small dry cargo vessel Gwyn of Graig Shipping Co Ltd. of Cardiff in July 1985, but she came to an untimely end when she sank in the North Sea in November 1985. All the crew were rescued safely, but the wreck was not raised until September 1986, whereupon she was declared a constructive total loss and was eventually sold for conversion into a suction dredger. Management of other vessels followed, including the Cotinga, which belonged to Hadley Shipping Co Ltd., followed by the Charles Cruz which, although owned by J E Hyde Shipowners Ltd, was on charter to Pegasus Line of Gibraltar. Originally, this vessel had been engaged in trade between Gibraltar, North Africa, Spain and the UK before being used as a feeder vessel in the western Mediterranean for Pegasus container operations until her sale in 1989. The year previously, the company chairman Frederick Everard had died, and was replaced as chairman by his eldest son F M Everard. Also in 1988, two Japanese tankers were purchased as replacements for the elderly Dutch-built tankers. They were renamed Averity and Amity, and were registered in the Bahamas. They were used in different activities, one going under charter to Burmah Petroleum Fuels Ltd., carrying motor spirit along the east coast, and the other going into general coastwise trade, mainly along the west coast of the UK. After a significant amount of preparatory work, an order was placed in October 1988 with the Richards (Shipbuilders) yard at Lowestoft for two tankers, which would be equipped with deepwell cargo pumps, segregated ballast tanks, a free-fall lifeboat and state-of-the-art communications and electronic equipment. The first of the two, the Agility, was delivered in March 1990, and the second vessel, the Alacrity, followed later in the year. Meanwhile, the shipyard, oil storage and road transport facilities at Greenhithe were all closed at the same time, and the company found itself with a significant amount of unused land at the Greenhithe site. The land was soon sold off to property developers, the office was closed and everything was moved to temporary accommodation located a short distance away to the west of the original site, which was soon razed to the ground. In 1989, the vessel Stability was transferred to the Bahamas flag, and she was followed by the vessels Speciality and Sagacity in 1990. The Stability was manned by a Polish crew, while the other two vessels retained their British crews.

Everards significantly extended the boundaries of coastal product tanker design in 1997 with the construction of the 3,700 dwt Asperity and a sister ship at the Keppel Singmarine yard in Singapore. This ship was designed without a centreline bulkhead but with a central trunk on deck for pipework and to provide a measure on longitudinal strength. The arrangement marked a departure from conventional design and was provided to facilitate quick cargo discharge operations and, hence, rapid port turnarounds. The Asperity, which was designed by F T Everard, was a new ship known as the most technologically-advanced coastal tanker in its class. The ship's design takes into account likely future maritime laws, oil company standards, turnaround time in harbours, fuel economy and manpower costs, and was the first of two vessels to feature advanced technology applications in tanker designs. In the period immediately prior to its takeover by James Fisher, F T Everard operated 11 "Clean Petroleum Product" (CPP) tankers, owning nine and chartering the other two, with a further four vessels, all product tankers, entering the fleet in 2007. Even as part of the merged Fisher Everard group, Everard's main business involves short sea trips for the major oil companies in Europe, predominantly in the UK and Ireland.

More recently, Everard invested in further newbuild vessels to renew its fleet, and orders for four 3,750 dwt product tankers, with two options, were placed with the Qingshan yard at Wuhan in China. The most distinctive feature of the new Everard ships was their diesel-electric propulsion systems, twin engine rooms and twin propellers, and they were described as being the most technologically-advanced vessels of their kind to have been built.

Although a diesel-electric propulsion system had been specified for several series of chemical parcel tankers and a number of shuttle tankers, this form of propulsion had not, prior to the construction of these vessels, been incorporated onboard such small tankers. However, this propulsion enabled the engines to burn fuel more efficiently while maintaining a service speed of 11.5 knots. Like the Everard vessel Asperity, the newbuild vessels were built with a main deck trunk arrangement, thus bringing in a greater degree of efficiency and safety to the loading and unloading of their sensitive cargoes. A number of advanced design features have been incorporated in the vessels, including a high level of automation and measures to prevent a single equipment failure resulting in the entire shipboard system becoming inoperable. In order to protect the environment, these double-hulled vessels were designed to minimise harmful exhaust emissions, noise and the risk of pollution. The F T Everard fleet took delivery in 2006-7 of the four new vessels of the 'Speciality'

The 1,696 grt Ability was built in 1979 by Goole Shipbuilders. In 2005 she was renamed Availability before being sold to Welwyn Management in 2008 and renamed Ancon Trader. She is seen here in Alderney in 2005.

The 1,930 grt tanker Agility was built in 1990 by Richards of Lowestoft. After the Fisher takeover she was sold to Aegean Shipping and renamed Aegean III. She is seen here arriving at Fawley in October 2005.

class, and all of these four oil products tankers now operate under the James Fisher Everard banner, namely Superiority, Speciality, Supremity and Seniority (all 3859 grt). The tanker Speciality was built by the Qingshan Shipyard in China, and was delivered to Everards in May 2006, with a gross tonnage of 3,859 grt and a deadweight of 4,426 tonnes, and an overall length of 95.14 metres. At the time of her delivery to Everards, she was described as the most environmentally-friendly small product tanker in the world by the December 2006 edition of the magazine "Horizons". Her crew of eight are mainly British, and she is registered at Nassau in the Bahamas. Like her sisters, Superiority is 95.14 metres in length and has a gross tonnage of 3,859 grt and a deadweight of 4,426 tonnes. She is registered in London, and has a multinational crew. Supremity, the last vessel of the class, was delivered by the Qingshan Shipyard at the end of September 2007. Her arrival in the Everard fleet cleared the way for the company to dispose of three of its older vessels, including the coastal vessel Alacrity, and it was reported that the sale of the Alacrity realised around £1.4 million, given its potential for several more years of use. Given their state-of-the-art bridge and navigational equipment, Speciality and her three sisters have been permitted to sail without paper charts in most European waters, using the state-of-the-art electronic ECDIS chart system. These developments ensured that Everards maintained its position as market leader in its sector and more advanced than any other company of its kind.

In December 2006, the Barrow-based company James Fisher took a major step in consolidating its position in the short sea market, when it announced the acquisition of the family-owned coastal tanker firm FT Everard. Everard was in a strong position, both in terms of financial status and market position, and could quite easily have maintained this position for many years to come, but the Board of Everard felt that with an increase in shareholders in the next generation of the family coupled with what was seen as a very fair and attractive offer by James Fisher, it would be justified in accepting the Fisher offer. The purchase price, as reported in the maritime journal Lloyd's List, was £23.7m in cash and the assumption of debts of £28m, and the eleven ex-Everard vessels were brought under the UK's tonnage tax regime as part of the expanded James Fisher fleet. Marine services group James Fisher made the biggest acquisition in its history, when it acquired the private tanker company F T Everard for £23.7 million plus £28 million of debt. James Fisher financed the transaction from its existing resources plus a debt facility from HSBC, and then implemented plans to sell and lease back the fleet which would then operate under the James Fisher Everard flag. Moving relatively small quantities of oil products around Europe for the major oil companies is a highly lucrative business said to offer a number of tax advantages. James Fisher shares added 36.75p or 6.92% to 567.75p, valuing the 160-year-old company at £280 million. The new expanded company now has the name James Fisher Everard, with members of the Everard family on the expanded company's Board of Directors. The fact that the two companies could merge their fleets in such a way as to further strengthen their position within the coastal and short sea bulk tanker fleet shows a significant degree of prudence within the shipping sector as a whole, and also illustrates the degree of how successfully they have been able to maintain their significant share of this market, and remain at the forefront of British shipping, even in times of economic uncertainty.

Following the absorption of Everards into the James Fisher Group, Michael Everard joined the Board of James Fisher as a non-executive Director, while William Everard joined as Executive Director. A few months later, William gave up his main responsibilities as technical director with the company, and in late May 2008 he was appointed to the Board of the Port of London Authority (PLA), the public trust whose responsibilities include ensuring